# THE EXPANSION OF EVERYDAY LIFE

# The
# Expansion of
# Everyday Life
# 1860–1876

DANIEL E. SUTHERLAND

The University of Arkansas Press
Fayetteville
2000

*Library of Congress Cataloging-in-Publication Data*
Sutherland, Daniel E.
    The expansion of everyday life, 1860–1876 / Daniel E. Sutherland.
      p.    cm.
    Originally published: New York : Harper & Row, 1989.
    Includes bibliographical references and index.
    ISBN 1-55728-596-9 (pbk. : alk. paper)
      1. United States—Social life and customs—1865–1918. 2. United
States—History—Civil War, 1861–1865—Social aspects.
3. Reconstruction. I. Title.

E168 .S957 2000
973.7–dc21

                                                    99-086670

*To the memory of Joe Gray Taylor*

# CONTENTS

Illustrations follow pages 50, 146, and 210.

# PREFACE

It is hard to imagine "everyday" life during the tumultuous era of the Civil War and Reconstruction. As the nation engaged in fratricide, battled for the South's political soul, conquered the Indians of the West, and unleashed all manner of industrial and technological changes, old patterns of life could not hope to survive. Yet daily life did continue, with people being born, receiving an education, surviving illnesses, taking jobs, marrying, building homes, raising families, and eventually dying. This book focuses on those ordinary yet essential functions of daily existence. Chapters have topical themes. Where appropriate, each topic stresses the differences and similarities between geographic regions, social classes, racial groups, and the sexes. While drawing on the insights of historians, I have been more concerned with those aspects of everyday life that seemed important to people living at the time. I have quoted liberally from letters, diaries, memoirs, newspapers, magazines, and popular songs of the era to convey a sense of everyday concerns.

The biggest difficulty with such a project is to define everyday life. Was it the life of a Pennsylvania farmer, or a New York merchant? A Texas cowboy, or an Ohio blacksmith? A white Chicago fireman, or a black Virginia tobacco worker? A stockbroker, or a domestic servant? A doctor, or a teacher? A female store clerk, or a male journalist? A soldier, or a minister? An immigrant shoemaker, or a native-born cab driver? All of these people played important roles in the era, yet each led a life different from the others. Who should be included? Who should be excluded? It was impossible to include all. It seemed wrong to exclude anybody. I finally decided to concentrate on what I perceived to be the majority group: "middle-class" American citizen. This decision forced me to limit, if not exclude, material on groups—such as Indians, the very rich, and the very poor—who differed markedly in habits, customs, and patterns of life from the majority. Without such limitations, the already difficult task of generalization would have been impossible. What remains, then, is the typical, the ordinary, and the majority.

To set the stage for this tale, a few words should be said about context. The era I seek to portray begins with the Civil War. It concludes with the great Centennial Exposition, which happened to coincide with the final throes of Republican political rule in the South, the period popularly known as Reconstruction. One president of the Confederate States of America—Jefferson Davis—and three presidents of the United States of America—Abraham Lincoln, Andrew Johnson, and Ulysses S. Grant—served during that time. Five new states—Kansas, West Virginia, Nevada, Nebraska, and Colorado—joined the Union. The population, in 1870, reached nearly forty million people, 86 percent being white (14 percent of that foreign born) and 12 percent being black. Despite a 6 percent increase in urban population during the 1860s, the nation remained overwhelmingly rural, with nearly 75 percent of the people living in "rural areas" (places with fewer than 2,500 inhabitants). The largest city, New York, had a population of 942,000 in 1870. Only ten other cities and towns had populations in excess of 50,000. The most numerous "urban" areas, numbering 309, were middle-sized towns of 2,500 to 5,000 inhabitants. Most Americans, however, resided in thousands of much smaller towns and villages and on the nation's 2,600,000 farms.

The nation's gainfully employed population of nearly thirteen million (85 percent male) suffered through a severe economic depression from 1873 to 1877, when unemployment ranged between 10 and 14 percent. It is impossible to talk of an "average" wage during the era, so wide were differences in wages based on occupation, geography, age, race, and sex; but, for purposes of contrast, "common" farm laborers earned $16.57 (with board) per month in 1870; town laborers earned $1.55 (without board) per day. The cost of living fluctuated widely, too, although prices, after soaring during the war, steadily declined after 1865. Given disparities in wages, inflation rates, supply and demand, manufacturing costs, quality of manufactured goods, availability of raw materials, sources of energy, and a dozen other economic factors, it is virtually impossible to translate the purchasing power of an 1870 dollar into modern terms. Still, with that caution in mind, we may imagine that one dollar in 1870 equaled approximately eight dollars in the 1980s. Most laborers received their wages in cash, although the form varied. Early in the Civil War, the federal government issued the first national system of paper money (popularly called "greenbacks") in denominations of $5, $10, $20, $50, $100, $500, and $1,000. The nation also minted an extensive system of copper, nickel, silver, and gold coins that, in addition to the standard denominations of today, included two-cent pieces, three-cent pieces, and $2.50, $5, $10, and $20 gold pieces. The legend "In God We Trust" first appeared on some coins in 1865. "Shinplasters" (paper notes of small denominations issued by municipalities and private companies) and "fractional currency" (postal-stamp-sized Treasury notes of three, five, ten, twenty-five, and fifty cents) also circulated freely, and some companies paid workers in scrip that could be spent only in company stores.

The era is difficult to capsulize. Every historical period is a mixture of change and continuity; every era is in transition. Still, two themes seem to characterize the 1860s and 1870s.

First, they were decades of physical expansion and economic growth. The westward movement, given a boost by completion of the first transcontinental railroad, hit its stride. Migration from farms and villages to towns and cities, if not a stampede, did quicken in pace. An accompanying shift from rural occupations and crafts to industrial pursuits and professions betrayed important changes in the nation's economy. A quiet world of farms and local attachments was increasingly disturbed by the thud and whirl of industry and the creation of national markets. Similarly, the pursuit of middle-class status became a driving force in everyday life. Economic growth, new technology, greater physical mobility, and national advertising (particularly through popular magazines) increased the variety of and desire for material goods. This desire, increasingly realized through the sale of mass-produced imitations of upper-class houses, furniture, clothing, and art, had, by the 1870s, begun to transform the appearance, even the character, of everyday life.

Was it a good time to be alive? For some, it was the best of times, for others the worst. People in all eras look back wistfully to what they vaguely imagine to be an earlier "golden age." Yet each period has its own advantages, its own improvements, its own reasons for optimism. Certainly the Civil War era was a turbulent time, and not everyone lived happily. Sectional interests collided tragically as North and South waged war and the political struggle for control of the South dominated public life. Southern slaves won freedom but not equality. The westward movement was marred by a painful clash of cultures, white man versus red man. Economically, prices declined steadily after the Civil War while wages tended upward, but the depression of the mid-1870s spoiled the prosperity for many workers. Moral and ethical values were in flux. The church, though still a vital social institution, suffered some erosion. The number of poor people increased, and the gap between poverty and comfort grew wider. The world had become a more confusing place; making one's way in life had become a more complicated process. Still, most Americans enjoyed an improved standard of living and probably found more to praise than to condemn.

This, then, is not the usual historical pageant of political elections, foreign affairs, and wars. Rather, it is a modest vignette of daily life. Let the era's poet of everyday life, Emily Dickinson (Walt Whitman is too monumental), set the tone with words penned in 1861:

> Read—Sweet—how others—strove—
> Till we—are stouter—
> What they—renounced—
> Till we—are less afraid
> . . . . . . . . . . . . . . . .
> Brave names of Men—
> And Celestial Women—
> Passed out—of Record
> Into—Renown!

# PREFACE TO THE UNIVERSITY

# OF ARKANSAS PRESS EDITION

Reader response to the *Expansion of Everyday Life* over the past decade has been gratifying. Students, teachers, scholars, writers, and the history-reading public have apparently found this modest presentation of ordinary people during the Civil War and Reconstruction both enjoyable and educational. I am glad it has turned out so, especially since the opportunity to write it came to me quite by chance. HarperCollins (at the time, Harper & Row), who published the original hardback and paperback editions in 1989, had initially asked my old boss and friend Joe Gray Taylor to write this volume for their Everyday Life in America series. Professor Taylor, who was not in the best of health and already saddled with several other projects, declined but suggested me as someone who might enjoy the task. And I did. My only regret is that Professor Taylor, to whom this book was originally dedicated—and so remains— passed away before I completed it.

The text of this reprint edition is unchanged from the 1989 publication. Some thought was given to expanding the narrative, but the arguments against it seemed to outweigh the potential advantages. Fresh vignettes and more details could have been added, but most readers have judged the length of the book to be "just right." The structure or principal themes of the book might have been reshaped, finessed, or otherwise altered, but, after due consideration, the existing themes of physical expansion, economic growth, and maturation of the middle class still seemed a convenient way to comprehend the era. Then, too, there were the problems (not to mention the expense) attendant to significantly altering a text that had been composed before the heyday of personal computers and electronic disks. However, by way of recognizing the large number of new books about the social history of the Civil War era, I have added an essay to the original bibliography.

Daniel E. Sutherland
Fayetteville, Arkansas
January 2000

# 1

A SOLDIER'S LIFE

$A$s JOHNNY REB marched off to war in the spring of 1861, he promised his mother he would return home by Christmas. He comforted his sweetheart with that assurance. He boasted as much to his friends and neighbors. Up north, Billy Yank did the same. Both men believed the war would be over in a few months. They disagreed only on its outcome. Few men could imagine the terrible truth: Americans had embarked upon sixteen years of continual warfare. They would fight first against each other, in four years of civil war. Then they would march westward to subdue hostile Indians beyond the Mississippi. Over 3.5 million men (1.5 million of them Confederates) led a soldier's life during the Civil War. A mere fraction of that number, fewer than 100,000, would serve in the army of a reunited nation after 1865. Yet all of these men, more men than ever before in the nation's history, shared a distinct way of life, a life most of them would not have chosen in happier times.

There was no typical Civil War soldier. Although the majority of recruits were native white country boys in their early twenties, both armies included dozens of nationalities, scores of occupations, and an age span of half a century. Foreign immigrants composed the largest minority in either army. Union forces included about 500,000 foreigners (25 percent of the army), mostly Germans and Irish. Numbers for the Confederate army are less certain, but tens of thousands of immigrants, most often Irish, donned the gray. North and South employed black laborers as teamsters, cooks, construction workers, and personal servants, but the Union army also recruited about 180,000 black soldiers (almost 10 percent of the army), with 134,000 of those men being recruited from occupied areas of the South. The armies recruited several thousand Indians, too, mostly for service west of the Mississippi River. Black and red men, while providing valuable service to the armies, rarely functioned as integral parts of those armies. Intense racial prejudice prohibited them from serving in white units. They received half the pay of whites, and their clothing, equipment, and supplies were frequently inferior to those of whites. Indians operated most often as scouts or on raiding parties. Negro troops tasted much combat, but they also drew more than their share of menial assignments, particularly heavy construction work on railroads and fortifications.

Women could not serve legally in the armies, but about four hundred Joans of Arc entered the ranks by posing as men. Authorities exposed most of these ruses, often when the women suffered wounds that required hospital care. Some women, however, managed the subterfuge for several years, even through the end of the war. "We discovered last week a soldier who turned out to be a girl," a shocked Indiana private recorded in his diary. "She had already been in service for 21 months and was twice wounded. Maybe she would have remained undiscovered for a long time if she hadn't fainted. She was given a warm bath which gave the secret away." Scholars believe the majority of these female recruits enlisted from the purest motives: patriotism, a sense of adventure, or, occasionally, to be near husbands who had enlisted. However, not a few women used their places in ranks to serve, sometimes for a profit, the physical needs of male comrades. One Union general was shocked to learn that one of his "men," a sergeant no less, had been delivered of a baby, "in violation of all military law and of army regulations."

The overwhelming majority of northern and southern recruits volunteered enthusiastically for service, particularly in the early months of the war, when northern and southern patriotism, fired by the heated oratory of politicians, reached fever pitch. Still, not a few fellows found their way to recruiting depots only after being pushed by the questioning glances of neighbors, disdainful jeers of uniformed swains, and resounding haughtiness of fair maids. A northern recruit marveled in his diary, "If a fellow wants to go with a girl now he had better enlist. The girls sing 'I am Bound to be a Soldier's Wife or Die an Old Maid.' " An Alabama lad who seemed particularly reluctant to place himself in harm's way suffered a stinging rebuke from his fiancée. Threatening to break their engagement, his darling sent him a package containing a skirt, a petticoat, and a note. The note commanded: "Wear these or volunteer." Most recruits required no such prompting. Not until 1862, a full year after the war began, did the Confederate States supplement enlistments with conscription; the United States did not draft men until 1863. Even then, conscription supplied only 20 percent of the fighting forces.

Young men determined to enlist made their way to a recruiting office in the nearest town. Most recruits, North and South, enlisted in one of the many regiments raised by their respective states for national service. The "Regulars" of the United States Army remained a tiny portion of the North's assembled forces throughout the war. The Confederacy had no regular army as such. Its entire military force consisted of state regiments, militias, and home guards. "With a nervous tremor convulsing my whole system, and my heart thumping like muffled drumbeats," recalled a lad about to enlist in a Massachusetts regiment, "I stood before the door of the recruiting office and, before turning the knob to enter, read and re-read the advertisement for recruits posted thereon." Excellent opportunities for "travel and promotion," declared the poster. Promises of good pay (eleven dollars a month), good companions, and unparalleled opportunities for glory, perhaps even fame, convinced the youth to enlist. He never suspected that one out of five recruits would be dead in four years. Following a cursory medical examination by an army surgeon, the recruit pledged allegiance to his country, swore to obey all orders and the articles of war, and mustered in for a three-year hitch.

New infantry recruits—the most typical common soldiers— quickly learned that army life meant organization. As they arrived at their local training camps, recruits found themselves thrust into a bewildering array of different-sized military units. They felt like minnows being swallowed by larger fish, which, in turn, were swallowed by still larger fish. And "swallowed" describes the process aptly. Recruits were first assigned to fifty-man platoons. Two platoons, they learned, formed a company, and ten companies formed a regiment. Both company and regiment served vital roles in the new soldier's life. The company became his military family. It provided him with his closest friends and served as the focus of training and daily routine. He marched in company formation, slept in a company bivouac, ate in a company mess, received punishments for minor offenses from his company commander. Company comradery would prove essential to discipline in combat. Stephen Crane called it a "subtle battle brotherhood," a "mysterious fraternity born of the smoke and danger of death." Companies formed the heart of the brotherhood.

The regiment served as a soldier's strongest link to home and preserved his identity as a Virginian or a Tar Heel, a Hoosier or a Buckeye. Regiments frequently designed their own distinctive insignia or adopted distinctive nicknames. Most regiments carried identifiable battle flags, generally handmade by the women of their neighborhood and presented to the regiment in emotional ceremonies as the boys marched off to war. Regiments also segregated most racial and ethnic groups. All blacks and most Indians fought in separated units, although commanded by white officers. Immigrants frequently fought in distinctive Irish, French, or German regiments. Sometimes a collage of ethnic groups united in a single regiment, as in the Louisiana unit that boasted thirty-seven different nationalities. Whatever their race or nationality, most recruits developed fierce loyalties to their regiments. Most men felt the same as a sergeant in the 1st Minnesota Infantry: "I would rather be a private in this regiment than a captain in any that I know of." Eventually, once their regiments were shipped to "the front," recruits assumed their places in brigades (composed of four regiments), divisions (three or four brigades), corps (two or more divisions), and armies (two or more corps).

Recruits next received their equipment, starting with the distinguishing mark of a soldier: his uniform. Uniforms varied in comfort, quality, and appearance. "My trousers were two long by three or four inches," complained one private, "the flannel shirt was coarse and unpleasant, too large at the neck and two short elsewhere. . . . The overcoat," he continued, "made me feel like a little nib of corn amid a preponderance of husk." Equally distracting was the variety of uniforms, "as various as the cities and states from which they came," reported General William T. Sherman. Some regiments sought an esprit de corps by issuing uniforms of their own design. Many militia units, particularly those that had been organized before the war, already had their own uniforms and refused to relinquish them. Consequently, northern regiments and militia companies sometimes wore gray uniforms while Confederates wore blue. At least a dozen differently styled hats could be spotted. Gaudiest of all were the "Zouave" regiments, which outfitted their men in uniforms patterned after the French Zouaves: with tasseled caps, or fezzes; short braided jackets; bright-colored vests; sashes; baggy pantaloons; and white leggings. It all produced a most brilliant spectacle, but left friend and foe alike thoroughly confused.

Each infantryman carried a knapsack stuffed with extra clothing, toilet articles, sewing kit, personal items (stationery, photographs, tobacco), and occasionally extra ammunition. Solidly folded and strapped around the top and sides of the knapsack were two woolen blankets and an oiled ground cloth. The bundle weighed from fifteen to twenty-five pounds, and an infantryman who had seen much campaigning soon discarded most of it. Few soldiers carried extra clothing after the first year of the war. They stuffed essential personal items into pockets. A single blanket, rolled lengthwise, covered by the ground cloth, and worn looped across shoulder and chest, accounted for the remaining original equipment. Haversacks, worn slung over a shoulder and across the chest, carried personal rations and eating utensils. Canteens, if not tucked inside the haversack, were worn in a fashion similar to the haversack. A cartridge box, percussion cap pouch, and bayonet scabbard hung from a leather belt buckled at the waist. Bayonets, more important than muskets as weapons in earlier wars, seldom drew blood in the Civil War. Rebs and Yanks used them more often as entrenching tools, can openers, and roasting spits. Most infantrymen in both armies shouldered either a Springfield or Enfield rifled musket. Both weapons were muzzle loaders, .58 and .577 caliber, respectively.

Once outfitted, soldiers settled down to the serious business of selecting their officers. Strange as it seems, privates in both armies generally elected their own company officers (lieutenants and captains). Some regiments elected all noncommissioned and commissioned officers, from corporals to colonels. The results could be chaotic. Some elections became mere popularity contests that resulted in the promotion of poor disciplinarians and inept leaders. In other instances, where new officers took their jobs too seriously, men grumbled about how rank had turned Tom or Henry into an old so-and-so.

This startling democratic process inevitably led some recruits to underestimate the importance of rank and discipline in their new lives. Discovering the truth could be a shock. One private, after his "needlessly fussy" sergeant had put the company through a grueling morning of drill, suggested that the boys be allowed to rest for a while. The recruit's audacious proposal cost him an extra hour of drill, but he had learned a valuable lesson: "I found that suggestions were not as well appreciated in the army as in private life, and that no wisdom was equal to a drill-master's."

Both armies reinforced discipline by instituting three levels of military justice. Company commanders disciplined men for minor infractions of military law and camp rules, including absence from roll calls, neglect of equipment, petty theft, neglect of duty, brawling, drunkenness, and insubordination. Punishment for these crimes generally amounted to nothing worse than extra duty, assignment to disagreeable duties, wearing placards that proclaimed offenses ("I Am a Thief"), carrying a knapsack full of rocks, or confinement to the guardhouse. Absence without leave became the most frequently reported infraction of the war. Slipping out of camp on "French leave," as the soldiers called it, was particularly tempting when armies camped near towns or chicken coops. Insubordination remained a problem through much of the war. Much early insubordination, as in the case of the "needlessly fussy" sergeant, simply betrayed the naïveté of young men adjusting to military life. Some soldiers, however, genuinely despised their officers and resented all authority. An Ohio soldier reacted to a disagreeable order by shouting back at his lieutenant, "You order me! You aint worth a pinch of shit!" Another Yankee told yet another lieutenant, "You kiss my arse, you God damned louse." Other officers heard themselves referred to as "dogs," "skunks," "greenhorns," and "whore-house pimps."

Courts-martial dispensed higher levels of justice. In regimental courts-martial, a board of three officers delivered judgments on more serious versions of the cases heard at company level, including extended absence without leave, threatening an officer, and theft. Hard labor, reduced pay, reduced rations, and more painful physical punishments could be ordered by the tribunal. Among physical punishments, hanging by the thumbs with toes barely touching the ground gained universal use, as did "riding the horse," which meant straddling a suspended log for hours at a time. General courts-martial, conducted by five to thirteen officers at brigade, division, or higher levels, heard cases for all capital crimes, including murder, rape, treason, desertion, cowardice, striking a superior, and sleeping on sentry duty. Courts could punish these crimes with imprisonment, hard labor, forfeiture of pay, dishonorable discharge, or death.

Of the tens of thousands of men disciplined during the war, only a tiny fraction suffered execution. Confederate records are incomplete, but federal files list 267 executions (mostly by firing squad, a few by hanging) in the Union army. More men than that received death penalties, but many of the condemned had their sentences reduced by higher authorities, usually to the relief of all involved. Over half of the men executed were deserters; murder ranked a distant second. Executions, however, served not only to punish the wicked but to warn the innocent. Entire regiments stood in formation to witness the death of comrades. The scene usually made a lasting impression. "I saw a site today that made me feel mity Bad," testified an Alabamian; "I saw a man shot for deserting there was twenty fore Guns shot at him they shot him all to pease."

Drill and camp routine supplemented the discipline of military law. Most recruits suffered only cursory drill at their receiving depots. Once at the front, with the enemy perhaps only a few dozen miles away, the pace quickened. "Right face," "left face," "inspection arms," "shoulder arms," "carry arms," "quick time march," "right about march," on and on it went. The procedure for loading and firing rifles alone included nine precise movements that companies repeated over and over again. "We are almost drilled to Death now," complained a Pennsylvanian to his friend back home; "My Dear Boy, Playing Soldier and Soldiering in reality is two very different things I can assure you." Ceaseless drum and bugle calls vibrated through camps, telling men when to wake up, when to eat, when to rest, when to fall in, when to fall out, when to sleep. Even Sunday, grieved the pious, was not entirely a day of rest. Sundays usually meant inspections of personnel and equipment. Not until after their midday meal could soldiers attend religious services or otherwise relax. Complained a Georgian: "A private soldier is nothing more than a slave and is often treated worse."

The average enlisted man's day in camp, where he spent fifty days to every one day in battle, went something like this. Bugles sounded at dawn, summoning men to the first of several daily roll calls. Men then had a half hour to wash, shave, or fall back into their blankets before another bugle call summoned them to breakfast. Bugles next announced sick call, with all respondents to be inspected by the regimental surgeon. Men without ailments carried out their first fatigue details of the day, most often cleaning their quarters and company grounds, chopping firewood, and hauling water. At 8 A.M., each company sent a guard detail to regimental headquarters to serve for the ensuing twenty-four hours. The remainder of the company fell in for drill, bayonet practice, or some other bit of military routine. These exercises lasted until the noon meal. A brief rest period— thirty to sixty minutes—was allowed after eating before the men fell in for more drill or target practice. At 4 P.M., sergeants ordered men to brush off their uniforms, polish their brass, black their boots, and clean their weapons in preparation for evening "retreat," which included personal inspection, tent inspection, another roll call, and evening parade. Supper followed the parade, and free time was allowed after supper until "tattoo" ordered men to their final roll call of the day shortly after dark. At 10:30 P.M., "taps" commanded lights out and an official end to the day.

The regimentation and monotony of these days in camp quickly eroded earlier attractions—real and imagined—of army life. Pretty local girls and sweethearts no longer brightened the soldier's weekends as they had at camps back home. The men had frequently traveled long distances from home, just as the recruiting posters had promised, but their journeys had not been very exciting or comfortable. Recruits found no glory in drilling, blacking boots, sewing uniforms, chopping wood, washing dishes, or any of their other humdrum daily chores. Meager wages did little to boost spirits. Union pay jumped early in the war to thirteen dollars a month and would eventually reach sixteen dollars. Confederate privates earned twenty dollars by mid-1864. However, severe inflation (particularly in the Confederacy) and irregular pay (sometimes months in arrears) wiped out any apparent gains.

Whether in camp or on the march, the average soldier spent an inordinate amount of time thinking about food. Food became his principal topic of conversation, the essence of his dreams, and the constant subject of letters home. Both northern and southern governments required an impressive allowance of food for their fighting men. Daily per-man quotas included twelve ounces of pork or bacon, twenty ounces of beef, twenty-two ounces of soft bread or flour, and twenty ounces of corn-meal or sixteen ounces of "hardtack" (flour and water crackers, two to three inches square and nearly a half inch thick). Additionally, each company was supposed to receive daily thirty pounds of potatoes, fifteen pounds of peas or beans, ten pounds of rice or hominy, eight to ten pounds of coffee, fifteen pounds of sugar, and specified amounts of tea, pepper, vinegar, and molasses. Unhappily, though not surprisingly, these standards proved nearly impossible to maintain once the fighting started. Early in the war, soldiers most often complained about the quality of food dished out by company cooks. "Our boys threaten a riot every day for the bad beef and spoiled bread issued to us," warned a Wisconsin soldier. As the war dragged on, however, quantity, not quality, became the soldier's principal gripe. "Some days we live first rate, and the next we dont have half enough," explained a Yankee private. "The boys say that our *grub* is enough to make a *mule* desert," wailed an

Illinois soldier, "and a *hog* wish he had never been born. . . .
Hard bread, bacon and coffee is all we draw." A loyal Reb
confessed that he would rather face Yankee bullets than army
chow. "If I ever lose my patriotism, and the 'secesh' spirit dies
out," he warned, "then you may know the 'Commissary' is at
fault."

"Hard" bread, generally in the form of hardtack, and coffee
became the universal staples of both armies. Most soldiers
found hardtack impossible to eat without first soaking it in
grease, coffee, soup, or water. Frying it in grease also helped.
Many soldiers so despised the crackers that they refused to
draw their ration, but the general reaction to hardtack came
from a Virginia soldier who, while admitting the crackers were
"notoriously poor eating," insisted, "When on the march and
pressed for time, a piece of solid fat pork and a dry cracker was
passable or luscious, as the time was long or short since the last
meal." Coffee, the other staple, ranked as the most popular
form of nourishment in either army. It became the oil that
lubricated the machine of war; hostilities could not have continued without it. When the federal naval blockade made genuine coffee a rarity down South, desperate Rebs improvised by
brewing parched corn, sweet potatoes, peanuts, and rye.

Luckily, American soldiers did not rely solely on their governments for provisions. Family members and friends sometimes mailed packages of delicacies to the front. Fishing and
hunting expeditions, undertaken both by individual soldiers
during their free time and by official regimental parties, supplemented the commissary. Foraging through the countryside produced all variety of livestock, fruits, vegetables, and cured
meats. Official foraging parties were supposed to provide re-
ceipts to farmers who "contributed" to army kitchens, but the
formality was frequently overlooked, and any number of unof-
ficial parties made this method of procurement little more than
a species of theft. Because most of the war was fought on southern soil, southern farmers and stock raisers suffered most from

foraging, but Confederate raids into Illinois, Indiana, Ohio, Pennsylvania, and Maryland gave Rebs adequate opportunities to practice their foraging skills. Indeed, few southern orchards, cornfields, vegetable gardens, chicken coops, pig pens, smoke-houses, or beehives remained safe from ravenous Confederate troops either.

Army sutlers became the surest legal means for private soldiers to supplement their diets. Sutlers were civilian merchants who, by permission of regimental commanders, sold all manner of foodstuffs and sundries to the troops. Pipe and chewing tobacco, cigars, stationery, socks, underwear, books, and writing pens lined the well-stocked shelves of sutler tents and wagons. Liquor was the only forbidden item. The sutler's biggest profits by far came from the sale of food, particularly sweets, fresh fruits, onions, canned goods, and dairy products. Apples, oranges, lemons, and raisins sold out quickly, as did candies, cakes, pies, ginger ale, and other "soft" drinks. The only draw-back of the sutler was price. Some merchandise, especially canned goods and dairy products, cost more than the average private could easily afford. Even early in the war, before inflation became a serious problem, federal sutlers sold butter at one dollar a pound, cheese at fifty cents a pound, condensed milk at seventy-five cents a can. The most affordable items—usually twenty-five cents apiece—were molasses cookies, cakes, and a mysterious pastry known only as "sutler's pies." "I have yet to see the soldier who can furnish a correct analysis of what they were made from," insisted one veteran of this last-named item, but he conceded that "the pies went down by hundreds." Not surprisingly, Confederate soldiers saw far fewer sutlers' wagons than did Billy Yank. Sutlers were businessmen, and they saw precious little profit in selling goods to an army where, by 1864, it took fifty Confederate dollars to buy a chicken. Johnny Reb most often contented himself with purchasing cider, pies, and cakes from local residents along the roadside.

A soldier's living quarters depended on the season, proximity of the enemy, and permanence of his camp. While on the march and during multi-day battles, soldiers frequently slept wrapped in blankets. More permanent, non-winter camps gave soldiers an opportunity to erect tents, some of them—the spacious Sibley tents—large enough to sleep twelve men. In winter, soldiers often constructed one-room log cabins, complete with fireplaces, wooden floors, cracker-box furniture, and cots. Less elaborate two-man dugouts could be fashioned from canvas and logs. Crude as these winter shelters may have been, they provided incomparable luxury when compared to the common soldier's quarters during most of the year.

Union and Confederate soldiers devised countless amusements to while away quiet moments in camp and on campaign. A hard day of soldiering always seemed less tedious, less wearisome, even less dangerous when a fellow could relax by a campfire with his mates. "The moon arises," explained a New York recruit. "Every tent becomes a little illuminated pyramid. Cooking-fires burn bright along the alleys. The boys lark, sing, shout, do all these merry things that make the entertainment of volunteer service." Checkerboards and decks of cards appeared as men settled down. Here and there friends huddled to discuss new rumors about their destination or the enemy's position. Some men darned socks, mended shirts, washed underwear. Serious-minded folk organized army chapters of fraternal societies and benevolent associations. The Freemasons, in particular, had extensive networks in both northern and southern armies. Introspective chaps savored the moment to read a newspaper (maybe a month old), write a letter home, drink a cup of "Rio," or quietly smoke a pipe and gaze at the stars.

Music proved to be the single most important means of warding off homesickness, buoying spirits, combating boredom, and relieving the weariness of a campaign. Soldiers whistled and sang while performing mindless chores around the camp. They joined in rollicking—sometimes ribald—route-step choruses as they tramped through the countryside. And, of course, men joined in songfests around evening campfires. Accompanists frequently appeared at the evening sing-alongs armed with an old harmonica, fiddle, or banjo. Sentimental songs about home became the most popular singing fare. "Home, Sweet Home" led the hit parade in both armies, followed by such tearjerkers as "Lorena" and "Annie Laurie"; but Union troops seem to have been nearly as fond of patriotic tunes, such as "John Brown's Body," "Yankee Doodle," and "The Battle-Cry of Freedom." Music occasionally inspired dancing. Some companies staged mock balls in which they observed the niceties of a formal dance but with all the "women" dressed in trousers. "From many of the [company] streets," reported a Wisconsin soldier, "the sound of a violin in the last agonies of the 'Arkansas Traveler' or the 'Campbells are coming' greets the ear and following the sound one finds a ring formed and a merry sett 'going in' on a quadrille." Other companies and regiments formed glee clubs to entertain officers and men, and most regiments and brigades had bands. While in camp, the bands performed evening concerts of popular and classical pieces for the troops and local residents. "I don't know what we should have done without our band," swore a Massachusetts soldier. No less an authority than General Robert E. Lee concluded, "I don't believe we can have an army without music."

Theatrical performances of one kind or another occupied the time of some soldiers. Budding thespians and other entertainers organized minstrel shows and dramatic productions. Some shows proved to be quite elaborate, performed not just for the camp but for local civilians and staged in local theaters. Sometimes the occasions served as benefit performances, proceeds going to crippled soldiers and impoverished civilians. Impromptu comedy routines were part of evening camp fare, too. "Brown . . . is a perfect mimic," recorded one soldier of his company's campfire clown, "facile, quick, good looking . . . has

a keen sense of the ridiculous & a good fellow for fun generally.
. . . I haven't laughed so much since I came in the army."
   Formal sports and games enlivened camp life, too. Companies sometimes challenged each other to shooting matches, foot
races, sack races, greased pig competitions, wrestling and boxing matches. Team sports, usually football, cricket, or baseball,
aroused spirited participation. Of course, some improvisation
was required. In most baseball games, for instance, a farmer's
fence rail or a stout stick served as the bat; a yarn-wrapped
walnut might be the "ball." Such compromises rarely dampened the players' enthusiasm. They raced about the field "just
like school boys." Tenpins proved a popular game where limited space curtailed more expansive activities. Impromptu
sports were also devised. A Union soldier wrote home to tell
how one company engaged in a great "rabbit hunt." Conduct-
ing the hunt "on strictly military principles," a few men moved
ahead as skirmishers. The rest of the company then fanned out
to beat the brush and flush out its prey. Whenever a bunny
broke from cover, the entire hunting party howled in triumph
and leaped to encircle it, flankers pinching in from the sides,
skirmishers seeking to turn the hare toward the main body. The
rabbit, "bewildered by the tumult on every side, would double
back at each point where a soldier opposed him, until his retreat
was effectively cut off, and he was either caught alive or felled
by a blow of a stick." The entire episode was punctuated by
roars of laughter and exaggerated cursing as soldiers tumbled
into bushes, tripped over each other, and flailed at their agile
prey. Everyone had a good time except the rabbit.
   Not a few soldiers craved nothing more than the sight, scent,
and sound of a female. Occasionally, local girls or the female
relations of officers visited the camps. Only infrequently did
private soldiers get close enough to these ladies to speak with
them, but the very presence of skirts and parasols was electrify-
ing. "Who could describe the effect of their appearance in
camp!" exclaimed a romantically inclined Virginian. "They pro-

duced conflict in the soldier's breast. They looked so clean, they were so gentle, they were so different from all around them, they were so attractive, they were so agreeable, and sweet, and fresh, and happy, that the poor fellows would have liked above all things to have gotten very near to them and have heard their kind words." Other men, far from content with looking, sought sexual gratification among the looser women in camp. Early in the war, numerous camp followers hired their services as cooks and laundresses to the armies. As campaigning became more rigorous and discipline more rigid, their numbers declined. Most often, then, soldiers had to seek out women while on furlough or in clandestine meetings without official leave. All evidence suggests they found plenty of frolicsome wenches. "The state of the morals is quite as low as the soil," complained one Reb in Alabama, "almost all the women are given to whore-dom & are the ugliest, sallowfaced, shaggy headed, bare footed dirty wretches you ever saw." The war had "demoralized everybody" along the Georgia-Tennessee border, regretted another Confederate. Young girls smoked, drank whiskey, and chewed tobacco, and "almost half of the women in the vicinity of the army, married and unmarried, are lost to all virtue."

Men encamped near large towns and cities naturally had the best opportunities to enjoy female companionship, whatever their choice in women. They could meet utterly respectable ladies at church socials, Sanitary Commission fairs, and other civilized occasions. If a man sought more than polite conversation, he headed for the fleshpots. Every town had them. The capitals of the warring nations, Washington and Richmond, had the most impressive array of bawdy houses, gambling dens, and gin houses. "Go to the Capitol Square any afternoon," reported a shocked Confederate from Richmond, "and you may see these women promenading up and down the shady walks jostling respectable ladies into the gutters." Washington, where larger numbers of men and a greater abundance of cash made prostitution even more profitable, was worse. Houses of ill fame occupied whole blocks along the south side of Pennsylvania Avenue. Soldier clientele christened their favorite houses with such colorful names as the "Wolf's Den" (operated by a Mrs. Wolf), the "Haystack," and the "Bake Oven." "I had a gay old time I tell you," reported a New England soldier after visiting Washington; "Lager Beer and . . . in the evening Horizontal Refreshments or in Plainer words Riding a Dutch gal." Memphis during federal occupation earned a reputation as the Gomorrah of the West. "Memphis," claimed an Ohio soldier, "can boast of being one of the first places of female prostitution on the continent. Virtue is scarcely known within the limits of the city." If one judges from the cases of venereal disease in the armies, more than a few men took advantage of the situation. Statistics for the Confederate army are incomplete, but Union records reveal that eighty-two out of every one thousand men suffered from some form of V.D.

To purge debauched souls, both armies experienced bouts of religious enthusiasm. "Many of the openly sinful are growing more temperate and reverent in their conversation and regard for religious things," rejoiced a soldier in Robert E. Lee's army. "There is less of cursing and profligacy, and much less of card playing in our Company now than formerly. The voice of prayer is often heard in camp among the men, and many commands now have regular, or at least, occasional preaching." Both armies were overwhelmingly Protestant, and the vast majority of Protestants belonged to evangelical denominations. Each regiment had a chaplain to conduct religious services and tend to private spiritual needs. Even without chaplains, religious soldiers held prayer meetings of their own. Nondenominational religious organizations, such as the American Tract Society and the Bible Society of the Confederate States, distributed Bibles, hymnals, Scripture readings, and moral tracts to soldiers. Many tracts were prepared especially for the soldiers. Such titles as *The Gambler's Balance Sheet*, *Satan's Bait*, *The Widow's Son Enlisting*, and *A Mother's Parting Words to*

*Her Soldier Boy* warned recruits about the temptations of camp life and beseeched them to fight as Christians in a noble cause.

Singing hymns became the most popular expression of religious enthusiasm in either army. Particular favorites, like "Sweet Hour of Prayer," "Rock of Ages," and "Amazing Grace," reinforced the values and exhortations of the tracts. "Almost nightly now," recorded one soldier in 1865, "before the tattoo is sounded, we hear the voice of song in our camp, religious and revival songs and hymns." Black soldiers, who saw the martial conflict as a holy war to free their race, were particularly vocal. "It used to seem to me," observed a white officer, "that never, since Cromwell's time, had there been soldiers in whom the religious element held such a place." Many former slaves enlisted in the Union army, and most of them shared the feelings of a Louisiana recruit who insisted, " 'Fore I would be a slave 'gain, I would fight till de last drop of blood was gone. I has 'cluded to fight for my liberty." Consequently, fervent prayer meetings and hymn sings became routine parts of Negro camp life. The black soldier's favorite hymns, including "What Make Old Satan Follow Me So," "Hold Your Light on Canaan's Shore," and "Wrestling Jacob," expressed his determination to fight for his people.

Outbreaks of evangelical revivalism expressed the most fervent brand of religious enthusiasm. The revivals, which began in 1863, occurred almost exclusively in the Confederate armies, and for several reasons. Most Confederate soldiers grew up in communities with strong evangelical traditions, where periodic revivals were common. Then, too, Confederate spirits began to sink in 1863, particularly after the twin military disasters at Gettysburg and Vicksburg. Confederates needed bucking up, and religious revivalism was a good way to do it. Coincidentally, southern preachers and religious societies began concentrated efforts to distribute religious literature and to win converts in 1863. The revivals, to a large degree, became natural responses to this spiritual assault. Finally, as the war dragged ponderously on, and as more and more men fell in battle, survivors became more aware of their own mortality. Luck and God's grace had brought them through the war so far, but no one could tell how long either blessing would last. It was best to be prepared. "All along the foot of Missionary Ridge we preached almost every night to crowded assemblies," recalled one Confederate chaplain, "and many precious souls were brought to God. . . . The soldiers erected stands, improvised seats, and even built log churches, where they worshiped God. . . . In all my life, perhaps, I never witnessed more displays of God's power in the awakening and conversion of sinners."

Whether he was prepared to meet his Maker or not, the most important brute fact of a soldier's life was the possibility of being killed, and, as the war continued, Billy Yank and Johnny Reb learned that there was more than one way to die. As best we can tell, close to 690,000 American soldiers died in the Civil War. Only about 160,000 of these men died on the battlefield, with another 80,000 later dying from wounds. As many as 40,000 perished in accidents, but far and away the largest number, about 425,000, died of sickness and disease. Modern notions about diet, sanitation, and personal hygiene were woefully lacking in both armies. Germs and bacteria had not been heard of. The primitive brand of hygiene practiced by doctors in hospitals and surgical tents produced far higher losses among the wounded than would be the case today, but even more shocking was the number of lives claimed by typhoid, malaria, dysentery, diarrhea, and pneumonia. Regimental camps became breeding grounds for disease. Camp streets were littered with refuse, food, and waste, some of it in advanced stages of decomposition. Flies, mosquitoes, fleas, and lice swarmed everywhere. Odors from piles of garbage, entrails of slaughtered animals, and human excretions smothered the air. Every camp had latrines, or "sinks," but these shallow trenches were shockingly near living quarters and generally left uncovered. In any case, men tended to relieve themselves wherever convenient.

Typhoid (known as "camp fever") and diarrhea became the biggest killers, the former claiming some 50,000 lives, the latter taking at least that many. "Typhoid fever is striking our men a heavy blow," revealed a Union officer; "233 of my regiment now down, and dying daily." "Tiford fever is Rageing here verry much," confirmed an Illinois private, "their has been several deaths of it . . . they hardley ever get over it." Diarrhea and dysentery disabled more often than they killed. Nearly every man in ranks suffered at least mildly from the "quick-step," as diarrhea was known; but the number of acute and chronic cases (1.1 million and 170,000, respectively) suggests the seriousness of the problem. The number of cases of acute and chronic dysentery totaled about 260,000. There seemed to be no escape. One of Robert E. Lee's men complained, "It is a very rare thing to find a man in this army who has not got the diorreah." From the other side of the battle line came this lament: "Sick with diarhea. Sickest I ever was. My bowels moved 18 times in 3 hours."

Men who escaped death on the battlefield or in hospital still ran the risk of "accidental" death. Some deaths were genuine accidents, generally caused by carelessness. Early in the war, men occasionally died while engaged in horseplay with "un-loaded" weapons. Loading and unloading ammunition could be hazardous, too. A group of federal soldiers, mistaking a railroad car full of "torpedoes," or sea mines, for barrels of pork, pro-ceeded to roll the mines down a ramp. As the second barrel rolled crashing into the first, an explosion heard twenty miles away rocked the platform. Not much remained of the forty men who died. Friends scraped together the remains and buried them in hardtack boxes. Pickets occasionally shot and killed their own men, the most celebrated instance being the death of Confederate general Thomas "Stonewall" Jackson. Other sol-diers died at the hands of their comrades, but not by accident. Unpopular officers, men who cheated at cards, and camp thieves became unmourned victims of assassination. Union loot-ers and foragers had to beware of outraged southern civilians. A resident of Culpeper County, Virginia, who discovered a Yankee soldier rummaging in his deceased wife's dressing bureau, split the vandal's skull with a wrought-iron shovel. With the help of his son, the man dragged the lifeless form to a nearby field and buried it in an unmarked and "dishonored" grave.

Ultimately, the average soldier joined the army to fight, but very few men marched into battle without being scared out of their wits. Civil War soldiers referred to the combat experience as "seeing the elephant," an expression derived from the nineteenth-century custom of allowing boys to water circus elephants in exchange for free admission to the big top. Those awesome elephants were the mightiest creatures a boy could imagine; one false move and he would be crushed. For boys transformed into soldiers, zipping bullets and screaming shells replaced the elephants; they became the price one paid for seeing "the show" of battle. The first time was always the worst. "The shock to the nerves was indefinable," recalled one veteran; "one stands, as it were, on the brink of eternity as he goes into action." "Oh! God," exclaimed a Reb, "I never saw the like. The men fell like grass. . . . I saw men running at full speed stop suddenly and fall on their faces with the brains scattered all around; others with legs or arms cut off." "The zip of the rifle balls has a peculiar stinging sound," explained yet another veteran, "and the shriek of bursting shells causes one to dodge instinctively; but I think that each soldier is impressed with the belief that he will not be struck. . . ."

To be struck and not instantly killed became the fear of some soldiers. To be downed, unable to move, but conscious of the carnage all around brought new horrors. "Now you are helpless," explained a Union soldier; "the bullets still fly over and about you—you no longer are able to shift your position or seek shelter. Every bullet as it strikes near you is a new terror." If not badly wounded, a man tried to crawl back toward his lines.

Others lay in anguish. "I am alone with my thoughts," recalled another soldier; "I think of home, of the seriousness of my condition; I see myself a cripple for life . . . and all the time shells are shrieking and minié bullets whistling over and about me. The tongue becomes parched, there is no water to quench it; you cry, 'Water! Water!' and pray for night, that you can be carried off the field."

Military life witnessed some important changes between 1865 and 1877. The most visible change occurred in the size and composition of the army. Confederate armies, of course, disbanded, but even the United States Army, by 1867, had been reduced to 54,000 men. Ten years later, the Regular army mustered barely 27,000. So far as we know, no women entered the new army. Only four black regiments survived the war, two less than the number authorized by Congress, and they remained segregated, poorly equipped, and commanded by white officers. Foreign-born immigrants constituted fully one-half of the new army. Irishmen, supplying 20 percent of the whole, led the way; Germans ranked second, with 12 percent. Most contemporaries agreed that these post-1865 recruits were significantly less honest, reliable, loyal, intelligent, and physically fit than Civil War soldiers. The new recruits enlisted not to defend some noble cause but because they were hungry, craved adventure, or had been given a choice between the army and jail. They were generally an unruly bunch to start with, and their distance from civilization, so often on the frontier, compounded the problem. The new army, charged a New York newspaper, was filled with "bummers, loafers, and foreign paupers," not to mention an uncomfortable number of criminals, perverts, drunkards, and toughs.

The newspaper exaggerated the situation, yet it seemed that the army did precious little to enlist more industrious citizens. A private's pay reverted to the 1861 level of $13 a month in 1871, besides being issued in greenbacks that had only 60 to 85 percent of the purchasing power of hard cash. Vigorous discipline, Spartan living conditions, and civilian contempt for America's "foreign" army placed a stigma on soldiers. Most recruiting officers, situated in northern cities, drew heavily on the urban poor. The bulk of enlistees identified themselves as unskilled laborers, many of whom had enlisted only because they could find no other work. The army's desertion rate became a national scandal. On average, over 18 percent of the army deserted each year between 1866 and 1877, and for several years after the big pay reduction of 1871 the rate climbed to over 30 percent. That contrasted sharply with the 10 to 12 percent desertion rate of the Civil War years. Of those men who completed their five-year enlistments, only about 1,000 reenlisted each year, giving the army a professional cadre of no more than 7,000 men at any one time.

In a sense, new recruits served in two different armies between 1865 and 1877. One army, stationed in the South, served the Congress and the Republican party as a political tool to "reconstruct" former Rebels. This army lived very much as the wartime army had lived. A second army, the Indian-fighting army, served in the West, and its daily life differed in several important ways from the Union army of 1861–65.

The assignment given the Indian-fighting army was formidable. A few thousand men—starting with just 5,000 in 1866—had to patrol hundreds of thousands of square miles and protect scattered white settlements and wagon trains from tens of thousands of hostiles. Men rode off to the Indian wars—for cavalry played a more important role than infantry in guarding the sprawling western territory—with even less training than the recruits of 1861. Especially glaring were deficiencies in horsemanship and marksmanship. Many "cavalrymen" went west without ever having mounted a horse, and economy permitted only a handful of cartridges per man each year for target practice. Even in so critical a campaign as George Armstrong Custer's ill-fated march to the Little Big Horn, one lieutenant complained, "Many of the men had never been on a horse until

that campaign, and they lost control of their horses when galloping into line." A sergeant in Custer's regiment asserted,
"The new men had very little training. They were poor horse-
men and would fire at random. They were brave enough, but
had not the time or opportunity to make soldiers. . . . Most of
the time they were on some other duty that gave them no
chance to learn how to fight." Yet this was one of the best
cavalry regiments in the army.

The routines, uniforms, living conditions, weapons, and entertainments of the Indian-fighting army did not change dramatically from the Civil War years. Soldiers carried
breech-loading Springfield carbines and Colt pistols, both of
them .45 caliber, instead of muzzle-loaded rifles. They usually
slept in permanent barracks instead of tents. The isolation of
western posts probably produced more alcohol abuse and offered men fewer opportunities to enjoy female company. A
sharper degree of social stratification within the army changed
the relationship between enlisted men and officers, the change
prompted, in part, by the presence of many officers' and enlisted men's families on western posts. Similarly, wider gaps
between the social origins and education of officers and enlisted
men meant that they had less in common. Officers were more
clearly "gentlemen," in contrast to the laborers and drifters
who filled their companies and regiments. In any case, officers
and men became more class—even caste—conscious, and the
rules governing their respective places became more uniform.

Perhaps the single biggest change came in the nature of the
fighting. For one thing, the frequency and duration of combat
diminished. Very few battles with the Indians lasted more than
a day. Casualties were usually light. Similarly, soldiers fought
fewer pitched battles. Indians avoided large detachments of
soldiers. They made war as raiders, from ambush, and in hit-
and-run attacks. Most fighting took the form of quick brushes
and skirmishes. In order to track down and confront their elu-
sive foe in vast western spaces, some military units spent as

much as half the year in the field. Necessarily, the army launched numerous winter campaigns to catch Indians napping in winter encampments. Consequently, the Indian-fighting army had to be more self-sufficient on its campaigns than Civil War armies. For infantrymen, this meant going out in "heavy marching order," the regulation burden of pack, rations, and weapons weighing fifty pounds. Cavalrymen carried an equal load, plus ten to fifteen pounds of grain for their horses, but then the horses, not the men, carried the weight. Foraging, other than hunting for local game, was nearly impossible.

When engaging the enemy, combat proved even more terrifying than during the Civil War. The terror came not from the weapons soldiers faced, but from the painted warriors themselves. "War is dreadful anyway," explained an army wife, "but an Indian war is worst of all. They respect no code of warfare, flags of truce. . . . It is like fighting to exterminate wild animals, horrible beasts." These harsh words expressed the feelings of most soldiers and civilians on the frontier. "Sargt. Williams of Co. 'G' got separated from the company and was shot in the head, stripped of his clothing, heart cut out, nose cut off, hacked and split and scalped with 16 arrows shot into his body," reported one soldier's daughter. "It was a horrible sight. Three men had arrows shot into their bodies which could not be removed without first shoving them through and cutting the fastening which held the barb and drawing the shaft back." A few lonely voices called for equitable and sympathetic treatment of the Redman, but such advocates of reason generally lived east of the Mississippi River. "I remember that I ducked my head and tried to dodge bullets which I could hear whizzing through the air," recalled a veteran of Custer's 7th Cavalry. The Battle of the Little Big Horn was his first combat, luckily not as part of Custer's ill-fated portion of the regiment. "I know that for a time," he continued, "I was frightened, and far more so when I got my first glimpse of the Indians riding about in all directions and firing at us and yelling and whooping like incarnate fiends."

Fear of being wounded on an open field likewise acquired a new, more terrifying dimension. Every white person on the frontier had heard stories—some true, others exaggerated—about the brutality of Indians toward white captives, of scalpings and hideous tortures. "When we fought with the Indians we had to fight for our lives," explained one veteran, "because they took no prisoners, or, if they did, only to torture them to death." "As the volume of the Indian fire seemed to increase," elaborated another man, " 'No surrender' was the word passed around the thin skirmish line. Each of us would, if he found it necessary, have blown out his brains rather than fall alive into Indian hands."

# 2

## HOUSES, HOMESTEADS,

## AND HOVELS

M EANWHILE, on the home front, non-soldiers worked, played, and otherwise attended to life's daily chores. Doing so, they found themselves in an array of different settings. The most important of those settings, be it ever so humble, was a person's home, and no one can claim to understand everyday life in the Civil War era without appreciating the diversity of American homes and communities. The single-family dwelling served as the ideal, but large numbers of Americans had to settle for something less. They made compromises by residing in apartments, boardinghouses, and tenements. Even when occupying their own homes, many families had to make do with rough cabins, sod houses, and decrepit shacks. Most soldiers lived in cleaner, more respectable dwellings. Equally important, dwellings could be found in a variety of settings: isolated on endless prairies, buried in busy cities, luxuriating in quiet suburbs, squeezed into company towns, nestled in picturesque villages, or standing proudly on the cultivated acres of thriving farms.

It is unclear how many families actually owned homes before 1890. No national statistics for home ownership exist before that date, and only 48 percent of Americans (37 percent in cities) could claim ownership at that time. Still, there is reason to believe the percentage might have been higher in 1870, before poor European immigrants began flooding American cities in the 1880s. A lower-middle-class family income ranged between $750 and $2,000 per year in the 1870s. The most skilled of the nation's manual laborers earned a little over $1,000. Beyond that level, most wage earners were "white collar" workers. For $750, couples could enjoy the privacy of their own suburban home. A comfortable, five-room cottage (twenty by thirty-eight feet) cost as little as $250, but that price did not include the land. Of course, food (usually half a family's budget), clothing (15 percent), and fuel would have to be paid for, too, and, once purchased, a house required furniture and maintenance. Mortgage terms were not easy either. A substantial down payment and 5 to 7 percent interest on a standard five-year loan required lots of scrimping and possibly help from relatives. Yet growing numbers of skilled manual laborers, clerks, merchants, and professional people seemed willing to make the sacrifice. Commodious, two-story houses, large enough for a family of five, could be purchased for under $10,000 (the upper salary range of the middle classes), and the average price of a home in 1870 was less than half that amount, at least outside large cities.

The size and appearance of a house announced the social position, aspirations, and "character" of its occupants, and the dawn of a "Gilded Age" following the war began a trend toward larger and finer abodes. "There is no country in the world where there are so many large and fine houses, in proportion to the number of inhabitants, as in these United States," asserted an observer in 1865. Not foreseeing the proliferation of grand millionaire mansions yet to come, this critic of the trend saw an increasing number of families earning $2,500 to $8,000 annually trying to rent fine houses for $1,200 to $4,000 or building houses that burdened them with monster debts. "We build our houses mainly for the purpose of being looked on," he lamented. "They are constructed to attract notice and impress the beholder with the idea of the importance of their inhabitants. Eager as we are for the reality of worldly success, we are still more intent upon making a show of it." Foreign visitors to the United States commented on the pretensions of American homeowners. "These houses in Cleveland were very good," admitted an Englishman of that typical midwestern town, "but some of them have been erected with an amount of bad taste that is almost incredible." The visitor marveled at square brick houses decorated by wooden quasi-Greek porticoes and Ionic columns, plain wooden abodes adorned with fancy scrollwork and gingerbread trim under eaves and around windows. "As a rule these [additions] are attached to houses which, without such ornamentation, would be simple, unpretentious, square, roomy residences."

The rage for owning homes is evident in the popular literature of the day. Dozens of "house pattern books," written by American and British architects, flooded the market. Similar guides had been around for many years by the 1860s, but never in such profusion and never with such broad appeal. "There never was a time," verified a prominent art critic of the 1870s, "when so many books written for the purpose of bringing the subject of architecture—its history, its theory, its practice— down to the level of popular understanding were produced as in this time of ours." Each volume offered architectural plans for a variety of different-sized and widely priced middle-class houses, ranging from five-room $500 cottages to twelve-room $18,000 villas. Pattern books also offered tips on proper ventilation, heating, lighting, and sewage systems. Several guides were serialized in popular magazines, like *Harper's Monthly, Harper's Bazar,* and *Scribner's Monthly,* further testimony to their popularity.

Other books and articles addressed specifically to the aspirations of the working classes offered tips on household economy that would allow people with modest yearly incomes to purchase homes. For instance, an 1866 article in *Harper's Monthly* explained how a newlywed clerk earning $2,000 a year (plus $2,000 in savings and a $2,500 loan at 7 percent interest) could purchase and furnish a two-story house in Brooklyn. The plan took into consideration the cost of a modest $500 lot (twenty-five by one hundred feet), moderately priced "cottage" furniture ($1,500), $400 annual payments on his loan, plus all living expenses, including $879.65 for food, $209 for clothing, $46.35 for trolley and ferry fare, $96 for a domestic servant, $12.50 for house insurance (one-half of 1 percent on $2,500), $9 for insurance on furnishings and belongings (three-fifths of 1 percent on $1,500), and $90 property taxes. The $400 annual house payment (with the mortgage paid off in eight years) was only slightly higher than the cost of renting the same house.

Taxes would not have placed an undue burden on most families, although they probably paid more than had their parents. Before the Civil War, the national government had relied primarily on tariffs and the sale of public lands for revenue. The war required new sources of money, eventually supplied by new income taxes, internal excise taxes, and special levies by towns, counties, and states. Many of the new taxes ended with the war, but some remained, and additional postwar taxes—such as increased land taxes—caused Americans to grumble more about their taxes than at any time since the Stamp Act. The loudest protests (mostly from the business community) came against the first national income tax. Initially (in 1861) a 5 percent tax on incomes over $1,000, the income tax fluctuated thereafter between flat and graduated rates (2.5 percent to 5 percent), and with exemptions of $600 to $2,000, until popular pressure forced its repeal in 1872. In any case, no more than 1 percent of the population ever had to pay the hated levy.

Declining construction costs for wood-frame houses also explain the ability of so many families to own houses. Balloon-frame housing (also known as "Chicago" construction, where the technique originated in the 1830s) held the key. In order to eliminate the high cost of skilled craftsmen and reduce the expense of building materials, balloon-frame construction substituted a light wooden frame of two-by-fours fastened with factory-made nails for the traditional foot-square beams augered and joined by mortise, tenon, and wooden pegs or handmade nails. Wall plates, studs, joists, and rafters, all made from thin-sawed timbers, also added to the lightweight construction. Such frame houses cost 40 percent less than square-beam houses, and could be delivered anywhere, promised lumberyards in advertising brochures, by freight wagon, railroad, or steamboat. One Chicago mail-order construction firm advertised everything from $350 three-room houses to $5,000 four-hundred-seat spired churches. Wealthy folk still constructed their houses from heavy timber, brick, and masonry, but less affluent Americans could now afford large, relatively inexpensive houses. Some observers insisted that such prefabricated houses betrayed a want of individuality in the American character. "Most of us prefer to get our houses ready made," scoffed one critic, "builders' planned and shaped on general principles like ready-made clothing, and warranted to be in the latest fashion."

The hard part was to identify the latest fashion. Architecturally, the United States became a Babel of styles during the 1860s and 1870s. Older styles, like Greek Revival, Gothic Revival, Renaissance, and Italian Villa, survived alongside new architectural notions, like Romanesque Revival, Eastlake, Eastern Stick, Second Empire, Château, and, toward the end of the period, Queen Anne. Likewise, interior designs offered a cavalcade of motifs. Renaissance, French, Italian, Asian, Moorish, and Turkish styles offered distinct varieties of furniture, wallpaper, carpeting, and accessories. Among the more conspicuous exterior ornamental touches on newly constructed houses were the wooden brackets, patterned after the Italian Villa style, that buttressed cornices, porches, and eaves. More flamboyant people preferred "gingerbread" scrollwork, carved in thin wood or cut from tin, to decorate rooftops, dormers, eaves, cornices, lattices, and porches. The fashion of painting houses in dark colors—brown, gray, green, and blood red—heightened the gingerbread effect, as did the dark brick and brownstone residences under construction in eastern cities since the 1850s. Economic prosperity, changing values, new building techniques, and a decline in craftsmanship produced such a jumble of exterior and interior styles from the 1860s to the 1890s that one scholar has dubbed this period the "Eclectic Decades."

A typical wood-frame, two-story, middle-class house of the 1860s and 1870s could be divided into three distinct sets of rooms: public rooms, private rooms, and workrooms. Public rooms, including parlors, family rooms, and dining rooms, opened into a hallway—furnished with mirrored hallstand, chairs, and marble-topped table—that ran the length of the first floor. Private rooms, usually located on the second, or "chamber," floor, included bedrooms, bathrooms, and privies. Workrooms included kitchens, pantries, and cellars. Household advisers urged careful planning and arrangement of rooms to provide the highest degree of comfort. "Merchants find the classification of their goods indispensable, or separate rooms for different classes of things," explained one builder with an analogy he thought would appeal to ambitious young homeowners. "And why not this principle equally requisite in a complete house?" By the 1860s, inexpensive factory-made replicas of expensive handmade furniture allowed families to maintain an interior that matched a house's boastful exterior. Similarly, American mills made good-quality wallpaper, carpets, and textiles at reasonable prices. "Taste" in interior decoration had become important, too, so furniture in each room "matched" and represented a coordinated "suite" rather than a hodgepodge of conflicting styles and different woods.

By showcasing a family's best furniture and most valued possessions, the front parlor became the centerpiece of any middle-class house. Yet, unlike most other rooms, front parlors served no "practical" daily function. Rather, families used them to receive visitors, entertain friends, and stage special occasions, most notably weddings and funerals. They regarded their par-

lors, as the word's origins in the French verb *parler* would
suggest, as a place for polite conversation, cordiality, and civiliz-
ing influences. No few words can adequately describe the glorious clutter of a middle-class parlor. "Providing there is space to
move about, without knocking over the furniture," declared
one authority on interior decoration, "there is hardly likely to
be too much in the room." A divan sofa, an overstuffed chair,
and one or more small cushioned chairs provided sitting space.
A marble-topped table, on which families displayed an ornate
Bible, plaster sculpture, or some other decorative piece, generally occupied the center of the room. A bookcase and a small
desk or secretary often stood along the wall. Wood furniture
most likely would be walnut or ash (mahogany or rosewood in
more expensive houses), elaborately carved with a rococo profusion of cartouches, scrolls, and brackets. Cushioned furniture
would be thickly upholstered, often tufted and tasseled, and
covered with mohair or brocaded fabrics. A gas chandelier,
usually with six globes, provided light in cities; kerosene, sperm
oil, or coal oil remained the lighting sources in the countryside.
Town or country, a sturdy, elaborately patterned, wall-to-wall
Brussels carpet (all the rage in the 1860s) added a final touch of
elegance. Diamond or square patterns were the favorite carpet
designs in the 1860s; in the 1870s, floral or geometric floral
designs became the fashion. Walls were papered more often
than painted above their six- to eight-inch baseboards. Families
that could afford a parlor piano or organ (two hundred dollars
and up) had one, and everywhere one encountered pillows,
doilies, assorted knickknacks, wall hangings, more knickknacks,
family photographs, a large, ornately framed mirror, and still
more knickknacks. The colors of all furnishings, whether carpets, furniture, wallpaper, or draperies, were generally dark
(reds, browns, tans), like the house's painted exterior.

Only in homes of the very rich did parlors fail to exact some
price in general household expense, comfort, and convenience.
*Harper's Bazar,* one of the nation's leading women's magazines,

flew into a rage at the amount of money families spent on furnishing their parlors. "Was there ever an American woman who, furnishing a house, did not first lay aside the money for the parlor?" asked one irritated contributor. "A parlor must be," he concluded, "even if after it there comes the deluge." Nor were common folk spared the inconvenience of fashion. "So far as space is concerned," observed a rural critic in 1876, "most people in the country should reverse the order of their parlors and kitchens." "Most farmers," he explained, "erect a nice and expensive house, with a costly parlor or two, and furnished with beautiful carpets, window shades and other adjuncts of a parlor, and go look into the—almost sacred—apartments about once a week. . . . What is the use of having a house without making fair and respectable use of it?" Other people complained about the discomfort of the parlor's furnishings. "A sofa, by courtesy so called, occupies irrevocably a well-defined space against the wall," grumbled another gentleman in describing a typical parlor, "but it is just too short to lie down on, and too high and slippery, with its spring, convex seat, to sit on with any comfort." This sofa, he submitted, was "the 'representative' man of the room," for it symbolized "the whole spirit of discomfort" that reigned "unmolested in every square foot of the apartment."

The dining room functioned as the next most formal room in urban homes, yet it saw far more daily activity than the parlor. Middle-class families in city and town ate all of their meals in the dining room; kitchens of this period served largely for the preparation of meals. A large oval dining table (usually walnut or mahogany) graced the middle of the room. A buffet, sideboard, and china cabinet stored china, silverware, flatware, and linen. The floor might be carpeted, although in the 1870s, as bare wood and parquet floors became popular, dining rooms were among the first rooms to lose their carpets. The same heavy draperies one found in the parlor shielded dining-room windows. Quite often, dining rooms, like front parlors, were illuminated by a gas chandelier. Otherwise, wall fixtures provided light. At least one large mirror graced the walls, as in parlor and hallway. Indeed, nearly every room in the house, save the kitchen, had at least one mirror. Mirrors hung on walls, chests of drawers, washstands, sideboards, cabinets, in hallways, and over mantels. Mirrors reflected light to expand and illuminate a space, and they suited the Victorian mania for personal appearance.

The "second," or "back," parlor had a relaxed, informal atmosphere. Also referred to as a sitting room or living room, it was the place where families spent most of their leisure hours at home, a place where people took off their shoes, played checkers, sang songs, or took a nap. The household's most comfortable furniture—club chairs, rocking chairs, slatback chairs, and chaise longues—filled this room. Cabinets and shelves held magazines, newspapers, children's games, and sewing materials. A smoking stand held Father's pipes. A large oval table, where family members could read, write, and play games, occupied the center of the room, and some families placed their piano or organ in the back, rather than front, parlor. Carpeting (ingrain or Venetian) and wallpaper tended to be less expensive than that used in the front parlor. Conversation tended to be more "gossipy" than "polite." Visitors only occasionally entered this sanctuary, and they were usually close friends who understood that this was "a room to live in." Other public rooms, including libraries, studies, conservatories, salons, music rooms, drawing rooms, and sitting rooms, served a similar dual purpose in the homes of more affluent Americans.

Most families also regarded public rooms as appropriate places to display their taste in art. Every respectable family was expected to display inexpensive framed lithographs or prints. Ideally, these prints endorsed praiseworthy moral or patriotic principles, values, or ideals. Color prints and varnish-finished lithographs, or chromos, selling at five to fifteen dollars, could be relatively expensive. However, by the 1860s, Messrs. Currier and Ives had revolutionized home decoration from their Spruce Street factory in New York by producing inexpensive black-and-white and hand-colored lithographs for fifteen cents to three dollars. Suddenly every household could afford images of idyllic landscapes, noble Redmen, historic events, cuddly pets, bowls of fruit, and family life. Currier and Ives's catalogue, by the 1870s, listed 2,800 subjects, and their advertisements proclaimed proudly: "These pictures are the cheapest Ornaments in the World." What Currier and Ives did for painting, John Rogers did for sculpture. His plaster statuettes, selling for six to twenty-five dollars, expressed the same values and virtues of family life, patriotism, humor, generosity, compassion, and sentiment. While clearly more expensive than the average lithograph, Rogers's work vastly expanded the ability of prosperous middle-class families to own decorative art that would give "a really elegant finish" to their parlors. A popular anecdote of the day had a tramp exclaim, "You can realize how poor we were, ma'am, when I tell you that my parents could never afford to buy Rogers' 'Weighing the Baby.' "

Bedrooms and their accompanying commodes and bathrooms provided the only genuinely "private" rooms. Besides allowing people to dress and undress, wash, and relieve themselves, bedrooms served as private sitting rooms for women who lacked separate facilities on the main floor. Certainly the furnishings and decorations of the misnamed "master's" bedroom reflected the mistress's tastes and wishes far more than her husband's. Builders recommended that one of its walls have two windows so placed that a lady's dressing table and looking glass, set between them, would secure the greatest possible source of light. Indeed, unlike the dark, almost morose, public rooms, bedchambers tended to be light and airy. One builder bragged that his bedrooms afforded "warm, cozy comfort" in winter and "cool, refreshing daintiness" in summer. People who could afford to do so stuffed bed mattresses and pillows with feathers, although some people swore by hair mattresses.

Less affluent folk contented themselves with shredded husks, combinations of cotton and moss, or straw (oat straw being preferred to wheat or rye). Everyone stored their linen and folded clothes in a chest of drawers, and most families placed hanging clothes on pegs in wardrobes (hangers were a gadget of the future), even though homes built after 1860 generally included built-in closets. Assorted small tables and straight-back chairs filled larger bedrooms. A washstand stood in one corner; a commode or chamber pot stood next to the bed.

Mention of commodes and washstands reminds us that most people maintained their personal appearance and attended to many hygienic needs in their bedrooms. In a world where indoor plumbing remained a novelty outside cities, this generally meant relying on a marble-topped washstand equipped with basin, pitcher, towel rack, slop jar, and footbath, the latter two items being secluded in a cupboard beneath the stand. Only a modest number of families had small "bathing rooms" on the chamber floor. These "rooms," actually no larger than a spacious closet, held only a bathtub. Bathers filled their tubs (about four feet long, of polished metal, and shaped somewhat like a rowboat) with cold water piped in from an attic cistern, sometimes as a shower. Hot water generally had to be carried upstairs from the kitchen. Lacking drains, most tubs had to be bailed out after bathing. Families without such modern arrangements continued to bathe in wooden or zinc tubs in kitchen, cellar, or yard. As late as the 1880s, a survey revealed that five of every six city dwellers, who were far more likely than most Americans to have plumbing and tubs, had "no facilities for bathing other than such are provided by pail and sponge." Although some Americans questioned the wisdom of too frequent bathing on grounds of health, it was mostly the inconvenience of the process that initiated a tradition of once-weekly Saturday night baths.

Similar technological problems delayed universal use of indoor toilets. Both a dry-earth and a water commode were in use by the 1860s, but neither gained universal popularity as a permanent household fixture. Increasing numbers of cities—110 by 1875—had sanitary sewage systems, but not every household in those cities had direct access to the systems. Also, most early sewers emptied directly into nearby rivers and bays. It was for these reasons that most hygiene experts recommended earth closets over water closets. Both types were constructed along similar lines: a wooden cabinet and seat (pine, oak, or mahogany, depending on income) that enclosed a galvanized iron pail or a waste shaft. The difference was the material (dirt or water) used to flush or bury the excrement. Commode closets built into new or remodeled houses were located in small spaces similar to bathing rooms. Otherwise, householders installed them in their bedchambers. Most families, however, continued through the 1870s to step outside to an old-fashioned privy during the day and rely on a chamber pot at night.

Coal-burning grates in fireplaces or coal- or wood-burning stoves heated most public and private rooms. Even newly constructed houses retained fireplaces in public rooms and most bedrooms, for the fireplace's long-standing association with family life made it an indispensable part of the "home" atmosphere. By the 1860s, however, coal-burning stoves had become fairly standard equipment in middle-class northern homes. A family usually placed its first stove—other than its cooking stove—in the back parlor. Master bedrooms and front parlors held the next priorities. Many households, especially in the countryside, kept a large "potbellied" stove in the front hallway. Some city houses even had hot-air furnaces, located in the basement, to circulate heat via ducts from one central source; but public opinion judged furnaces to be less efficient than stoves. Most furnace-heated homes required a second furnace in order to pump heat to the chamber floor, and even that plan offered only minimal help on very cold days. "The coldest day for sixty years," complained a northern furnace owner in January 1866, with the wind blowing "lancets and razors." The gentleman stoked his furnaces full blast and built a raging fire in every fireplace. Still, the temperature indoors reached only thirty-eight degrees. Furnaces could be expensive, too, anywhere from seventy-five to three hundred dollars, as compared to ten dollars and up for a stove.

Public and private rooms—although more frequently the latter—also provided fine examples of American "patent furniture." Patent furniture was convertible, collapsable, or folding furniture, furniture that moved, and nineteenth-century America's middle classes adored it. Wealthy people did not require patent furniture. They enjoyed the means and space to purchase and display solid, substantial, traditional furniture. Middle-class households, on the other hand, remained somewhat cramped. Patent furniture provided, without overcrowding, ease and comfort in limited space. A sofa or lounge that converted into a bed (a double bed at that), a bed or bathtub that became a wardrobe, a bench that doubled as a table, all of these fit middle-class tastes and needs.

Another consideration in the design of nineteenth-century furniture—patent and otherwise—was posture. In a word, nineteenth-century posture (and not just in the United States) was relaxed. Whether sitting or lying, Americans liked to stretch, slouch, rock, twist, and move. They remained mobile even in repose. They demanded reclining chairs, lounges, folding chairs, rockers, adjustable chairs (many of them quite modern in appearance), and, by the 1870s, hammocks. Besides allowing relaxed and informal posture, many of these chairs provided movement of their own. Rocking chairs, by the 1860s, had become "a constant" in American life. They seemed to be everywhere—on porches, in nurseries, in living rooms, on lawns. Swivel, or "office," chairs served only as a derivation of the rocker. Furniture catalogues referred to them as "piano-stools," "library chairs," "easy chairs," and "revolving chairs" when they first appeared in the 1850s. Originally intended for home use, they were upholstered and padded as plushly as any drawing-room chair, yet they permitted even more flexibility than rockers and a wonderful variety of sitting postures.

A household's third set of rooms, its work and production areas, were tucked out of sight in the rear or basement of a dwelling. The kitchen, the hub of any home's work area, had survived a mobile career in many parts of the United States. In the South, kitchens had frequently stood as separate outbuildings, in order to spare families unnecessary heat and slaves in the "big house." In northern and southern cities, kitchens had traditionally been placed in basements, where some builders insisted on placing them into the 1870s. Increasingly, however, kitchens found their way to the ground floor, in the rear of a family's public rooms. Household advisers who still worried about excessive heat from cooking stoves recommended placing the stove, along with accompanying pots, pans, and other cooking paraphernalia, in a "stove room," separated from the kitchen by sliding doors. The basement continued to accommodate laundry rooms, storage areas, and living quarters for servants.

Wherever they put their kitchens, Americans equipped them with the latest "modern" conveniences. Cast-iron cookstoves, fueled by either coal or wood, provided enormous savings of time and labor over the open-faced hearth. Kitchen ranges not only roasted, baked, and boiled food, they heated water for washing, bathing, and cleaning. In houses with indoor plumbing, the fire box of the range could be fitted with water pipes that fed warm water directly into an adjacent copper storage tank. From there, the water could be piped to upstairs tubs and wash basins. Gas stoves were available by the 1850s, but the danger of explosion or asphyxiation retarded universal acceptance. "Refrigerators," in the form of large wooden boxes lined with tin or zinc and cooled by blocks of ice, stood in most middle-class city kitchens by the time of the Civil War. One household adviser, as early as 1840, proclaimed, "They are a convenience which no family should be without." Most rural families chopped their ice from frozen winter streams and lakes and stored it in underground icehouses. Townsfolk generally purchased ice from local companies that delivered it to their homes. A boon to urbanites came with the manufacture of artificial ice, the first artificial ice plant opening in New Orleans in 1865. Indoor kitchen sinks, usually with hand pumps, formed the third necessary item of kitchen equipment, even in rural kitchens. However, many sinks, most of them made of zinc, lacked drains, and so had to be lifted and carried outside to be emptied.

Remaining kitchen furnishings were sparse. Generally large, plain rooms with whitewashed walls and varnished wood floors (sometimes covered by an oilcloth), kitchens contained a worktable, a few chairs, a slop bucket, and cupboards. In the cupboards and on shelves along the walls, cooks kept a variety of containers for storing and preparing food. Especially useful were earthenware crockery (for mixing and preserving), iron ware (cooking pots and pans), tin ware (baking), and wooden ware (mixing bowls and utensils). Spices, gourds, pans, and sometimes meat hung overhead or along the walls. A pantry closet sometimes provided storage space for bins of flour and sugar (purchased in bulk) and shelves for preserved fruits and vegetables and canned goods. Only in small houses, without dining rooms, did kitchens have tables and chairs for taking meals.

Farmhouses varied with the prosperity of the farmer. Comfortable farm families owned large, two-story houses of six to eight rooms, furnished much like the homes of clerks and shopkeepers in town. Poorer farmers and tenants lived under more Spartan conditions. In any case, farmers usually had more pressing concerns than maintaining a large house, even though their families tended to be larger than urban families. An accepted adage of rural America insisted that where a farmer's house looked more impressive than his barn, his wife ruled the roost. The result was a four- to six-room clapboard frame house, frequently unpainted and with an exterior chimney built of stone or crossed sticks and mud. In the South, for example, where more than a third of the farmers were tenants and sharecroppers, one- and two-room cabins became the norm. The most primitive abodes contained pine tables and chairs, a trunk or chest to hold clothes, and a cupboard to hold dishes and pans. Board shelves nailed to the wall substituted for a cupboard. Corn shucks filled mattresses, and children frequently slept in a loft or two or three in a bed.

Even fairly prosperous farmers had a mixture of old and new furnishings. Their best furniture, which might include family heirlooms and one or two pieces of factory-made furniture, stood alongside rough-hewed, homemade pieces. Most farm families ate in the kitchen, usually at a large oak or pine table, and they usually had to choose between having a parlor or a living room because they could not afford both. If they preferred to keep up appearances by outfitting a parlor, the kitchen became the living room, the place where Father figured accounts, Mother sewed, and the children played games or did schoolwork. But many commentators on rural life encouraged farm families to forsake their elaborate front parlors (conversion to informal sitting rooms became a popular alternative) as symbols of urban waste and pretension. "Some one," admitted a farm wife, "whose ideas are placed on large roomy dwellings may think the little five room house almost two small for comfort. But it is large enough for two, and let me whisper it, quite ample enough for my modest supply of furniture." All farmers depended on oil lamps for lighting. Bathing rooms and water closets were rare.

It was an age, too, when many people still built their own houses. Poor folks in city slums and frontier settlers fashioned dwellings from whatever materials were handy: shacks made from tin and scrap wood; frame shanties made from logs or lumber; tents made from canvas, blankets, or potato sacks; prehistoric-type hovels made of stone and earth. "Flimsy, rickety, filthy little hovels" was how a visitor described one such collection of mining town homes. Western bunkhouses and miners' cabins had a similarly casual look. Many were plain log cabins. Others were constructed of planks, and may or may not have received a coat of whitewash. Similarly, their dirt floors may or may not have received a covering of boards. Sawdust sprinkled six inches thick and covered with a gunny sack would serve equally well. Furnishings likely consisted of wooden chairs with seats woven from rope or rawhide. Board beds supported mattresses filled with straw. It all depended on the ambitions of the inhabitants.

The traditional log cabin did not appear as frequently as it had in pre–Civil War days. This may be explained, in part, by increased settlement on prairies devoid of timber. It may also be explained by the rapid growth of railroads into new areas of settlement. Indeed, many new communities sprang up *after* a railroad had been built. In some instances, railroad companies sponsored and promoted towns along their rights-of-way by hauling not only potential settlers to the site of settlement but the timber and materials needed to build a town. In more isolated areas, settlers built log cabins by traditional means. They notched their logs at the corners and laid them in rectangles twelve by sixteen feet to a height of five or six feet. They cut doors and windows in the finished structure and added a roof of split timber or tree bough. Finally, they filled chinks between the logs with earth or clay and gave windows a covering of greased paper.

Sod houses and dugouts, the prairie settler's answer to the log cabin, dotted the landscape of Kansas and Nebraska. Dugouts usually served as temporary shelters, until larger, sturdier sod houses could be built. Settlers literally dug out the side of a hill or ravine until, after two or three days of hard work, they had cleared a space about ten by twelve feet. They covered the open side with square turfs, canvas, brush, or whatever material was handy. Some families found this arrangement sufficient for their needs and made permanent homes of their dugouts, perhaps widening the interior space. More ambitious people cut sod bricks about a foot thick, two feet wide, and three feet long to build houses or to construct additions to existing dugouts. They laid the sod bricks—dubbed "prairie marble"—much as one would lay clay bricks, filling cracks and joints with dirt instead of mortar, to form the walls of a one-room dwelling sixteen by twenty feet. A mixture of white clay and water made "as nice a finish as yu'd ever hope to see" for interior walls. When possible, settlers laid board floors. Door and window frames were set in the walls during construction with sod placed around them. Sod served for the roof, too, usually as sheathing for a layer of brush and grass supported by pole rafters. The average "soddy" required about an acre of sod and weighed nearly ninety tons.

Both dugouts and soddies took some getting used to. While cool in summer and warm in winter, they leaked, lacked adequate ventilation, smelled musty, and seemed perpetually dark. "They wet up when it rains, they dust off when it gets hot," recalled one man who had been raised in a Kansas soddy. "Mama said she wasn't going to have neither, that she had brung a big roll of rag carpet . . . to cover the ceiling so's she could keep the dirt out of our victuals." After first installing Mama's most prized possession, her stove, Papa unrolled the carpet and hung it "like a canopy to cover the ceiling." A Nebraska settler reported the same experience, and decided that only people with money and possessions from the East could hope to live comfortably in a sod house. "With doors and windows in place," he insisted, "with furniture brought from the old home . . . , with perhaps a carpet on the floor and an organ or piano and good furniture, a nice home could have been established. . . . But this is a roseate picture of the very few homes where the settler had brought some money with him."

Rural homes, on the other hand, enjoyed a big advantage over urban residences: their locations. The "healthy" home be-

came an important consideration by the 1860s. The same concern with sanitation and hygiene that had inspired creation of
the wartime Sanitary Commission led architects, builders, and
average citizens to associate health with household designs that
provided plenty of sunshine and fresh air. Simply put by one
household adviser, "When 'the wise woman buildeth her
house,' the first consideration will be the health of the inmates."
This concern sent Americans—and not just farmers—scurrying
to the countryside. Cities were noisy, crowded, dirty, dangerous, and expensive places to live. Even a modest rowhouse
extracted hundreds of dollars a year in rent, and the exorbitant
price of urban land made a city house an impossible dream for
all but the most affluent people. Why not, asked growing numbers of folks, move to the suburbs, where a family of four, even
on the outskirts of New York, could buy two acres of land and
a commodious house for $6,000? How much more pleasant,
urged one builder, than "the narrow house in the crowded
street, where every sense is offended—with no open sky or
distant horizon tinged with the glories of the dying day or rising
morn—no grassy lawns, or waving trees or fragrant banks of
flowers."

Flower gardens and surrounding grounds made the suburban
home "a haven of repose." "The velvety lawn, flecked with
sunlight and the shadows of common trees," insisted one observer, provided not only an inexpensive pleasure but "a very
elegant refreshment for the business-wearied eye." By living in
the restful suburbs, a weary city worker, buffeted and bruised
by the hectic, grueling competitive whirl of daily labors, could
retire each evening, "take off his armour, relax his strained
attention, and surrender himself to perfect rest." As early as
1868, a visitor to Pittsburgh saw "villages springing up as far as
twenty miles away to which the business men repair, when, in
consequence of having inhailed smoke all day, they feel able to
bear the common country atmosphere through the night."
Lawn mowing became a relaxation in its own right, and chil-

dren's magazines promoted lawn games that allowed families to relax out-of-doors while remaining under the influence of the "home spirit." Urban orphan asylums and juvenile homes tried to place their charges in rural and suburban families, where nature and the ideal (Christian) home environment provided the best possible antidote for the youngsters' earlier unfortunate lives. A variety of domestic animals, including ducks, chickens, hogs, horses, and cows, as well as the more usual dogs and cats, roamed the grounds of many middle-class homesteads in both city and country. Outbuildings, including woodsheds and stables, added a further bucolic touch to suburban homes, not as artificial decorations but as functional parts of daily life.

Architects and home decorators tried to reduce artificial barriers between nature and the family. Windows became larger and more numerous. Hanging plants, climbing ivy, moss, and potted ferns invaded public rooms. Homemade rustic picture frames, fashioned from tree branches and "garnished" at the corners with acorns, pine cones, coral, or sea shells, enjoyed a vogue. "Then there is a bracket covered with moss," expounded a woman in describing one decoration in her sitting room, "with a bird's nest on the shelf, while fastened a little above, the mother bird [made of cotton batting] is perched with wings spread, looking into the nest." Describing her window curtains, she continued, "Across the top where they are gathered, is a band of autumn leaves, pressed, and pasted in place. On the curtains are large ferns, gracefully curved, and also pasted." Some furniture companies even manufactured rustic tables and chairs from varnished tree limbs and roots.

Porches and verandas became larger and more functional, almost serving as outdoor parlors. Porches surrounding two, even three, sides of a house became quite popular, as did the fashion of outfitting them with a variety of gliders, swings, rocking chairs, and wicker furniture. Summer meals could be taken on the porch, too, particularly as wire screens and mosquito netting became available. The origins of these defenses against flying insects are murky. A material to cover windows and doors known as "wire cloth" came on the market shortly after the Civil War, but the innovation caught on slowly, and most houses, let alone porches, remained fly-blown into the 1880s. More popular was mosquito netting, which back-porch diners found particularly useful. Mark Twain, who enjoyed taking summer meals in the evening air, wrote ecstatically to the manufacturer of his "portable folding fly and musketo net": "There is nothing that a just and right feeling man rejoices in more than to see a mosquito imposed on and put down, and browbeaten and aggravated,—and this ingenious contrivance will do it. It is a rare thing to worry a fly with too. A fly will stand off and curse this invention till language utterly fails him."

City folk tried similar tricks. They had no front or side yards, and backyards were invariably cramped (less than twenty-five feet deep) and exposed to rear alleys, privies, accumulated garbage, and scavenging pigs and dogs—hardly a place to enjoy an evening meal. Thus, city dwellers came to rely on public parks for their pastoral setting, and the development of such parks became an important part of city planning after the Civil War. The appeal of Central Park in New York or Fairmount Park in Philadelphia—just two of the best-known efforts to incorporate nature into city life—is understandable. Large numbers of city dwellers had been born and raised on farms or in small towns, and they missed the serenity of those early, simpler days. They believed that grassy parks muted the starkness of city canyons and lent otherwise intimidating surroundings a small-town atmosphere. Similarly, the concept of residential neighborhoods, enclosed by parks and tree-lined streets, became an important consideration in city expansion and development. "The streets are handsome, and are shaded by grand avenues of trees," observed one man on a visit to Cleveland, Ohio, "—not little paltry trees as are to be seen on the boulevards of Paris, but spreading elms." "Discordant elements," like factories, mills, lumberyards, and railroads, were segregated from residential districts. Additionally, social distinctions between exclusive, merely respectable, and downright slovenly neighborhoods appeared to a more marked degree than ever before. The center, or "downtown," of a city became more obviously a business or commercial district, perhaps residing cheek by jowl with a slum or lower-class residential neighborhood. The middle and upper classes moved outward and clustered on a city's fringes, where trees and grass kept them in touch with a sentimental past.

A more serious sacrifice required that most city dwellers give up all thought of owning their own homes. High property taxes, high land prices, and burgeoning populations produced housing shortages in the largest cities. People who chose to live in the city or who were forced by economic circumstances to live there had to satisfy themselves with something less than a traditional, detached single-family dwelling. Rowhouses offered one solution to the problem in places as diverse as Baltimore, Cincinnati, Philadelphia, and Pittsburgh. These tall, narrow-fronted, identical-looking structures, standing like "books on a shelf," occupied entire city blocks. The standard rowhouse, most often made of brick or stone, measured sixteen to thirty feet across, ran as much as seventy feet deep, stood three to five stories high, and contained as many as a dozen rooms. A substantial income was necessary to rent and maintain the best of these dwellings, although some enterprising builders erected low-rent wooden rowhouses for the working classes. The rowhouse's principal drawbacks, other than cost, were its numerous stairs and claustrophobic placement.

Less popular than rowhouses but far more numerous were boardinghouses. It has been estimated that during the nineteenth century 70 percent of the nation's citizens boarded at some time in their lives. Tabulated another way, as many as 20 percent of urban households may have taken in boarders during the period. Bachelors and young married couples, in particular, sought boardinghouse accommodations in order to avoid the expense of housekeeping and the worry of servants. Apprentices, young artisans, and clerks sometimes lived with employers in lieu of part of their wages, and many private families took in boarders to supplement their incomes. Impoverished "gentlewomen" and widows seem to have presided over an inordinate number of these establishments. Whoever operated them, boardinghouses ran the gamut, from elegant to slovenly. A few people converted mansions of the hitherto rich into fashionable rooms and fed boarders on canvasback duck. At the lower end of the scale, people could board in tents, sod houses, or lumber shacks, where they sat on kegs and boxes and dined on beans and salt pork.

Few people seem to have approved of boardinghouse life. It was criticized for being an "unnatural and artificial" way of living that destroyed "independent home-life." "Let us keep house no matter how little we have to begin with," pleaded a young woman to her fiancé. "There is too much of the quiet, the closeness, the nearness to be given up in boarding." A child, asked where her parents lived, replied, "They don't *live;* they BOARD." Boarders generally lived in a single bedroom, although couples and families might have suites with two or more rooms. Everyone ate at a common table, and, in large houses, most occupants shared a common, sparsely furnished parlor. Out West, in Virginia City, Nevada, where miners frequently stayed in boardinghouses, a standard room measured ten by twelve feet and rented, during the boom days of the 1870s, for forty to sixty dollars per month, including board. Each room contained a bed, a chest of drawers, a wash bowl, and a pitcher. A cast-iron stove supplied heat, and a kerosene lamp (sometimes supplemented by candles) provided light. Toilets stood out back.

An urban compromise between rowhouses and boardinghouses was the apartment. Apartments first appeared in the United States before the Civil War in New Orleans and New York. Having originated in Paris, they were scornfully referred to for many years as "French flats." They seemed foreign not only in origin but in concept. Like boardinghouses, apartments seemed to undermine family life. The working poor in eastern and midwestern cities had lived in cheap tenements for over a decade by the 1860s, but middle-class Americans worried, even when escaping the menagerie atmosphere of boardinghouses, about the social and moral implications of living with numerous and totally unrelated families under the same roof. Nonetheless, the idea caught on by the late 1860s, when a six-room apartment on New York's East Eighteenth Street (in the first building in the U.S. constructed exclusively as an apartment complex) rented for one hundred dollars a month. That was far less than the rent charged at the best boardinghouses and about the same as an expensively maintained rowhouse. Most important, the new apartments allowed family privacy and "independent housekeeping, in good but not extravagant style."

Elsewhere in urban America, things were less cheery. Inner-city tenements, serving as home for many members of the working classes, pockmarked nearly every city in the country. A New York slum, in 1872, stretched across a neighborhood that only a dozen years earlier had been a "home of middle-class good repute." As the city expanded outward, the middle classes had fled uptown and to the suburbs. Enterprising landlords turned old residences and nearby abandoned warehouses into one- and two-room apartments to be rented at profitable rates to immigrants, itinerants, and the poor. "The population is dense," explained one observer of Gotham's inner city, "and as little addicted to cleanliness as godliness. The streets . . . are generally matted with the foulest garbage, thrown from the houses in defiance of law and decency. . . . In winter huge heaps of ashes are added to the piles of kitchen and grocer garbage, both intermingled with fouler filth. . . ." Personal habits of the residents only partly explain this dreary scene. Most cities, including New York, cleaned streets, collected garbage, and provided sewage facilities only where neighborhoods paid for those services. Tenement residents could not afford such luxuries, and landlords refused to pay for them.

As for the buildings, "few of them have more than three floors," observed one man, "not more than two with an attic. All of them have the first floor, which is raised only one or two steps above the pavement, divided into a hallway and two rooms; and the upper floors are on the same plan, except that half the hallway, front and rear, is partitioned off to make those last abominations of builders known as hall rooms." Typically, a family of five lived in a ten-by-twelve-foot living room and a bedroom six by four feet with "no regard . . . paid to ventilation or domestic conveniences." Almost without exception, such tenements lacked water and gas, again because landlords refused to invest in utilities. Many buildings leaned on their foundations, had unsafe stairways and decaying floors, and looked "dirty and dingy beyond description." Furniture, if such it could be called, consisted of a few wooden chairs, a table, and perhaps a bedstead.

A few reformers, particularly in areas heavily populated by foreign immigrants, urged that public monies be used to construct safe, clean tenements for the poor. "Shall we make no room for any portion of these industrious, freedom-loving people?" asked one midwestern newspaper. "Shall we drive them to building huts in the alleys and to squatting upon the outskirts of the town?" Despite the concern, most towns and cities witnessed the growth of shantytowns on their fringes, in a netherworld between city and suburbs. In fact, the earliest "suburbs" had been formed by these poor squatters, the new, middle-class suburbs being erected beyond. Some heaps of shanties grew so large that they formed separate towns, with hundreds of residents and their own post offices. Most shanties consisted of a single room, "built of slabs, old boards, timber from torn-down houses, old tin rolled up and spread out again." "If the owner possesses a horse, a cow, or a pig," reported one observer, "the animal has a room as good as his owner directly alongside the dwelling." Respectable citizens, from "across the tracks," shunned the shantytowns as morasses of "poverty, misery, beggary, starvation, crime, filth, and licentiousness."

In "company towns," where certain mining and textile firms single-handedly carved communities out of the countryside, much of daily life, even provisions for housing, depended on company rules and regulations. Combinations of boardinghouses, semi-detached rowhouses, tenements, and single-family cottages provided an array of housing styles in these towns. Some sat proudly along clean streets and neatly trimmed lawns; others were packed into narrow thoroughfares or set precariously on bleak hillsides above the town. Not all companies owned every building or even all the land in their towns. Some companies encouraged workers to purchase plots of land and build their own houses. A few companies even sponsored building and loan associations to finance the dreams of ambitious employees. "Nearly three hundred houses have been erected," reported a visitor to Lawrence, Massachusetts, in 1876, "chiefly as boarding-houses for the young people, which have large rooms for meals below, and numerous smaller apartments for lodgers above." On the other hand, continued this same person, "The heads of families have been encouraged to build houses for themselves, the Company making loans to them at 6 per cent. to enable them to do so; and it is believed that about 40 per cent. of the men permanently in the Company's service have houses of their own." Such instances, however, were more the exception than the rule. "There was not so much as a pig pen or the paling of a garden fence that did not belong to the company," complained a resident in a Pennsylvania mining town. Far too often company housing formed "depressing rows of hideous barracks . . . looking for all the world like a row of institution children."

# 3          LIFE AT HOME

REGARDLESS of what they looked like, American houses provided a focus for family life. "It may not immediately appear, to every one," reasoned one commentator in the 1860s, "that a house is not necessarily, in any true sense of the term, a 'Home.' It is, however, the shell, the hive in which busy hands and anxious hearts combine their toil and hope." From sunrise to sunset, the typical American functioned as part of a family, and that family pursued many of its most important daily activities in the home. The details of those activities varied, depending on a family's social status, where it lived, and how its breadwinner spent his working hours. The war and an expanding urban economy had weakened the family cohesiveness of earlier decades, yet family life remained a powerful force, and much can be learned about Americans of the Civil War era by examining their daily routines at home.

American families of the 1860s and 1870s averaged about five people. This was slightly smaller than families had been in earlier decades and slightly larger than families would be in decades to come. City families, on average, tended to be smaller than rural families. The typical family included parents and children (the nation had seventeen million children aged sixteen and under), but it was also quite usual to have an elderly relative—grandparent, aunt, or uncle—living in the home. Toss in a servant or two, perhaps a boarder here and there, and the population of a middle-class household could be formidable. Clearly, Americans preferred married life. With an adult population of barely twenty million people in 1870, nearly fourteen million lived as man and wife. Thus well over three-fourths of the nation's population lived in a family environment.

The typical middle-class household, whether in town or country, began to stir before daylight. Mothers, daughters, and perhaps servants hurriedly dressed before reviving cooking stove embers to start breakfast and heat water. In cold weather, they would also stir fires in bedroom grates or stoves before waking the rest of the family. In smaller houses, where kitchen stoves provided the principal source of heat, people often dressed in the kitchen on cold mornings. Farmers usually arose with their wives, for routine daily chores like milking cows, feeding livestock, chopping wood, and drawing water had to be accomplished before breakfast. Breakfast provided a mere interlude to the day's heavier work. Day laborers and mill hands, who usually had to be at work by 6 A.M., had little time to spare either. Only businessmen and professional people could grab a few extra winks; their workdays did not begin until 8 or 9 A.M.

Children followed the same morning pattern as their parents. Rural children helped their fathers and mothers with early morning chores in house and barnyard. Most children found this an irksome way to start a day, and cold winter mornings became a particular "time of trial." "It required stern military command to get us out of bed before daylight," recalled an Iowa farm boy, "to draw on icy socks and frosty boots and go to the milking of cows and the currying of horses." His toilet, he confessed, "was hasty—something less than 'a lick and a promise.' " In town, children might be called on to feed the stove, carry hot water to Father's washstand, or make sure the biscuits did not burn. "I was the coal breaker for our family," recalled a small-town Pennsylvania boy. "Each day, after the chamber work for the cows and horses was done, I had to break the coal to be used for the next twenty-four hours. I was taught how to do everything around the house as well as to mend my own clothing."

Breakfast, based on a rural tradition that required hardworking farm folk to be well fortified before going to the fields, could be a hearty meal, even in town. Beefsteak or pork, eggs, fried potatoes, fruit pie, hotcakes, and coffee provided the nucleus for many a middle-class breakfast. Porridge proved popular in cold weather, but dry cereals, most notably those developed by Dr. John H. Kellogg, of Battle Creek, Michigan, became available in the 1870s. Each region of the country had a favorite form of hotcake. Buckwheat cakes, rice cakes, corn cakes, griddle cakes, buttermilk cakes, sourmilk cakes, flapjacks, slapjacks, hominy cakes, and a variety of fritters and waffles were indispensable. So were fruit pies and doughnuts, the latter being cut in solid shapes. Not until the end of the century did doughnuts become round with a hole in the center. Tea and chocolate appeared occasionally as breakfast drinks, but coffee, in some places the beverage for every meal, dominated. Most children drank milk, but they did not monopolize the beverage. European visitors expressed amazement at the quantities of milk enjoyed by Americans of all ages.

The clothes families wore to breakfast depended on income, occupation, and geography, but certain styles and fashions remained fairly universal during the period. All but the poorest or most isolated families purchased some ready-made clothing by the 1870s, and store-bought fabrics and paper patterns made it easier to sew a variety of shirts, blouses, undergarments, and children's clothing at home. Women's magazines fairly burst with new designs, and the "paper pattern business," by 1867, had become a thirty-million-dollar annual industry. The result was a curious standardization of American clothing. "The uniformity of dress," concluded *Harper's Bazar,* "is a characteristic of the people of the United States. The man of leisure and the laborer, the mistress and the maid, wear clothes of the same material and cut."

Still, one could detect differences. Rural men and town laborers donned plain daily garb. Coarse, heavy fabrics—most often
cotton, canvas, or denim—served for shirts, pants, and jackets.
The Levi Strauss Company introduced a rugged brand of
denim trousers in the 1850s, first colored brown. By the mid-
1870s, Levi's were blue and copper-riveted. Most men held up
their pants with suspenders, or "braces," but many westerners
preferred broad leather belts. Loose-fitting vests, usually
woolen, became popular for both work and dress. Businessmen
and professionals wore loose-fitting suits. Suit coats, usually
wool, had broad shoulders and wide sleeves. Pants had baggy
tube legs. Shirts fit loosely at neck and cuff, although stiff paper
or starched cuffs and collars gave a quite rigid appearance. The
"best people" still wore white shirts exclusively, a sign that they
did not earn their living by sweat and heavy labor. Increasingly,
however, bright colors and bold stripes adorned men's shirts,
even the "sporting" shirts of gentlemen. Neckties—most often
flat, broad bow ties, but with satin cravats growing in popularity—came in every conceivable color. All men wore hats. Silk
or beaver top hats remained popular among professional men,
but many styles of new felt hats, from broad-brimmed "slouch"
hats to natty "bowlers" and "derbys," won favor. Many men
wore straw hats in summer. Beneath all, most men wore ankle-
length drawers, closed at the front with buttons.

Women's dress also boasted variety. Rural women wore fairly
plain floor-length dresses of calico, gingham, or linsey-woolsey.
They seldom owned extensive wardrobes, usually only two or
three dresses, with one of those reserved expressly for Sundays,
holidays, and special occasions. Rural women were also partial
to large, functional sunbonnets, quite different from the frilly
headgear, full of feathers, flowers, and other ornamentation,
worn by city women. The latter, including working-class girls
who purchased cheap imitations of middle-class apparel,
tended to be more fashion-conscious. They wore skirts and
dresses elaborately trimmed, looped, and flounced in cascades

of fringe, lace, braid, and ribbon. Underneath all this "daintiness," urban women wore scalloped and embroidered drawers (knee length), chemises, and petticoats that came in glorious colors and stripes. "Underclothing has reached a luxury unknown in any age," declared one fashion magazine by 1876. In order to show off the gorgeous colors and beautiful trim, women began hitching their skirts and raising their hemlines an inch or two above the ankle.

Women also wanted clothes that displayed their figures to best advantage. "A well-developed bust, a tapering waist, and huge hips are the combination of points recognized as a good figure," observed an 1873 fashion commentator. During the 1860s, seeking to achieve the desired effect, women cinched themselves into corsets and encircled themselves with hoops, cages, and crinoline petticoats. Crinoline, a fabric of linen and horsehair, puffed out a woman's skirts and added to the "erotic" and "seductive" look of fashionable dress by further exposing undergarments and "limbs." The fashion caused havoc and hilarity. Newspapers daily reported crinoline rigs catching fire as they brushed against fireplaces and stoves. Popular songs ridiculed crinoline-clad women who obstructed traffic in crowded rooms and on public conveyances. Mercifully, the "reign of crinoline" lasted only about a decade in its most extreme form. By the 1870s, women preferred less expansive muslin petticoats. Women still seeking to make an impression turned to the bustle, the first one appearing in 1868. Made either of horsehair with a series of ruffles across the back, or of cambric with wire supports running through the casing, bustles broadened the beam and swept dresses out in the rear. The "crinolette," a half hoop or system of petticoats, served the same purpose. This made women a hazard in only one direction, and as the expanse of skirts and petticoats receded, fashion magazines began to speak of a more "natural form." On the other hand, the new fashion retained a "charming" (translated "sexy") look, as its clinging, form-revealing lines guided the male eye backward from the bust to the outward thrust of the bustle. One historian has declared this "Grecian blend" fashion, generally worn in combination with high heels to further accentuate bosom and buttocks, "the most erotic style of the century."

Footwear varied according to purpose. For general wear in town, men and women wore leather-soled, high-topped shoes, quite often with fabric tops. They could either button their shoes on the sides or lace them in front, the latter being the newer and increasingly preferred style. Another innovation was the gored shoe with elastic sides that eliminated the need for both buttons and laces. "Sports" shoes—for croquet, archery, and lawn tennis—appeared during the 1860s. These early versions of sneakers were laced, fabric-topped, and rubber-soled for both men and women. Workmen and farmers wore heavy-soled, hobnailed work shoes, although many farm families went barefoot in warm weather. The latter were not necessarily poor, but they associated footwear with "dress up" occasions, and so reserved their shoes for church and social functions. In town, women wore higher heels in the 1860s than they did in the 1850s, but the 1870s saw the trend reversed. Regardless of style, sizes remained limited. No manufacturer made half sizes or distinguished between "left" and "right" shoes. Only two widths—slim and wide—were available. Socks and stockings were cotton or woolen, mostly black, brown, or white. Women could purchase silk stockings, but they were quite expensive.

In addition to dress, town and city women paid considerable attention to their toilet—dressing and "shampooing" their hair (rather than simply washing it), experimenting with colognes and perfumes, caring for their complexions, and doctoring natural hues with cosmetics. Long hair remained popular throughout the era. In the 1860s, women swept their hair back in a "waterfall," secured with a net behind the neck. If their natural hair lacked the length or body to produce the desired effect, they added a hairpiece (usually horsehair) to the arrangement. These sleek coiffures gave way in the 1870s to piles of hair swept up on top of the head, embroidered with cascades of curls, ringlets, bandeaux, braids, and cadogans, and cut across the forehead in bangs or crimped in tight bundles of curls. Growing numbers of women dyed their hair, too, the most fashionable tints being Venetian blond and Titian red. Various washes for the complexion gained favor, many of them home-made concoctions of lemon, cucumber, and horseradish. "Virgin's milk," a solution of benzoin, glycerin, and water, earned loyal devotees; and a mixture of benzoin, honey, and alcohol was supposed to eliminate wrinkles and cleanse greasy skin. A pomade made from oil of bitter almonds, fresh butter, lard, and mutton suet was recommended for dry skin.

Most of these potions won social approval, but excessive use of cosmetics shocked people, who associated painted faces with women of easy virtue. Respectable women seldom applied anything more than modest amounts of rouge (for lips and cheeks), face powder, and occasionally eyebrow coloring. "If women, prompted by no other motive than that of pleasing men, paint their faces," warned a gentleman in 1874, "I solemnly declare to them, in the name of the masculine sex, that they are going a false route and will only render themselves horrible." Not all men shared his view. One adolescent of the 1870s remained fascinated by his "distinctly modern" aunt's "daintily-drapped dressing table," piled high with "pots of face creams, boxes of powder, and even rouge." "She spent long hours applying ice packs to her lovely throat and bosom," the smitten youth recalled, "brushing to lacquered brightness her black hair, and even doing calisthenics each morning."

A man's toilet did not take very long. His only real task was shaving, and more than likely some portion of his face sported a growth of hair. Mustachios, lamb-chop sideburns, and, to a lessening degree, full beards were both fashionable and practical. Etiquette books regarded facial hair as natural, expressive, healthful, dignified, handsome, and virile. "Shaving," one manual declared, "renders the face effeminate." Even those portions of the face kept smooth often felt the scrape of a man's straightedge razor only every other day. Fashionable men splashed on a little cherry-laurel water for after-shave.

Men and women who bathed took a morning, more often than an evening, bath. By the mid-1870s, Americans were furiously debating the benefits of daily bathing. Even advocates considered the hygienic value of soap and water less important than the therapeutic effect of washing. "They will tell you that they are not themselves until they have taken their daily bath," observed one gentleman of the bathing advocates; "that it not only keeps their pores open, and their circulation perfect, but their mind clear, and their disposition buoyant." Nonsense, said the critics: "A wet towel applied each morning to the skin, followed by friction in pure air, is all that is absolutely needed; although a full bath is a great luxury." Some medical experts deplored the use of bathtubs—"zinc coffins," one physician called them. Far better, he said, to cleanse the body thoroughly while standing on an oilcloth bathing mat in front of a wash basin. Debate also raged over the value of cold versus hot baths, and the merits of bathing as a form of "exercise" for people of "sedentary habit."

Once dressed, bathed, and fed, fathers headed for work. If working in town, and living fewer than three or four miles from their jobs, they probably walked. Even people who owned private carriages—the "distinguishing mark" of a prosperous family—often found it more convenient to walk or rely on public transportation. Poorer folk, who could ill afford the ten-cent round-trip trolley fare charged in most cities, sometimes walked as many as five miles to work.

Many children headed for school, but not all of them. Only about half of the nation's school-age population of twelve million attended classes, and many of these children attended only at night, after having worked all day to help support their families. Racially, more white than colored children attended school regularly; ethnically, more native-born than foreign-born children attended. Farm children, particularly boys, joined their fathers and the hired hands in planting, harvesting, and construction work during most of the year. Rural students began classes only after fall harvest (December) and finished before spring planting (March). A statistical study of Massachusetts schools, one of the best state systems in the country, showed that students in rural communities attended classes forty fewer days than urban students in 1870. On the other hand, growing numbers of poor urban children abandoned education for labor. "It is safe . . . to say," reported the Massachusetts labor board in 1874, "that, at least twenty-five thousand children between the ages of five and fifteen do not receive the slightest education either in our public or private schools." In the nation at large, hundreds of thousands of schoolchildren—one hundred thousand in New York City alone—labored to supplement family incomes. Poor urban families had little choice. A father who earned $450 dollars a year and paid as little as $25 a month for rent—a sum that provided only the most Spartan quarters for a family of four—had already exceeded his budget. The family could make ends meet only if the children and, quite possibly, the mother contributed an income.

Some boys and girls, with both parents working and no older siblings to look after them, became latch-key children. A New England cotton mill worker admitted to leaving his ten-year-old daughter at home every morning when the rest of the family went out to work. "She gets her own breakfast from what we leave for her on the table," he explained. "Then she washes herself, or comes to the mill and I wash her." She went to school at nine o'clock, but joined her father at home for lunch. After eating, the father returned to the mill and the daughter returned to school. "After school," continued her dad, "she comes to me at [the] mill, and I give her the house-key. She goes home, unlocks and waits for us to come home."

Larger numbers of women than before worked outside the home, too, for the Civil War unleashed a modest revolution in female employment. No massive or permanent movement into traditionally male jobs occurred, but the ancient dictum that woman's place was in the home had less validity than before the war. More women sought careers and identities other than as wives and mothers, and more wives found it necessary to work outside the home. Even some middle-class mothers, many of them widowed by the war, had to earn a living.

Still, the vast majority of mothers remained guardians of home and family life. Statistics on the marital status of female workers are unavailable before 1890, and the number of female workers in 1860 is unknown. However, between 1870 and 1880, working women composed less than 20 percent of the labor force and only 10 percent of the female population. Most Americans, male and female, still believed that Providence had created "spheres" of human endeavor, and that home and family marked the "undisputed sphere of woman." "[A house] is not only the home center, the retreat and shelter for all the family," asserted an observer, "it is also the workshop for the mother. It is not only where she is to live, to love, but where she is to care and labor. Her hours, days, weeks, months and years are spent within its bands; until she becomes an enthroned fixture, more indispensable than the house itself."

What was more, the wife/mother/housekeeper's burden was growing heavier. Changes in family relationships that had begun in the decade before the war grew steadily during the 1860s and 1870s. At the risk of oversimplifying matters, it is fair to say that mothers were playing more important roles as household leaders while fathers relinquished some of their leadership. Family bonds generally grew stronger during the 1860s and 1870s, but as more men entered non-agricultural occupations (over five million, and nearly half the male work force in 1870), they spent more time away from home and less time with their children. Fathers showed love and tenderness toward their children, but, except for discussing "manly" issues of finance and career with sons, they seldom advised their children. Even punishments, long a fatherly prerogative, gradually passed into female hands. "Mothers," declared one of the many popular household advice books of the period, "have as powerful an influence over the welfare of future generations as all other earthly causes combined." Similarly, a man's relationship with his wife changed. Men had long been expected to provide for their families, just as wives and mothers assumed responsibility for taking care of the household and its inhabitants. In the past, however, when more men worked at or near their homes as farmers and artisans, men and women had frequently shared each other's prescribed roles. By the 1860s, non-farm households no longer functioned as the center of life. They served, instead, as the center of *family* life, apart from the everyday world of work. "Home" had become a "refuge to which men could retreat from the world."

Once husbands and children had left the home, housekeepers devoted their mornings to daily tasks: making beds, emptying chamber pots, washing breakfast dishes, and preparing the midday meal. In large families, marketing could also be a daily morning activity. Heavier weekly chores followed and, depending on their difficulty, extended through the remainder of the morning and into the afternoon. Normally, women devoted one day each week to laundry, ironing, sewing, dusting and cleaning, and baking, but some women used Monday—the traditional laundry day—strictly as an organizational day. "Any extra cooking, the purchasing of articles to be used during the week, the assorting of clothes for the wash, and mending such as would otherwise be injured—these, and similar items, belong to this day," suggested a writer in 1869. Most mothers also reserved part of several afternoons or evenings for sewing. Evening meals had to be prepared, too, although in many parts of the country these were light repasts consisting entirely of cold food.

Technology played only a minor role in easing housework. Kitchens had been "modernized" by cookstoves and gadgets like eggbeaters, apple parers, pea shellers, and coffee grinders, but most other labor required plenty of muscle and elbow grease, and even the new gadgets frequently proved unreliable. Numerous carpet sweepers had been patented by 1860, but they were crude, often bulky, and always expensive machines that did not find widespread use before the 1880s. The first American patents for laundering and wringing machines dated from 1805, with some dramatic improvements in the 1850s and 1860s. Still, the first recognizably "modern" hand-cranked washing machine did not become available until the 1870s, and its operation required strong shoulders and back. Women had to prepare their own starch, bleach, and cleaning compounds, too, and proper treatment of different fabrics and stains was very nearly a science. A boom in commercial laundries, commencing in the 1870s, offered another solution to the miseries of "blue Monday," but wise husbands learned to "eat a cold dinner on wash day without grumbling." Not surprisingly, many families, even those with modest incomes, hired laundresses to come in once a week to "do up" the wash.

Numerous housekeepers depended on servants to help with more than just the laundry. The justification for employing servants was complex, but most reasons stressed the importance of maintaining well-ordered households and contented families. Servants, by performing the monotonous, disagreeable, and backbreaking chores of the household, allowed families to spend more time enjoying life and middle-class housekeepers to fulfill their full range of responsibilities. In the context of a budding "Gilded Age," servants became important status symbols of middle-class success. Ambitious young clerks and merchants, along with their wives, sought to advertise their improving financial fortunes by employing one or two servants, even when, as in outfitting their parlors, it played havoc with household budgets. By 1870, the servant population was large enough for one in every eight American families to have domestic help, and in cities the ratio was usually twice that high.

Working-class housekeepers lacked both servants and household gadgets. Consequently, even though they managed smaller homes than the middle classes, mothers on modest farms and in tenements labored many hours. Working-class neighborhoods in cities frequently lacked paved streets, which meant families tracked more mud and dirt into the house, and the grit and grind of railroads, factories, and mines floated into working-class quarters more often than into suburban homes and downtown apartments. On laundry day, the wives of mechanics and carpenters had to wash clothes saturated with dirt, grime, and grease. Perhaps the single biggest chore for these women was getting water. Without indoor plumbing or sewage, every drop of water used in the house—for drinking, cooking, bathing, and cleaning—had to be carried indoors and dirty water carried out. Urban families living on the third or fourth floor of a tenement made many treks each day to public faucets.

Rural women faced similar housekeeping challenges. Imagine the difficulty of keeping a sod house or dugout spick-and-span, with dirt filtering down from the ceiling or, in rainy weather, floors and walls awash with mud. "How happy we were to have the sun shine again," rejoiced one dugout resident. "I spread all my household goods out to dry. . . . But alas, the next morning the rain was pouring down again." Housekeeping conveniences may have been few in town, but they were almost totally lacking in rural districts. Few frontier families enjoyed the luxury of even a cookstove. Until wells could be dug, farm women hauled water from nearby creeks and rivers. Barnyard wells eased but did not eliminate the strain. One rural woman declared dish washing the worst daily chore. "The sweeping and dusting is discouraging enough," she admitted, "but there is this consolation. It isn't the same dirt which you swept before." Cooking, by comparison, seemed "awful tame," and it, at least, contained a creative element. Washing and ironing offered "dreadful monotony," but they were weekly chores with some variety, according to the material being washed or ironed. "But those dreadful dishes!" she exclaimed. "You rinse, scald, wash and scour again, and put the dead pictures of discouragement upon the same shelves and the next morning there they sit ... staring, mutely and appealingly, the same white plates, cups, saucers and bowls, and away you go."

Rural housekeepers also had numerous outdoor chores. Feeding chickens, milking cows, even working in the fields formed part of many daily routines. A few diary entries recorded by a Wisconsin woman in 1865 suggest the variety:

> Saturday, March 4. Scrubbed and did my ironing.
>
> Monday, March 27. Did our usual work. In the afternoon yoked up the oxen and drawed logs for firewood then went to sugar bush with Mother and brought down some sap on the little sleigh and had a queer time driving oxen.
>
> Friday, March 31. Moved about twenty bushels of potatoes with Ma's help and put them in the cellar.
>
> Monday, April 3. Emma and myself carried in fifty bushels of turnips out of the pit. We did not think it was so hard a job until after we got at it.

Unfortunately for farm families, fewer and fewer rural women wanted to "hire out" to do housework; more and more sought jobs in towns and cities. "No one wanted to be a servant," recalled a woman who grew up in rural Kansas. "Each woman and every girl expected to be in a house of her own with at least three men on hand to fetch water and cut wood, etc. Thus we were often without a hired girl." "Women are paid high wages, are very incompetent, and daily grow more inefficient," came the lament from New England. "It takes three women to do what one used to do, and house-keeping is getting to be a grievous burden." The shortage forced rural men and children to do their share of the housework. "Female hired help was not to be obtained," reported one husband. "I assisted my

wife all I could—probably did as much housework as she did."
Just as rural boys spent more time on the farm than in the
classroom, so rural schoolgirls spent more time than their city
cousins learning housework and helping with outdoor chores.
Nevertheless, the brunt of rural housekeeping fell on farm
wives. Like the mothers of tenement families, farm women
aged more quickly than middle-class women in town. Shoulders
became bent. Hair grayed prematurely. Skin turned brown and
leathery in the sun and wind.

Special occasional chores sometimes interrupted daily routines in town and country. Candle making, for example, while
becoming more and more rare, was still a necessary activity in
some frontier and isolated rural regions. "It was a job I sincerely
loathed," recalled a woman familiar with the process, "from the
boiling of the fat to the extracting of the finished candle out of
its mould, scalding my fingers and scratching them with jagged
tin every step of the way. There was not a redeeming feature
in the whole business." Similarly, soap making was a tedious,
day-long task that required boiling and stirring a disgusting
mixture of potash (made by pouring water over wood ashes),
salt, fat, and bacon rinds.

The most dreaded seasonal chore was "spring cleaning." Oh,
what horror that phrase held for housekeepers! In all but the
simplest dugouts or tenements, spring cleaning meant one or
two weeks of upheaval, chaos, and pronounced indigestion. No
one can say how this annual rite of domestic mayhem began,
but it soon grew into a monster. Every piece of furniture in
every room had to be moved, either outdoors or to a different
room. Carpets had to be taken up, drapes taken down, and
every square inch of floor, wall, and ceiling dusted, mopped,
washed, polished, or otherwise refurbished. Rugs, looped across
outside clotheslines, were beaten unmercifully, raising a storm
of dust reminiscent of a cyclone touching down on the open
prairies. Upholstered furniture was similarly aired and beaten,
while wood furniture—indeed, every wood surface—was oiled

and polished. Heavy feather mattresses had to be aired outside for two days so that each side could be alternately drenched by the dew and dried by the sun. Most families also used the opportunity to put winter clothes into storage and haul out summer and fall wardrobes. Not surprisingly, many churches held bazaars during this chaotic season to take advantage of the sifting of old clothes and worn-out household furnishings.

The other principal seasonal event was "canning," a peculiar name for a process that should more properly have been termed "jarring." Canning took place at different times through the summer and early fall, depending on when particular fruits and vegetables ripened. Once harvested, tomatoes, peaches, corn, strawberries, cucumbers, and other foods had to be cleaned, cooked, strained, and drained. The prepared foods, some in the form of jellies and relishes, were then transferred to glass jars (the most popular brand being the Mason jar, introduced in 1858) still warm from boiling and sealed with molten paraffin. It was hard, hot work, but when winter came and all those "fresh" fruits and vegetables added zest to a dull diet of meat and potatoes, everyone blessed the effort. The ritual was widespread, even in towns and cities where families managed to keep backyard gardens and fruit trees.

Whether attending to daily or seasonal chores, most housekeepers interrupted their workday between noon and one o'clock to welcome their families home to dinner. Children, when possible, came home from school. Fathers, unless working a considerable distance away, also joined the family circle. In rural areas and small towns, this had been the tradition for many years. Dinner was the principal meal of the day, a time for families to relax and converse, though the tradition seemed to be dying in large cities by the 1870s. "The family dinner at midday, and the evening tea of inland towns, at which parents and children gather about the tables and learn to know one another through the interests and feelings of every day," lamented one city dweller in 1875, "are almost unknown in the same grade of social city life." Urban families whose busy schedules infringed upon the traditional midday rendezvous made supper, taken between six and seven o'clock, their principal meal.

Growing numbers of urban businessmen, clerks, artisans, and laborers further marked changing times by eating "luncheon" at saloons, oyster bars, and small restaurants that specialized in serving large numbers of patrons in the shortest possible time. Strangers to this American custom found it repulsive, suggestive of "a piggery at swilltime." "The noise, the bustle, the hurry, in such a place," complained one man, "can only be compared to that which occurs when the animals are fed at Barnum's caravan." Customers "do not eat," he insisted, "they feed." Most men took no more than ten minutes to gulp down a meal, pay, and leave. Many saloons and oyster bars served a "free lunch" of "mammoth size" meat and cheese sandwiches, boiled eggs, and pig's feet to patrons who purchased a five-cent mug of beer. By the 1870s, "Hamburg steak" had appeared on menus as a sandwich. More affluent and leisured men might spend twenty to thirty minutes to enjoy a fifteen-cent plate of beans, potatoes, ham or corned beef, bread, and coffee. "You will recognize an old restaurant *habitué*," one observer chuckled wryly, "by the leanness of his face, general debility, depression of spirits, and the habit of belching wind like a blacksmith's bellows."

Families eating at home enjoyed a variety of fresh and processed foods. Canned goods, refrigerated railroad cars, and factory-made dairy products provided more and cheaper goods to larger numbers of people. Americans bought five million canned goods in 1860, thirty million in 1870. The largest volume of canned goods was sold in the West. Although one New Jersey grocer offered fourteen varieties of canned fruits, vegetables, and seafood in 1867, most easterners suspected canned goods of being unhealthy. Equally important, many women regarded them as signs of deficient cooking talent. Refrigerator cars made fresh fruits and vegetables available for a longer part of the year and with a wider distribution. National brand names—including Pillsbury flour, Van Camp's beans, Quaker oats, and Chase and Sanborn coffee—established new standards of quality and nutrition. The old general store remained an institution in rural areas and small towns, but people quickly recognized that food sold from open barrels, crates, and boxes was too often soggy, stale, dirty, adulterated, and uneven in quality. The first chain grocery store—the New York–based Atlantic and Pacific Tea Company—won almost instant approval when it opened its doors in 1864. By 1880, the company had over one hundred stores scattered throughout the country.

The nation at large remained a meat-and-potatoes country, those two staples appearing at nearly every meal; but wide variations flourished. Among meats, pork remained popular with both rich and poor in the South and parts of the West. In rural areas of the South, pork constituted at least half of the total diet. As fresh beef became more widely distributed, northerners considered pork (other than cured hams) a "lower-class" meat. Corned beef, both hashed and with cabbage, was popular everywhere. Only northeasterners and southwesterners ate much lamb or mutton, but everyone loved turkey and chicken, although the latter would nearly always be fried in the South and boiled in the Northeast. Preference of potatoes neatly divided North and South. Northerners preferred Irish potatoes; southerners had a passion for sweet potatoes. Both sections enjoyed their potatoes in many different forms, including mashed, boiled, stewed, baked, scalloped, and "German fried." By the end of the Civil War, city restaurants had introduced a popular new dish: "French fried" potatoes. Most of the nation outside of rice-producing regions remained indifferent to rice.

Among other foods, Americans had definite preferences. They loved cheese. Increasingly, they ate factory-made cheddar, home manufacture of cheese having all but disappeared by 1880. Americans did not hold the same regard for green or yellow vegetables, and, in any case, they prepared them badly. Most cooks, from a long-standing distaste for raw vegetables, boiled them nearly to extinction. This attitude contrasted sharply with the nation's passion for raw fruit, which people ate, when possible, at every meal. The most popular and most adaptable vegetable proved to be corn. Only the rich bothered with green salads, although the middle classes experimented with salads made from potatoes, tomatoes, and cabbage. Celery seemed to be the only exception to the national distrust of raw vegetables. Foreign visitors expressed amazement at the "prodigious" amounts of celery Americans consumed, and at the way they "almost incessantly" nibbled at it "from the beginning to the end of their repasts."

Americans consumed baked goods—whether made from wheat or corn—in staggering quantities. A Vermont farm wife recorded making 421 pies, 152 cakes, 2,140 doughnuts, and 1,038 loaves of bread in a single year. Northerners ate more wheat bread than westerners or southerners, biscuits being a more popular form of preparing wheat in the latter two regions. Regional tastes and available fruits dictated pie fillings. New Englanders swore allegiance to pumpkin and mince, westerners demanded raisin and apple, and southerners enjoyed citrus fruits, pecan, and sweet potato. Cakes, too, came in a variety of styles, including layer, pound, gingerbread, sponge, coffee, and coconut. Strangely enough, all this baking failed to stimulate a boom for commercial bakers. Americans distrusted commercial bakers and felt guilty about using them, just as they felt guilty about using canned goods. "Whether on the score of health, of cleanliness, or economy," insisted a woman in 1869, "it is impossible to urge too strongly the importance of making bread at home."

Regardless of their ingredients, home-cooked dinners were heavy meals, not just because of the quantities of food families consumed, but because of their preference for fried foods. Meat, potatoes, eggs, even vegetables were fried in butter, lard, and bacon grease for most meals. This diet seemed all the heavier because of the speed of an American meal. The only leisurely portion of the noon meal came when fathers reclined for a short nap before returning to field, shop, or office. Otherwise, Americans, even at home, bolted their food. Manners often fell by the wayside. "There was very little ceremony at these meals," recalled one farm boy of the noon repast. "Man and boy went to the table as they came from the field, wet with sweat. . . . Napkins were 'against the law,' and steel knives were used to help out the three-tined forks. . . . The farmwife's universal greeting to her ravenous workers was, 'Now boys, help yourselves. What you can't reach, yell for.' " Small wonder, what with all the grease and haste, that "dyspepsia," or indigestion, was the most universal physical complaint of the nineteenth century.

The noon meal completed, men headed back to work and their wives attacked afternoon chores. Women without servants frequently kept their daughters home from afternoon school sessions to help them. In the countryside, during those few months when children attended school at all, boys and girls attended classes for only half the day. Afternoon was also a popular time for leisured ladies to visit neighbors and friends for afternoon tea, attend to charitable and civic duties, or seek "self-improvement." "Housekeeping does not exclude those other employments that have of themselves so large a share in the world," explained a household adviser. "Music, drawing and painting, and also literary pursuits, they all have their place in the model housekeeper's domain, and help to make life and home beautiful." Patronizing the arts, attending lectures and lyceums, and participating in the newly popular women's clubs required time. Temperance societies, charity bazaars, and organizations promoting relief for the homeless and indigent demanded attention. Less formally, afternoons also became a popular time for gossiping with neighbors over backyard fences.

Whatever their afternoon routines, family members assembled once again as fathers and husbands drifted home from shop, field, factory, and office after laboring their normal ten-to twelve-hour day, six days a week. Men with particularly gritty jobs in mines and factories would take time to wash and change clothes before the family sat down to eat supper between six and seven o'clock. Families that had indulged themselves at dinner usually ate light meals, composed of such fare as cold meats, potato salad, and fresh fruit. After washing supper dishes, families settled down to enjoy a few quiet evening hours before going to bed. Most evenings they sat in the living room or, if on a farm, gathered around the kitchen table. On warm evenings, the porch or veranda became a natural place to gravitate toward. In town, neighbors out for a stroll might stop to chat. Otherwise, Father smoked while the family conversed or meditated. Boarders, most of whom had spent the day at work, might join the family, too. Only a few families, however, would be so liberal as to invite servants to join them. Most servants and hired hands spent evenings in the kitchen or their own living quarters.

Evening entertainments at home suited each family's tastes and inclinations. Schoolwork for the children; the day's newspaper for Father; letter writing, more sewing, or *Harper's Bazar* for Mother would be a likely pattern. Most people spent some time reading, and in many families Father or Mother read aloud from the latest popular novel or periodical. Americans certainly had a wide variety of literature from which to choose. Women relished the latest sentimental novel of Mrs. Southworth, Augusta Jane Evans, or Louisa May Alcott, and everyone began chuckling at the humor of Mark Twain, who first gained widespread popularity with *Innocents Abroad* in 1869. Dime novels, chronicling the exploits of Buffalo Bill, Ned Buntline, and other adventurers, appealed to many readers. The number of weekly and monthly periodicals, with annual subscription rates as low as two to four dollars, reached record proportions after the war.

Nearly six thousand newspapers and magazines were being published in the United States by 1870, with 1.5 million copies issued annually. Many publishers devoted their journals to specific topics, such as fiction, religion, children's literature, medicine, finance, agriculture, education, art, music, sports, politics, humor, fashion, gardening, labor reform, and etiquette. Women readers, who set the tone for a large share of the market, could choose from general home journals, such as *Ladies' Repository* and *Wood's Household Magazine;* society journals, like *Boston Home Journal* and *Fifth Avenue Journal;* fashion, dominated by *Harper's Bazar* and *Demorest's Monthly* (which included a tissue-paper dress pattern in every issue); and women's rights journals, like *Woodhull & Claflin's Weekly* and Susan B. Anthony's *Revolution.* The most popular general magazines, such as *Harper's Monthly, Atlantic Monthly,* and *Scribner's Monthly,* included fiction, poetry, and articles on politics, fashion, gardening, childrearing, home decoration, history, biography, travel, and current events. Many periodicals, especially weeklies and ladies' magazines, were also copiously illustrated with woodcuts.

More energetic families used evenings at home to stage puppet shows, perform magic tricks, act out charades, play board games, or accompany the family pianist by singing the latest popular songs. "Round games," new versions of which seemingly appeared every week, were popular. "Yes and No" (described as an "improved form of 'Twenty Questions'") gained a popular following, as did "Authors" (a homemade card game that had a variation known as "Poets"), "Gossip," "Who Am I," and "Quotations and Authors." If Father was a "club man," he slipped away a few evenings each month to attend meetings and club functions. When he returned, the family might pause to pray or read the Scriptures before retiring. One man recalled how his family concluded each evening by singing some "beautiful old Presbyterian hymns" before kneeling to pray "in sincere and reverent tones."

Evening entertainments in rural areas and among the laboring classes could be even simpler. Rural fathers might return to the barnyard, even after dark, to tend to some chore by moonlight or lantern. Children might be ordered to study lessons they had missed by not attending school. More often, education would continue in less formal fashion, with Mother, if she was literate, overseeing the children's progress. "Mother found no time to read," recalled one westerner. "But she guided and directed somewhat the children as they learned to read. . . . Her mind was filled with the lore of the Bible as she had learned it when a child, with Mother Goose rimes, with words and music of gospel hymns and popular songs, with the sayings of Poor Richard, and some German rimes and folklore." Many families were too tired to do anything but go right to bed. A New England carpenter, who generally went to sleep at nine o'clock, admitted that, although he sometimes read his daily newspaper, he was usually "too much exhausted at night to go out for any recreation or amusement." Residents of boardinghouses and hotels, having no home life as such, might visit places of amusement or simply roam the streets.

Weekend routines differed in some notable ways from weekdays. Most men still went to their jobs on Saturdays, although farmers frequently had business to attend to in town. Children, having a day off from school, pitched in to help Mother around the house. Girls generally helped with housekeeping and cooking, especially the latter, for many families prepared both weekend meals on Saturday. This relieved women from cooking on the Sabbath and gave hired help a day off. The small number of families with three or more servants generally arranged work schedules so that at least one servant could wait at table. Boys drew outdoor chores, such as chopping wood, tending animals, maintaining outbuildings, or performing some other yard work.

Weekends also offered a chance to relax. Once Saturday morning chores had been completed, children spent the rest of the day playing outdoors. Seasons dictated activities. Sledding and skating were both popular winter pastimes in northern climes; baseball and swimming were the warm-weather equivalents for boys. Girls played with dolls year-round. In rural districts, hunting and fishing provided both sport and food. Several new crazes, including bicycling, lawn tennis, archery, roller skating, and croquet, caught the fancy of townsfolk during the 1860s and 1870s. Croquet, as one of many new games played on country and suburban lawns, became the most popular outdoor family sport of the era. Families played croquet on Saturday evenings, Sunday afternoons, holidays, whenever fair weather favored them. The gaily colored pegs, balls, wickets, and mallets marked the yard of a middle-class family. Some towns even formed croquet teams, just as they did baseball teams, to challenge surrounding communities. So great did the vogue become that manufacturers issued playing sets with candle sockets on the wickets to permit night playing.

Croquet's popularity, like that of most of the other new family recreations, grew from the ability of men and women to play the game together. It became an acceptable means of courting, as couples socialized and flirted in full view of watchful parents and neighbors. Several popular songs, recognizing these ulterior motives, made sport of the young men and women who played "the courting game":

> I saw the scamp—it was light as day—
> Put his arm around her waist in a loving way,
> And he squeezed her hard. Was that croquet?

Saturday evenings found many families entertaining friends at home, either formally in the front parlor or casually in the living room. Visitors joined in much the same amusements families pursued on weekday evenings, with perhaps more attention given to music and dancing. Weekend calls also gave both hosts and guests an opportunity to practice proper middle-class social behavior. For guidance, they relied on the period's many etiquette books. From these invaluable manuals they learned, for example, that the conversation of well-bred people should avoid religious and moral topics, which usually led to "angry, endless, and useless contests." Similarly, parlor conversation was expected to avoid certain types of language or expression, including "affectation," "low expression" ("a dialect peculiar to low people"), "provincialisms," and "unmeaning exclamation" ("O my! O mercy! &c."). If the evening's entertainment included a supper party, people had to keep pace with changing table manners. *Scribner's Monthly* reported, in 1874, that "some things that were in vogue a generation or two ago, are no longer deemed polite." Most obviously, introduction of the four-pronged fork had made eating from one's knife unnecessary and vulgar. Similarly, the time had passed for cooling tea and coffee in a saucer before drinking it.

Of course, much of this concern over etiquette radiated from urban homes. Country folk tended to be less ceremonious, less concerned with formalities than hospitality. An Englishman visiting the upper Mississippi River valley in 1861 found "no stiffness or uneasiness" in the manners of the settlers. Rural and small-town Americans never hesitated to "drop in" on a neighbor or to welcome passing strangers into their homes. The contrast could create problems for people who moved from town to country or from farm to city. "We hear bitter complaint among strangers, used to provincial customs," testified one gentleman, "of the coldness and lack of sociability of New Yorkers and Philadelphians." Transplanted city dwellers, on the other hand, expressed shock at the audacity of overfamiliar neighbors and the "back-door, inane, country gossips" that characterized village life. Even people moving up the social ladder in their own towns had to learn new ways. "Each social clique," warned a nineteenth-century Emily Post, "has its own unchangeable ideas in regard to what is or is not etiquette in the manner of calls."

Sunday was supposed to be a day of rest. Most Americans, particularly in rural districts, still adhered to that ancient dictum; but the tradition began to erode after the Civil War. Erosion became particularly evident on pleasant spring and summer days, as croquet, baseball, picnicking, and carriage rides punctuated the Sunday afternoons of many families. Ideally, families dressed in their best clothes and spent the morning at Sunday school and church. Afternoons began with the dinner prepared on Saturday, and the remainder of the day was devoted to quiet pursuits: napping, letter writing, reading, or visiting relatives (to be distinguished from Saturday night visits to non-relatives). Frequently, a brief early evening church service for adults and older children concluded the day.

Before turning in, middle-class families donned nightshirts and nightgowns. Nightcaps, a much earlier fashion, won a brief revival in the 1870s, but most people regarded them as out of date. Household manuals advised people to wear the same material in their nightshirts that they wore next to their skin during the day, be it cotton, flannel, linen, or silk. Most families slept with open windows, even in winter, because they believed the flow of fresh air protected their health. "How many thousands are victims to a slow suicide and murder," wondered one household adviser, "the chief instrument of which is want of ventilation. . . . No wonder there is so much impaired nervous and muscular energy, so much scrofula, tubercles, catarrhs, dyspepsia, and typhoid disease." People with indoor sewage pipes and toilets worried about "sewer gas," which backed up from clogged pipes to poison household air. With wider concern for oral hygiene, more people brushed their teeth before going to bed, although the practice was still far from universal. People applied various household mixtures to their teeth with fingertips, a bit of sponge, or a small brush. One popular recipe consisted of a boiled compound of water, lemon juice, salt, and burnt alum.

# 4

## CHURCHES, CHARITIES,

## AND SCHOOLS

A MERICAN home life rested upon the twin pillars of religion and education. Churches and schools, serving as the nation's most important public institutions, shaped and expressed essential national values, beliefs, and assumptions. Religion was most important. Few Americans doubted that God actively intervened in everyday affairs. Recalled one old-timer of the era, "It was God who sent you children, made the potatoes turn out well, put the blight on the orchard trees, and caused the roan mare to sicken and die." And the Almighty's power extended well beyond the family farm. His abiding influence, Americans believed, in no small measure caused the Civil War, as well as a startling burst of charitable activity during and after the war. As for schools, even remote rural and frontier communities considered a schoolhouse an immediate priority, along with a church, in building a legitimate settlement. In fact, the same building sometimes served both God and McGuffey.

"The first thing almost which strikes a newly arrived traveler in the United States," observed an English visitor in 1862, "is the immense number of churches. . . . The country is dotted over with the wooden steeples, whose white painted sides, I must own, sparkle in the bright sunlight uncommonly like marble." Not all of America's 72,000 churches (in 1870) fit that idealized image. Many citizens, particularly those worshiping on the frontier and in rural areas, gathered in log shacks, barns, carriage houses, town halls, saloons, or beneath God's open skies. The nation's multiplicity of religious sects ("more numerous . . . than in any other part of the Christian world") also added variety to America's religious landscape. Yet, the Englishman's larger point could not be obscured. Religion served as an important part of America's social structure. Church attendance, like being married and owning a house, conferred respectability and implied an honorable character. Even without the churches, which by themselves could not hope to measure the true strength of the nation's religious moorings, Americans were a pious lot.

True, probably no more than half the nation attended church regularly. Americans in the 1860s and 1870s were more worldly, more materialistic than their parents and grandparents. Charles Darwin had thrown religion on the defensive, and not a few people, generally rough men in rugged occupations, cared for neither science nor religion. As a resident of one Colorado mining town observed, "In Leadville there was no Sunday." No doubt, too, many people practiced the formalities of religion without feeling its spirit. One English visitor in the 1860s called American religion "rowdy." "By that I mean to imply that it seems to me to be divested of that reverential order and strictness of rule which . . . should be attached to matters of religion," he explained. "One hardly knows where the affairs of this world end, or where those of the next begin." Elaborating still further, the Englishman concluded of Americans, "They are willing to have religion, as they are willing to have laws; but they choose to make it for themselves."

Still, even half a population of nearly forty million is a hefty number, and most Americans, whether or not they attended church regularly, considered themselves Christians. "The Cross," claimed one man, "is everywhere the symbol of . . . faith." Americans, remarked another observer, regarded "the general acceptance of Christianity to be one of the main sources of their national prosperity, and their nation a special object of the Divine favour." Roman Catholics had formed the nation's single largest religious community by the time of the Civil War, but their prominence was somewhat misleading. Only four thousand churches and chapels served four million Catholic souls by 1870, and most Catholic houses of worship stood in northern cities, where the clamor of over two dozen other denominations with many millions of members muted their influence. In any case, Protestant Americans, most notably Methodists, Baptists, and Presbyterians, with tens of thousands of churches in all parts of the land, claimed the largest block of the faithful and formed the most vibrant religious force in the country.

Most denominations deemed church attendance a family activity. Parents, children, and grandparents all took seats in the sanctuary (sometimes in rented pews) for worship services. Hymns, Scripture readings, and sermons formed the heart of Protestant services. Foreign visitors rarely failed to be impressed by the common sense of American sermons or the central role of music in worship services. "There is more frequent and more melodious singing," concluded a visitor comparing an American service to one in Britain. "It is not thought sinful to comply with the exhortations of the Psalmist: 'Rejoice in the Lord, O ye righteous.' " Other visitors noted the singular contributions of choirs and professional soloists to worship services, contributions that sometimes excluded participation by the congregation. A not uncommon worship pattern, followed by a Presbyterian church in Chicago, opened with an organ prelude and a mixed quartet singing a sanctus. Next came a prayer, followed by a chant, an Old Testament Scripture reading, another prayer, a New Testament Scripture reading, a hymn, the sermon, the offering, another hymn, and the benediction. In poorer churches, where hymnals proved too expensive for wide distribution, congregations repeated the words of unfamiliar hymns as dictated by their ministers; but most regular churchgoers knew dozens of standard hymns by heart. Some ministers complained about the number of people who departed services following the singing (and before the offering), although other clergymen, on occasion, allowed the singing to go on so long that they had to shorten or postpone their sermons.

The sermon tended to be "topical" rather than an exposition of Scripture, as growing numbers of preachers abandoned the formal essays, long homilies, and dry dogmatism of earlier years. "The modern preacher," submitted one observer, "preaches more and argues less." The inspired preacher applied Christian ideals to everyday life. "He shows men to themselves," insisted one commentator, "and then shows them the mode by which they may correct themselves." Fewer preachers tried to frighten people into good behavior with threats of fire and brimstone. Rather, they sought to "make men better" by shaping their character. A Scotsman praised American preachers for being "more direct, homely, and practical" than British clerics. "The difference," he concluded, "is in their being less . . . clerical in tone and manner and more human."

Sunday schools and prayer meetings provided additional religious inspiration and instruction for both children and adults. Congregations selected their Sunday school teachers very carefully. Leading men of the community—lawyers, merchants, and the like—usually got the call. Large churches constructed assembly halls adjacent to their sanctuaries to host Sunday school classes, as well as social events and public lectures. In smaller churches, teachers divided space in the sanctuary for their classes. Sunday school lessons, like the preachers' sermons, centered on important moral and ethical principles, special emphasis being placed in children's classes on parables. Sunday schools paid particular attention to children. Without regular, ongoing conversion in the junior ranks, churches soon would have died out. Yet many children lacked natural religious enthusiasm. "I had had church and Sunday school regularly," recalled one man of his youth, "and I did believe in God and

Christ. . . . Religion, however, had been a duty, not a reality; church was, like school, like other requirements, a mere matter of the dull routine of life." Similarly, many Protestants complained that the only people who attended prayer meetings were church officials—all men—and the leading ladies of the church, who dragged along "such of their families as they can induce to accompany them."

Rural communities, too small to command the services of a full-time preacher, relied for spiritual guidance on circuit riders. Depending on the section of the country, riders could have as many as a dozen appointments on their circuits, but four to six was more usual. A preacher with six appointments could generally manage, with some hard riding, to squeeze three sermons into a day, thus meeting with each congregation every two weeks. Like the postman of yore, neither rain, nor sleet, nor dead of night could stop the dedicated circuit rider from making his appointed rounds. Bachelor riders frequently had no fixed home, but ate and slept a week at a time in the homes of his widely scattered flock. Nor was he an idle guest. During the week, when not otherwise engaged with funerals, marriages, and visits to the sick, he helped with chores around the house and in the fields. His presence was a godsend, so to speak, to devout people who hungered for a permanent preacher in their community. "Today is the Sabbath," wailed a discontented Wisconsin woman. "O that the Lord would raise up a people in this valley who will delight to do His work. O that we might have Sabbath and sanctuary privileges once more." Itinerant circuit riders, if not the ultimate answer to such prayers, at least provided balm for grieving hearts.

Camp meetings and revivals offered a popular means of invigorating languid spirits and wayward communities. The nation had experienced two great upheavals, or "awakenings," of evangelical enthusiasm before the Civil War. A third, brief wave swept through some cities in the late 1850s, to be resumed in the postwar years. But local revival meetings followed the dictates of faith rather than fashion, and fervent revivals echoed through the American countryside pretty regularly. Meetings lasted from a few days to several weeks. Autumn was the most popular season for revivalism, after crops had been harvested and the winter's wood supply gathered. Revivals thus served as thanksgivings for the harvest and as boisterous, yet acceptable, celebrations of a year's hard work. Meetings could be held in churches or out-of-doors. Hundreds, sometimes thousands, of worshipers traveled for miles in wagons, by horseback, or on foot to reach the site. They slept in wagons, tents, or rude shelters fashioned from timber and brush. Their abodes generally encircled a central meeting area. Within this clearing they constructed a raised, bough-covered platform for the preacher and rows of plank or split-rail benches for the congregation. Some worshipers also constructed a rail fence through the middle of the clearing to separate men from women. The entire encampment glowed each evening from the light of hundreds of campfires and lanterns.

Most encampments scheduled three meetings a day, one each in morning, afternoon, and evening. Preachers saved their hottest fire-and-brimstone exhortations for these assemblages. "The sermon was followed with singing and prayer," explained a witness at a revival on the Kansas plains; "during the exercises the power of God came down among the people, Sinners cried for mercy, Saints rejoiced and shouted aloud the high praises of the Lord of Hosts. The songs and shouts of the Lord's redeemed continued for several hours." But preachers measured their success only partly by the volume of singing or hysterical expressions of devotion, such as "jerking" or "losing strength." Their real object was to reclaim backsliding sinners and draw new members into the fold. Preachers who failed in these tasks believed they had failed God. "Again the conviction that I am a failure as a preacher almost crushes me," confessed a despondent Illinois revivalist. Yet, on another occasion, having inspired several members of his audience to approach the altar, the same man praised God: "The spirit was upon me in extraordinary power."

Some people questioned the effectiveness of camp meetings. One fellow acknowledged the air of enthusiasm and goodwill at the meeting he attended. "Once or twice during each day," he affirmed, "according to the number of converts, they waded into the creek, and amid shouts of 'glory' were baptized." Yet, the meeting had another side. "Lots of people," he observed, "went to the meetings who were not members of any Church, and the whole thing partook very much of the nature of a week's picnic. There was plenty to eat and drink, and considerable amusement was to be found by the not too serious part of the community." Even the faithful and the newly converted soon lost their bloom of rejuvenation. "When the revivalists had departed," observed our eyewitness, "and the excitement had abated a bit, the new members slacked down to their former level, and but little effect remained in a short time of the enthusiastic revival."

Even without the revivals, churches played important social functions by providing a focus for family and community life. Worship services, Sunday schools, and midweek prayer meetings provided convenient and eminently respectable occasions for young men and women to become acquainted. One Pennsylvania swain, having praised the "very practical and profound sermon" delivered by his minister, went on in his diary to record other events of the day. "It was a very awkward maneuver to approach her and ask for her company to another service," he confessed in describing post-service activities in a church stairway. "But I accomplished it casually, and she could not refuse. We went at once to another church, chatting and enjoying ourselves marvellously. . . . We returned in the evening talking all the time but more gravely than before."

The venerable "church social" served any number of functions, most often helping to raise money for some worthy cause. Donation, or "pound," parties, held at least once a year in small towns and rural areas, allowed congregations to supplement their ministers' meager salaries with contributions of money and groceries. Church festivals and fairs became the most ambitious social projects, generally serving to raise money for missionary societies or to pay off church mortgages. Nearly all of these social occasions had a lavishly prepared meal as the central attraction. That at least persuaded local bachelors to turn out. Additionally, churchwomen sold or auctioned donations of food, candies, preserves, quilts, clothing, books, and similar articles. Booth games provided entertainment for the more liberal denominations. People bought chances (usually a dime or nickel) to dip into a grab bag for some ridiculous toy. They paid to peep into a pasteboard box labeled "What a Young Man Hates" (they saw a boy's mitten). They might even pay in order to cast votes for the prettiest girl at the fair, contests that could make as much as a hundred dollars. Nearly all denominations forbade liquor and tobacco at their festivals.

Unfortunately, in the opinion of some Americans, church and the Sabbath had become a little too sociable. "Religion," recalled one cynical commentator, "had largely ceased to be a fact of spiritual experiences, and the visible church flourished on condition of providing for the social needs of the community." Even more to the point, fewer people took seriously the ancient law that Sunday should be a day of rest. Shops and offices still closed on Sunday; shovels and rakes still rested idly against barns and fence rails. However, afternoon outings and recreations increasingly replaced quiet and meditative hours at home. The war undoubtedly helped to accelerate this trend. Returning veterans had long since departed from old and familiar routines, and life on the home front had been forced into alien patterns by war's necessities. Ferry boats, horse cars, and trains had to be maintained, in some instances so that the faithful could attend worship services. Moreover, growing numbers of European immigrants, whose observance of the Lord's day had never been quite as strict as in America, inspired a less rigid

"European" or "Continental" Sabbath in some places. "The theater, the horse-race, baseball, the cricket-ground, the lager-beer saloon, have nothing in them that can take the place of the institutions of religion," complained one gentleman. Despite such disapproval, Sunday strolls, picnics, and carriage rides had become part of Sunday afternoons by the 1870s, particularly in towns and cities.

Many city dwellers, caught in the snares of poverty, crime, and ill health, questioned the benevolence of God and the value of religion. Divisions appeared between affluent, middle-class churchgoers, who rented family pews and paraded in sartorial splendor on Sundays, and working-class families that had little to offer the church but a rapidly eroding faith. "[How] can I afford to be a Christian and hire a pew and dress up my family in such a style on Sunday that they won't be snubbed for their shabby appearance by genteel Christians?" asked an embittered Bostonian. Things were even worse in New York. "A vast mass of the population is completely outside of the influence of any religious body," warned a concerned church leader. Factory workers, after long hours of weekday labor, usually sent their children to Sunday school, but they stayed home to rest or catch up on household chores. Asked why he did not attend church regularly, one cotton mill hand replied in 1871, "I really have not time, because if I went to church, my woman would have all the work to do, and it would take her all the day Sunday, and that would be seven days' work."

Religion's pivotal role in the era came during the Civil War. While agreeing on fundamental religious truths, Americans remained subject to all sorts of political, social, and economic prejudices. Different perspectives among Methodists and Baptists, the nation's largest Protestant denominations, led those churches to divide, North and South, in the 1840s. The principal cause for this rupture was the slavery issue, and as slavery became an increasingly important moral issue in public debates of the 1850s, most congregations began taking sides. When the

war came, patriotic duty and religious faith seemed indistin-
guishable. Northerners and southerners entered the war with
an unshaken belief that God was on their side. "The conduct of
the government of the old United States towards the Confederate States is an outrage upon Christianity and the civilization of
the age," sputtered a Georgia Presbyterian who expressed the
feelings of most religious separatists. "The church must be divided," he insisted. "To continue the union of the church after
we are divided nationally is contrary to the usage of the Church
of Christ in all ages." A New York Episcopalian, inspired by the
sight of his nation's flag flying atop a church steeple early in the
war, decided, "This flag is a symbol of the truth that the Church
is no esoteric organization, no private soul-saving society; that
it has a position to take in every great public national crisis, and
that its position is important." By the end of 1861, southern
Catholics, Episcopalians, and Presbyterians had joined Methodists and Baptists in separating from their northern brethren.
Lutherans followed suit in 1863.

Whichever side God was on, the churches shaped the principal role northern and southern civilians would play in the war.
Beyond the ordinary, inescapable rhythms of daily life—working, playing, sleeping, eating—people on the home front fought
the enemy by aiding their soldiers in whatever ways possible
and by seeking to alleviate the pain and suffering caused by
inevitable upheavals in civilian affairs. Their work, defined and
directed by the churches and religiously inspired organizations,
gave numbers of civilians, most of them women, a feeling that
they could contribute personally to the war effort. "The first
shock of war broke the enchantment to which the national
heart was succumbing," explained a northern clergyman, "and
called the whole people to the unwonted task of doing and
suffering something for the public good." North and South,
churches rallied their respective sections by filling in wartime
the role they played best in peacetime: a touchstone for uniting
faith and family. The churches helped to make the war "a
family affair."

Aiding their troops became the first and chief object of northern and southern civilians. As young men rushed to enlist and marched off to war, their womenfolk began sewing, stitching, and knitting. Alone in their parlors or as groups assembled in churches and schools, women in every community made flags, socks, underwear, mittens, anything that might prove useful to local companies and regiments. Some young women at first felt embarrassed to be sewing "drawers" for young men, and quite a lot of giggling accented early sewing circles. Novelty, however, soon gave way to purpose. One cerebral young lady, who had "lived wholly among books," suddenly blossomed into a dynamo when her southern town called for sewing volunteers. "Now she has devoted herself most enthusiastically to working and knitting for the soldiers," observed a neighbor, "and her Italian and French has given way to drawers, shirts, and socks." A Philadelphia family soon converted its house into a "vast workshop," with so many sewing machines being operated that it sounded "like a factory." To increase efficiency, most communities soon organized formal aid societies. Even the smallest rural societies could produce a startling amount of clothing. In just one month, the Society of Center Ridge, Alabama, with about two score members, contributed 422 shirts, 551 pairs of drawers, 80 pairs of socks, 3 pairs of gloves, 6 boxes of hospital stores, 128 pounds of tapioca, and $418 in cash to the Confederate government.

The United States Sanitary Commission, founded in 1861, coordinated the most widespread relief effort in the North. Despite its official-sounding title, the Sanitary Commission was a voluntary civilian organization that assisted the army's medical department by caring for wounded and needy soldiers. Its title was descriptive, however, insofar as "sanitation" served as the commission's initial and dominant concern. Organizers knew that disease and sickness killed more men than bullets in nineteenth-century wars. Sanitation and good health, more than any other factors, decided the victor. The commission prodded the government into enacting rigid standards for camp drainage, waste disposal, hospital cleanliness, hospital supplies, diet, food preparation, and personal hygiene in the army. Leaders and organizers of the commission were mostly professional men from northeastern and midwestern cities, but thousands of plain folk donated their time and services to the commission, and tens of thousands contributed money. Local "Sanitary fairs" raised money by selling homemade pies and jellies, handcrafted quilts and baskets, and chances on lottery wheels or raffles. Children joined "Alert Clubs" to canvass neighbors and raise minimum monthly subscriptions of twenty cents per household for the commission's work, or to collect groceries, liquors, jellies, and crackers from local merchants for boys at the front. Schools held "onion days" and "potato days" to collect produce for the army, and many farm families used part of their land to plant "Sanitary potato patches." Residents of an Illinois town delivered 500 bushels of potatoes to the commission.

Southern military relief was not nearly so productive, particularly not at the national level; but Confederate citizens proved no less responsive to their charitable responsibilities. In addition to sewing and knitting, local aid societies collected clothing, medical stores, blankets, groceries, and other supplies needed by soldiers in the field. "We had no Sanitary Commission," explained one Confederate. "We were too poor; we had no line of rich and populous cities closely connected by rail. . . . With us, every house was a hospital." Southern fairs and bazaars were, of necessity, smaller and less profitable than the monster affairs held in New York and Philadelphia; but they certainly boosted morale and made southern civilians feel as though they could make useful contributions to the Confederate nation. "To go there," insisted one woman at a bazaar in Columbia, South Carolina, "one would scarce believe it was war times, [for] the tables were loaded with fancy articles—brought through the blockade, or manufactured by the ladies." Only the prices—$2,000 for a doll, $75 for a cake—betrayed an inflationary economy. Local newspapers gave wide publicity to such affairs, and they frequently listed the names of citizens who contributed to various fund-raisers as a means of stimulating public enthusiasm and participation.

The most striking, not to say shocking, examples of civilians donating their time and talent to the war effort were the thousands of women who served as nurses. With no professional nurses available (schools of nursing did not produce their first graduates until the mid-1870s), Catholic sisterhoods, such as the Daughters of Charity, and laywomen of all denominations volunteered their services. Some people worried about the propriety of sheltered and refined ladies working amidst the blood, excretions, and bare bodies of a hospital ward, but patriotism, compassion, and a determination to be useful led many women to defy public opinion. Clara Barton, one of the North's most famous nursing volunteers, responded to critics by saying that tending wounded and dying soldiers was no more "rough and unseemly for a *woman*" than fighting was "rough and unseemly for *men.*"

Nurses paid a price for their heroics, particularly when working at the front. Hunger, exhaustion, carnage, and disease formed part of their daily regimen. "I thought it best not to trouble you with an account of how we have been living lately," reported a Union nurse in Virginia, "everything cut off, nothing but coffee . . . bread and [tough] meat." She continued: "One day it was past all bearing. I was positively so hungry I could have eaten cat's meat. I sat over the fire after supper, tired and hungry and wondered if the good I did was balanced by my suffering." Nurses also had to cope with the sight and sounds of wounded and dying men, some of them suffering from ghastly wounds. "The horrors of that morning are too great to speak of," confessed a nurse after her initial exposure to the ragged refuse of battle. "While those awful sights pass before me I have comparatively no feeling except the anxiety to alleviate as much as possible. I do not suffer under the sights; but oh! the sounds and screams of men. It is when I think of it afterwards that it is so dreadful." These courageous women found the work frustrating, too—never enough soap, bandages, medicine, or space, and little appreciation of their efforts by doctors or the public. Most nurses stuck it out because of the supreme contentment derived from their work. Having distributed a rare shipment of delicacies—including buttermilk, loaf bread, and wafers—to her patients, a Confederate nurse confessed, "It did my heart good to see how the poor men enjoyed such things. . . . They were very grateful and urged us to come and see them again."

After the armies, the dependents of soldiers were the next most important object of public charity. "Another army besides that in the field must be supported—the army at home," explained a Mississippian. "Their preservation and their comfort are as essential to our success as that of soldiers in the field." Most states and communities offered some form of assistance to the families of servicemen, but many people refused the aid— such as it was—because applying for public assistance bore a stigma of pauperism. In the North, for example, recipients of government charity had to meet stringent eligibility requirements for the sake of a few dollars a month ($5 in New York for a mother and four children; $4 in the Midwest). Luckily, public-spirited neighbors, generally rallied by local churches and ladies' aid societies, worked to alleviate want. Rural residents near Dayton, Ohio, contributed 225 wagons of firewood, 20 wagons of flour, and 60 wagons of farm produce to the families of local soldiers. In an Illinois town, rival political factions publicized their delivery of groceries and firewood to soldiers' families. Such generous personal contributions supplemented relief funds and enlistment bounties paid by states, counties, and towns. The bounties, offered to attract volunteers to the army, were meant to help support a soldier's family while he served his country.

In the South, even in areas untouched by the tramp of armies, rampant economic inflation, poor transportation, and military confiscation left many people hungry and naked. "I can't manage a farm well enough to make a surporte," complained a Georgia woman requesting the government to discharge her husband. "If you dount send him home," pleaded a Virginia mother in the same situation, "I am bound to louse my crop and cum to suffer." It is hardly surprising that Confederate desertions increased dramatically in the last twelve months of the war, when soldiers received letters from home that read: "Christmas is most hear again, and things is worse and worse. . . . I don't want you to stop fighten them Yankees till you kill the last one of them, but try to get off and come home and fix us all up and then you can go back and fight them. . . . We can't none of us hold out much longer down here."

Soon, it failed to matter. As the Confederate cause faltered and died, no one doubted that God had, once again, arranged the outcome. "The prayers of both," perceived Abraham Lincoln, "could not be answered." Northerners celebrated with parades, bonfires, and fireworks. Churches throughout the North erupted in an orgy of bell ringing and prayerful services of thanksgiving. The war ended with a whimper in the South. The only bonfires came from the still smoldering remains of southern towns and plantations; the only fireworks erupted from burning Confederate arsenals. Southerners had suffered not just physically—from want of food, clothing, and shelter—but spiritually, from faith destroyed. "Oh, our God!" cried a North Carolinian. "What sins we must have been guilty of that we should be so humiliated by Thee now!"

Of all the denominations divided by the war, only Catholics and Episcopalians reunited before 1877, and deep antagonisms, even hatreds, continued to rake unreconciled churches. A northern Presbyterian believed that southern clergymen ought never be allowed to serve as "teachers or rulers" in the church, and rank-and-file southerners ought to be permitted back into the fold only "upon proper sense of their sins, and upon proper confessions and promises." "Instead of giving the rebels place and power again," submitted a New England preacher, "they ought to be taken by the nape of the neck and held over hell till they squalled like cats." Southerners saw things differently. A southern Presbyterian charged that vile abolitionists had, with "calculated malice," goaded the South into war. "What!" he exclaimed, "forgive those people, who have invaded our country, burned our cities, destroyed our homes, slain our young men, and spread desolation and ruin over our land! No, I do not forgive them." Baptists and Methodists felt the same way, and, insofar as these two groups and the Presbyterians constituted nearly 95 percent of southern church membership, the churches could hardly be relied upon to engender a spirit of sectional forgiveness. When a southern clergyman asked a young girl if she knew what evil men had crucified the Lord, she replied without hesitation, "Oh yes, I know, the Yankees."

Yet, if stunned and confused by the war and its aftermath, the churches did not remain paralyzed. The wartime role they had assumed in charitable and benevolent work remained an important focus of their activity. The war had made Americans more aware of pressing social and health problems in their communities. A new breed of revivalist preacher, men like Dwight Lyman Moody and Samuel Porter Jones, who aimed their campaigns of conversion and rebirth at the nation's cities, kept the issue of charity in the fore of daily religious life. The Sanitary Commission's concern for personal hygiene and public health led to increased awareness of sewage and sanitation problems. Increased consumption of alcohol during the war inspired the formation of the Women's Christian Temperance Union. The YMCA and the newly created YWCA expanded their activities, both geographically and conceptually. Wartime orphans, the aged and indigent, the physically and mentally handicapped, all aroused public sympathy and private relief efforts. Natural disasters, such as crop failures in the South, infestations of grasshoppers in the West, fires in Chicago and Boston, and epidemics of smallpox, cholera, and yellow fever in towns and cities throughout the country, inspired unprecedented response to aid suffering communities. The severe economic depression of the mid-1870s produced further efforts on behalf of the suffering poor. Soup kitchens and homes for the indigent opened in the larger cities. In New York, for example, the combined efforts of several charitable bodies fed seven thousand people a day during the harsh winter of 1873–74. "With all our terrible faults," marveled one man, "I believe we are the most generous people in the world."

Probably the most visible change in American religion came with the establishment of independent Negro churches in the postwar South. Prior to and during the war, most blacks had worshiped at white churches, albeit in the basement and at different hours from the white congregation. If white Americans saw the war as a religious crusade, black Americans saw Union victory as the Second Coming. When "Babylon," as some blacks called the Confederacy, fell, newly freed slaves packed local churches to praise the Lord for their deliverance. Others, unable to join in group celebrations, shouted individual thanks. "I jump up an' scream, 'Glory, glory, hallelujah to Jesus! I's free!'" recalled a Virginia slave. "'Glory to God, you come down an' free us; no big man could do it.'" Another black exulted, "Golly! de kingdom hab kim dis time for sure."

Southern Negroes had created two new segregated churches by 1870: the Colored Primitive Baptist Church and the Colored Methodist Episcopal Church. Other blacks joined two churches that had been formed earlier in the North: the African Methodist Episcopal Church and the Zion Church. Whatever the denomination, churches became an important institution in black life. Asked to identify the people living in an adjacent community, an Alabama black replied, "The nationality in there is Methodist." And, indeed, their churches did represent something akin to surrogate nations for black Americans. Church buildings functioned not only as houses of worship but as schools, lecture halls, and political centers. Black ministers assumed even more important roles in black communities than white preachers did in white communities. In the absence of large numbers of black doctors, lawyers, and politicians, preachers were the only professionals in many neighborhoods. They provided not only spiritual guidance and moral leadership but, quite frequently, political direction and financial counsel.

Black churches differed little from white churches in doctrine and organization. In addition to regular Sunday services, they offered Sunday school classes, weekly prayer meetings, lectures, church socials, fund-raising festivals, numerous benevolent societies, and periodic revivals. Like white revivals, black revivals sometimes went on for days and weeks at a time, which caused some complaint among white employers. "Revivals may be very good in their way," admitted one man, "but when our cooks and washerwomen throw down their work and hurry off to the church to spend the week, they get to be a nuisance."

The biggest difference between black and white congregations could be seen in the higher level of religious enthusiasm in black churches. While most white churches held two Sunday worship services, black churches generally held three. While most white services lasted about sixty minutes, black services lasted twice that long. While white choirs and solo singers assumed sole responsibility for singing parts of the service, everyone joined in the singing at black churches. Most striking of all was the emotional pitch of black evangelical worship. Whites demonstrated emotional extravagance in their revival meetings, but black churchgoers made demonstrations of zeal an integral part of all services. Blacks called it "getting religion." "For fully ten minutes the preacher walked the pulpit, repeating in a loud, incoherent manner, 'And the angel will read this letter,'" observed an awestruck white observer. "This created the wildest excitement, and . . . was the signal for loud exclamations from the various parts of the house. 'Yes, yes I wants to hear the letter.' 'Come, Jesus, come, or send an angel to read the letter.' 'Lord, send us the power.' "

The noise and extravagance dismayed white missionaries and even some sophisticated black clergymen, but the average black congregation knew what it wanted. Shouting, waving, and clapping hands demonstrated love of God and purity of spirit. "I goes ter some churches an' I sees all de folks settin' quiet an' still, like dey dunno know what de Holy Sperit am," explained one black woman. "But I fin's in my Bible, that when a man or a 'ooman gets full ob de Holy Sperit, ef dey should hol' dar peace, de stones cry out." "Not make a noise!" she exclaimed further, warming to her subject. "Why we make a noise 'bout ebery thing else; but dey tells us we musn't make no noise ter praise de Lord. I don't want no sich 'ligion as dat ar."

Whether black or white, regular churchgoers or Christmas-Easter perennials, most Americans endorsed religion as a "good thing," and so did they education. Schools and school systems varied widely, but if we ignore for the moment private, parochial, trade, and professional schools, which served the needs of relatively few, most American contact with education came through the common schools. By 1876, all states had public elementary school systems, and the private academies that had traditionally provided post-elementary education were steadily giving way to public high schools. On the other hand, much of the country regarded education beyond the basics of reading, writing, and arithmetic as unnecessary. Consequently, the average American received just four years of formal education.

A community usually raised its first school by subscription, with the teacher receiving one to two dollars per month for each student. Teachers, like rural preachers, generally "boarded around," living one to four weeks with each family. Only after state-supported schools were established did teachers receive a regular salary ($25–$30 per month). By 1870, female teachers outnumbered male teachers two to one in settled areas, partly because women worked for lower wages than

men. Most rural teachers lacked the education of their counter-
parts in town. Rural districts tried to attract normal-school graduates, but they often settled for whatever reasonably
well-educated person came along. Standards could be shockingly low. "I taught my school in the old Presbyterian church,"
confessed a female teacher in Oregon. "Of my sixteen pupils,
there were three who were more advanced than myself, but I
took their books with me nights, and, with the help of my
brother-in-law, I managed to prepare the lessons beforehand,
and they never suspected my incompetency." A Pennsylvanian, after rejoicing in winning a sixteen-dollar-per-month
teaching post, confided to his diary, "I shall give myself regular
lessons and I am going to study a great deal this winter. I am
studying algebra and grammar at present."

A typical one-room schoolhouse was a rectangle with two or
three windows on each long side and a single door at one end.
The door opened into a vestibule partitioned off from the main
room. Rows of pegs or hooks on either side of the door provided
places for students to hang their wraps. A cast-iron stove in the
middle of the room provided heat, and the sun provided light.
The teacher's desk stood on a raised platform at the end of the
room nearest the door. In the most primitive schools, students
sat on plank benches and wrote their lessons on wood-frame
hand slates. Occasionally, long boards extended the width of the
room in front of each bench to provide a writing surface. Most
rural schools lacked writing paper, blackboards, maps, globes,
or any of the other equipment associated with modern class-
rooms. Existing equipment remained crude. Blackboards, for
example, consisted of plaster or wooden boards painted black.
A bit of sheepskin served as an eraser. Textbooks supplied
knowledge, the most important volumes being Noah Webster's
"blue-back" speller and William McGuffey's *Eclectic Reader*. A
variety of arithmetic, history, and geography books supplemented these two standards, the total cost of textbooks for six
years of schooling amounting to about ten dollars. Many parents

tried to reduce even this modest sum by passing on outdated textbooks from one child to the next, so teachers sometimes had to contend with as many different readers, spellers, and geographies as they had students.

A typical rural schoolday began at 8:45 A.M. with a prayer, a Scripture reading, and a patriotic song. It lasted until 4 P.M., with an hour for recess and dinner at noon. Without copybooks and blackboards, most learning was the result of student memorization and recitation. Teachers stimulated students, who could range in age from six to twenty, with a number of time-honored gimmicks. For instance, students learned the multiplication tables, states of the Union and their capitals, and other tiresome facts by singing in verse. "State of Maine, Augu-us-ta, Massachusetts, Spri-ing-field" went nicely to the tune of "Yankee Doodle." Spelling lessons procecded à la Webster, with students called upon to pronounce and spell by syllables and to give each word's meaning. Short words, such as *baker* ("b-a, ba, k-e-r, ker, *baker*"), posed few difficulties, but *incomprehensibility* caused many a stammer and stutter. Most students hated to recite aloud for fear of exposing their ignorance to snickering classmates. Long "speak-pieces," in which students recited passages from famous orations, such as "Webster's Reply to Hayne" and "Catiline's Defense," held particular terrors. "I rose in my seat with a spring like Jack from his box," recalled one gentleman of his schooldays. "My limbs were numb, so numb that I could scarcely feel the floor beneath my feet and the windows were only faint gray glares of light. My head oscillated like a toy balloon, seemed indeed to be floating in the air, and my heart was pounding like a drum."

Students also learned more than the three Rs at school. Strong ties bound school, church, and home in the Civil War era. Parents expected that children would develop a strong moral sense, be exposed to polite behavior, and develop their "character" at school. A Minnesota teacher, recognizing the parents' desires, insisted to a friend, "Let us not only strive to teach thoroughly the several studies which they [the students] may pursue but to instill into their minds and hearts those principols [sic] which will make them noble men and women." One student recalled that the rules of behavior in his classroom were far more intricate and difficult than any subject he ever encountered. On the first day of school his teacher presented the class with a list of eighteen forbidden actions. "They ranged all the way from plain and fancy whispering to fighting in class." The teacher explained each rule carefully, and impressed his class with the importance of obeying them, but it all proved too much for the children. "That first day, we succeeded in breaking all his rules but one," recalled one sprite. "That was the busiest day I ever spent in school."

Yet discipline was essential, both because parents expected it and because lone teachers, facing their array of scholars, could not function without it. Everyone in the community—students, teachers, and parents alike—expected a battle of wits between teachers and students at the beginning of each new term. Teachers who lost the battle generally lost community support. "On the first day of school the teachers regularly brought either a strap or a yardstick," recalled a former farmboy, "and as a preliminary explained its uses." Bigger boys often tried to bully physically unimpressive male teachers, and any female could expect varieties of harassment—frogs in her desk, spitballs behind the ear—until she or the class gained control. A Kentuckian remembered how "Miss Lou" tamed his unruly class. "We were all dreadfully afraid of her," he admitted. "She ruled despotically; to cross her meant one certain thing—a thrashing, tho' you might be the biggest fellow in school." While boys generally caused the most trouble, not all girls were made of sugar and spice. A Connecticut teacher, in 1867, punished one chronically mischievous girl so harshly that "she had black marks across her hand, a bunch on her head, and one of her ear rings tore out." Another boy remembered how his teacher, if unhappy with a recitation, would "grab me and hold me be-tween his knees and pull my ears and hit me over the head."

McGuffey knew what parents wanted, too. The stories, poems, and essays in his readers offered students proof from the best of Western literature that virtue triumphed over evil, that thrift and piety won out against extravagance and irreverence. McGuffey reaffirmed the American belief that all problems were susceptible to faith and industry. "Wealth, rightly got and rightly used . . . power, fame, these are all worthy objects of ambition," assured his *Fourth Reader,* "but they are not the highest objects, and you may acquire them all without achiev-ing true success." In verse, his *Second Reader* promised:

> A little child who loves to pray,
> And reads his Bible, too,
> Shall rise above the sky one day,
> And sing as angels do.

He ridiculed pomp and wealth, and praised the virtues of rural over city life:

> Then contented with my State,
> Let me envy not the great,
> Since true pleasures may be seen,
> On a cheerful village green.

He extolled family and home life:

> We are all here!
> Father, Mother,
> Sister, Brother,
> All who hold each other dear.

Most rural schools, being ungraded, had no formal examina-tions or report cards, but teachers devised numerous ways to stimulate students. Winners of spelling bees and year-end quizzes in geography, history, and arithmetic—usually con-ducted at a public exhibition on the last day of class—received certificates and awards (usually a book or lithograph). One teacher admitted that he held public examinations as much to please parents as to evaluate students. "The parents who attended these exhibitions of stuffed memories," he chuckled, "were struck at the proficiency of the progeny, and retired with the impression that their children knew a great deal because they had parroted off so much that was all Greek to them."

Schools in town and city differed from rural schools in important details. Besides accommodating scores or even hundreds of students, city schools enjoyed more elaborate facilities, including a school assembly room, "recitation" rooms for individual classes, maps, globes, blackboards, student desks, and copybooks. By the 1870s, more schools had instituted written examinations, grading systems, and formal requirements for passing from one grade to the next. Students received report cards, and they were expected to attend classes regularly and to arrive on time. Town and city teachers were more thoroughly trained and more often female than in the countryside. The presence of so many females also inspired a different system of discipline. While rural teachers continued to rely on corporal punishment and humiliation, city schools introduced "moral suasion." Plenty of "fast boys, young rowdies," as one teacher called them, remained, but the troublemakers, rather than being punished by the teacher, were more frequently expelled from school. The number of intermediate and high schools grew steadily after 1870. Rather than leaving school at age thirteen or fourteen to enter a trade or earn an apprenticeship, middle-class urban children increasingly spent their teenage years in school. Working-class children, on the other hand, continued to leave school at an early age to help support their families or, in the case of girls, to help mothers with housework and the care of younger siblings.

One Illinois town, hoping to modernize its "promiscuously" mixed ungraded school, demonstrated the sort of changes in vogue. Residents first replaced their stuffy, dark, "dilapidated and forlorn" schoolhouse, which had produced a generation of "slovenly and unhappy inmates," with a new "model" school, one not only "neat and attractive in appearance" but including "all the attractions of a pleasant and happy home." The new school featured separate cloakrooms for boys and girls and a well-lighted classroom with neat rows of iron-mounted desks. The "neatness, order and taste" of this environment, insisted the district superintendent, would ensure "progress of study, accurate recitations, . . . courteous manners, refinement and true politeness." The school adopted new rules governing student punctuality, absenteeism, and social behavior. By the late 1860s, the town boasted an entire school system, with four primary schools, a Negro primary school, and a high school.

Mention of black schools raises the specter of segregated education. Not until after the Civil War did most northern communities provide public monies for black education, and even then the funds supported separate schools. The South's problem, compounded by its immense new free black population, merely reflected the North's lesser dilemma. Only four southern states—Florida, Louisiana, Mississippi, and South Carolina—established racially integrated schools after the war, and not even those systems survived the 1870s. Southern blacks, therefore, opened their own schools, at first with help from the Freedman's Bureau, black churches, and northern-sponsored benevolent societies, later with state revenues. Certainly southern blacks seemed enthusiastic about acquiring an education. "Everybody wants to learn to read," observed a Virginia teacher of the freedman's new passion. Blacks associated education with broader social and economic opportunities, and saw it as a representation of their new status as free citizens. "Charles, you is a free man they say," spoke up one gentleman, "but Ah tells you now, you is still a slave and if you lives to be a hundred, you'll STILL be a slave, cause you got no education, and education is what makes a man free!" The range of ages in a rural white school was uniformity itself compared to the toddlers and grandparents who flocked to black schools. Parents, realizing the importance of education in the white world, sent their children, and older blacks accompanied the youngsters so that they might at least learn to read their Bibles. A group of adult Georgia freedmen promised their new teacher, "We work all day, but we'll come to you in the evening for learning, and we want you to make us learn; we're dull, but we want you to beat it into us!"

The climax of any school year was the commencement ceremony. Even the smallest communities celebrated commencement day as a joyous and important occasion. Children passing to a higher grade felt distinguished and a little more grown up. Young ladies and gentlemen being graduated, whether from high school or the sixth grade of a rural school, felt ready to tackle the world. Rural activities included a spelling bee and other demonstrations of the students' intellectual prowess. Town and city schools organized formal degree-conferring ceremonies. At the Tiffin, Ohio, high school commencement exercises of 1869, the five graduates—all girls—sat on the stage of the town hall along with their teachers, the local superintendent, and members of the local school board. The audience filled every available seat, and the town's symphonic band contributed both stirring marches and melodious waltzes. Each graduate presented a formal philosophical address to the assembly, the subject of the class valedictorian being "What am I? Whence came I? Whither do I go?" The audience showered each girl with flowers as she concluded her speech. The ceremonies ended with the new graduates standing together on the stage and singing their class song.

The popularity of education beyond high school grew but slowly before 1880. Many professions, including teaching, medicine, and law, could still be entered without a college diploma or even formal high school education. The nation had some five hundred colleges and universities in 1870, but only fifty thousand students and slightly over five thousand faculty members.

Some colleges, particularly in the early postwar South, had only a dozen students, and, with few schools resting on firm financial ground, dozens of colleges closed every year. Entrance requirements and academic standards remained low. Only a few colleges offered courses beyond the level of modern high schools, and many students were only in their mid-teens. Methods of instruction did not advance much beyond the tradition of recitation. One Harvard graduate of the early 1870s complained, "I never really studied anything, never had my mind roused to any exertion or to anything resembling active thought."

This is not to slight dramatic improvements in college education during the period. Several important colleges, including Harvard, modified their old "classical" curriculum of Latin, Greek, ethics, and rhetoric to include modern languages, science, history, literature, and economics. Students could take electives, too, rather than strict schedules of prescribed studies. Entrance requirements stiffened in some places, and fledgling graduate schools appeared. Women also found more opportunities for higher education, as numerous midwestern state universities opened their doors to both sexes, and several women's colleges, including Vassar, Smith, and Wellesley, breached the gates of eastern educational conservatism. Changes in curricula produced more money for libraries and laboratory equipment. Yet, a college education remained a fairly unimportant commodity, as most Americans churned happily along with their grammar school basics.

# 5       RITES OF PASSAGE

H IDDEN WITHIN the maze of daily routines, numerous milestones and rituals marked life's journey for Civil War–era Americans. Birth and death loomed large as the most fundamental rites of passage, but many other rituals, most of them representing births or deaths of one sort or another, figured prominently in daily life. Several such rites, including those associated with war, religion, and education, have been mentioned in preceding chapters. Others worthy of mention include emigration, adolescence, courtship, marriage, parenthood, divorce, and death. Whether a source of joy or sorrow, rejuvenation or despair, each of these challenges helped to define the lives of millions of people.

Emigration provided two types of "passage." On the one hand, it marked a physical passage from one place to another. On the other hand, it meant a fresh start, a new stage of life. Americans had been known as a mobile people long before the Civil War. By 1876, after only a century of nationhood, they had spread across and very nearly conquered an entire continent. The most obvious and traditional migration routes had been westward. The populations of Texas, Kansas, and California totaled 909,000 in 1860; by 1870 those same states had claimed 1,800,000 inhabitants. Not all Americans drifted westward. They went wherever opportunity beckoned. Northerners moved south to exploit the political and financial possibilities of postwar upheaval. Southerners moved north seeking the same objects in prosperous Yankee communities. Americans were on the move, leaving defunct farms for virgin territories, stagnant villages for booming towns. Wherever they wandered, they felt, as did one Ohio woman moving westward, that they had entered "a new world, one of freedom, happiness and prosperity."

The most typical emigrants were homesteaders moving westward in search of fresh farm land. They reached their destinations by a variety of means, including horseback, stagecoach, railroad, steamboat, and wagon; but most homesteaders, burdened with families and piles of possessions, traveled by wagon. They dubbed their wagons "prairie schooners," because from a distance their billowing white canvas or heavy muslin tops looked like ships sailing on a sea of grass. These springless schooners—generally four feet wide, twelve feet long, and capable of hauling up to twenty-five hundred pounds of clothing, furniture, cooking utensils, and farm equipment—rumbled across the continent in groups of a dozen or more until the 1870s. Only then did wagon traffic begin to wane, as railroads began to carry a larger proportion of settlers. Long-distance travel by stagecoach died at the same time for the same reason. Still, western trails leading out of Kansas City, Leavenworth, Omaha, Independence, and Saint Joseph—the most popular points of departure—seemed as crowded as eastern highways. "Sometimes hundreds [of wagons] would pass my office in a single day," reminisced a midwesterner. "The occupants were usually young families. . . . Their objective was Kansas or Nebraska where they hoped to establish themselves in homes of their own instead of renting farms in the older states." Some people embarked on the rugged journey well into the 1890s.

A family of four required about six hundred dollars' worth of equipment—wagon, mules or horses, food—to reach California, although the sale of the wagon and animals at journey's end could recoup about half the amount. Even people bound for

Kansas or Nebraska needed several hundred dollars' worth of farming equipment and traveling rig to have a reasonable chance of success. California-bound emigrants began their journey from the Mississippi River in April or May. By April, the grass had usually grown high enough to support livestock along the way; a June departure left barely enough time to finish the journey before winter snows closed mountain passes. Women and young children endured most of the journey sitting in the rolling, swaying, creaking wagon. Men and older children walked alongside to guide the horses or mules. Groups of wagons drew into a circle at night to protect pilgrims and livestock from storms and marauding Indians. When space permitted, travelers slept in their wagons, but more often they slept beneath them or in hastily pitched tents.

Few people started the trek without misgivings. "On the evening before [starting]," recalled one emigrant, "the whole family, including my mother, were gathered together in the parlor, looking as if we were all going to our graves the next morning." "How our friends crowded around us at parting," remembered another of her tearful farewell. "Some cried and talked of Indians and bears." One woman recorded tersely in her diary on the day of departure: "STARTED FROM HOME." Things did not get any easier on the trail. A five- or six-month journey to California or Oregon sapped the strength of even determined folk. Women, especially, had a hard time. One settler marveled from her new western home at how she and so many other women had been "able to endure it." Countless women, recording their experiences in diaries, included daily entries like this one: "Felt very tired indeed—went to bed early." A young woman traveling through Kansas in 1867 noticed the fresh graves of numerous emigrants who, overwhelmed by hunger, heat, cold, fever, and Indians, had never reached their destinations. "But hundreds of such mounds have marked the advance of pioneers," she reflected. "And what stories of grief do they suggest to those travelers who have passed that way."

Untold numbers of southern blacks lent credence to the liberating influence of emigration. Southern slaves experienced the most fundamental rite of passage imaginable when they became free men and women after the war, but subsequent struggles to enjoy the fruits of emancipation weighed heavily on them. Many ex-slaves, after being held in bondage for so many generations, had a hard time understanding the meaning of "freedom." Many, too, found it hard to accept a printed proclamation as sufficient proof of their new status. They needed to prove to themselves that the day of jubilee had indeed arrived, and the best way to do that was to move. "The negroes don't seem to feel free unless they leave their old homes," reported a North Carolinian, "just to make it sure they can go when and where they choose." A North Carolina black affirmed that leaving his master's plantation seemed the best way "ter find out if I wuz really free."

It seldom mattered where or how far they moved. Most blacks remained fairly close to their old homes, migrating perhaps to a nearby town or the next county. The idea was to "test" their freedom by leaving the house or plantation that represented the physical limits of their old world. Like many rural whites, they often headed for towns and cities, where they mistakenly assumed jobs would be plentiful and life more exciting. Most émigrés soon returned, having discovered "dat freedom ain't nothin', 'less you is got somethin' to live on. . . . Dis livin' on liberty is lak young folks livin' on love after they gits married. It just don't work."

European immigrants arriving in America began their new lives with a similar passage. Approximately 4.2 million foreigners entered the United States between 1861 and 1877, the vast majority (two-thirds) arriving at New York City. Expecting a land of milk and honey, they more frequently encountered hunger, sickness, and exploitation. Their arrival began with bureaucratic delays. Ships entering New York harbor could not land their passengers without first being inspected by port health officers. If doctors found any sign of contagious disease or sickness, they quarantined the ship and allowed no one to disembark until the danger had passed. When passengers finally did come ashore at docks along the Hudson or East rivers, customs officials listed and enumerated them before sending the dazed refugees to Castle Garden, a former opera house on the southern tip of Manhattan that had been converted into the nation's central immigrant depot in 1855. There, officials subjected immigrants to further paperwork and assisted them in exchanging money, buying railroad tickets to the interior, and arranging meetings, if need be, with representatives of churches and welfare agencies.

After processing, some immigrants found friends or relatives waiting for them outside Castle Garden. More often, they found themselves alone in a very large city. Most immigrants did not linger long before continuing their journeys—usually but not always westward—by train or boat. For instance, steamboat passage from New York to Boston cost just five dollars, and from there immigrants could disperse to nearby mill towns, like Fall River, where they provided a large portion of the work force. Some immigrants arrived with promotional literature circulated by American "emigrant agents" stationed in Europe that encouraged settlement in particular states. In other instances, agents accosted people as they left Castle Garden with inducements (sometimes free passage) to travel to towns in the South, New England, or the West. Employment agencies had representatives standing by to enlist immigrants seeking immediate work in the city, and all sorts of confidence men and "sharpers" swarmed around the depot trying to turn a quick buck off the naïve foreigners. The most numerous employment agents sought cheap domestic servants.

The nation's young people, whether native born or immigrants, faced many of the same rites of passage faced by modern adolescents. In fact, the term *adolescence* acquired an increasingly precise meaning after the Civil War. A faster-paced world and a shift from "occupations" toward "professions" increased academic expectations for boys. New cultural, intellectual, and economic roles increased the opportunities of women for employment, and the emergence of female-directed families saddled them with new responsibilities. The myriad of social rites and rituals leading to adulthood for both sexes seemed formidable. Perhaps most difficult of all for adolescents, amidst mounting pressures to mature and succeed, was encountering the opposite sex. Girls began inspecting their ripening bodies, entering menstrual cycles, and paying more attention to fashions. Boys inspected their upper lips for budding mustaches and took more care when dressing for Sunday school. Girls and boys felt the urge to masturbate, and both sexes were plagued by acne (Fowler's Solution, an arsenic-based medication, provided one remedy).

Girls probably had the toughest adjustments. Their bodies changed more vividly and visibly, and they bore the brunt of the responsibility for keeping relationships with their beaux comfortably platonic. Morality and custom demanded that they disguise their attraction to the opposite sex lest they acquire a reputation for being "fast." Some young women resented the double standard. "As long ago as I can remember," protested a resident of Circle Valley, Utah, in the 1870s, "I longed to be a boy, because boys were so highly privileged and so free. Thousands of things for which I heard girls gravely reproved, met only an indulgent smile when done by boys." "I hated being a little girl," recalled a midwestern woman. "All of a girl's duties were irksome to me.... On the other hand, a boy's work exactly suited me."

Young women also suffered a disadvantage as a result of misleading and conflicting advice about their bodies. Some sexual and medical advice manuals told them that nice girls had little sexual feeling. Some writers encouraged frigidity as "a virtue to be cultivated and . . . a condition to be desired." Woman's role in the sexual act, they explained, was to become impregnated. "The *best* mothers, wives, and managers of households," declared one male writer, "know little of sexual indulgence. Love of home, children, and domestic duties are the only passions that they feel." Nonsense, declared other authors. The principal purpose of intercourse in marriage may be regarded as "procreation of the species," but sex must also be cherished as one of life's "few legitimate pleasures." Indeed, rather than portraying women as reluctant partners in sex, some wise and apparently experienced authorities suggested that many women actually garnered more physical satisfaction from sex and displayed more endurance in intercourse than did men. "Perhaps most men learn this lesson soon enough for themselves," explained a writer in 1873, "but a strongly passionate woman may well-nigh ruin a man of feebler sexual organization than her own."

Adolescent girls suffered further from a dearth of reliable information about how their bodies functioned. "Purity manuals" advised them to endure their menstrual cycles—"love's eternal wound"—as a necessary (but unmentionable) function of womanhood. They were to expect that menstruation would leave them weak and in a delicate condition. For a period of fifteen to twenty days each month, suggested one writer, a woman "was not only an invalid, but a wounded one." Small wonder general opinion regarded women as physically frail and unsuited for the rigors of an active life. Authorities similarly misunderstood female masturbation and associated it with ill health. Practitioners of this "solitary vice" (also called "self-pollution," "self-abuse," and the "soul-and-body destroyer") could expect to suffer bouts of indolence, backaches, nervous exhaustion, and a generally "languid manner." Likewise, girls were to guard against too strong an affection for others of their own sex. If one had to kiss, caress, or hold hands with other girls—these acts in and of themselves not thought to be unusual—one was supposed to reserve such displays of affection for "hours of privacy," and certainly "never . . . before gentlemen."

Adolescent boys and young men felt pressure, too. Masturbation remained for them as well as for their sisters and sweethearts a sinful act of self-abuse. Advertisements, even in small rural newspapers, offered conscience-stricken boys remedies for "impure thoughts" and assured them that by ordering quickly they might yet be cured without "use of the knife." Boys felt confused by the explosive urges aroused in them by young ladies and by the social ramifications of this new stage in their lives. They heard radical feminists like Victoria Woodhull and Tennessee Claflin call husbands selfish, unfeeling swine who used their wives' bodies to satisfy their own lust. Such attacks confused them. Did not women lack, according to leading authorities, "real desire," and were not men advised in some manuals to make short work of intercourse (a few minutes at most) in order to preserve their energies? And what about fellows who felt more drawn to men than to women? Some young men admitted to courting and establishing intimate relationships with young women in order to block undesirable affections for male companions. "I am anxious to fall in love [with a woman]," confessed one fellow to his diary, "to see whether I would love Ed as much then as now."

Most men and women of courting age circumscribed their sexual activities to fit the most conservative advice of the day. The number of premarital pregnancies remained small during the nineteenth century, well below 10 percent of all pregnancies, and this despite the frequently unreliable contraceptive devices of the day. Parents, perhaps surprisingly, seldom chaperoned or otherwise monitored their children's love affairs. Chaperoning, a largely European custom, held little appeal for Americans until the very end of the century. American girls, especially, enjoyed a large measure of freedom as to where they went and whom they saw. Foreign visitors to the United States expressed amazement at the amount of freedom young people of all ages enjoyed. They described younger children as "painfully precocious" and "obnoxious," and young adults as "bold

and flirtatious." Some Americans agreed. A contributor to
*Harper's Bazar,* in 1868, worried about the "want of respectful
reserve among young people of both sexes, their interchange of
slang phrases, their audacious and dangerous flirtations." Much
of the flirting and courting took place in public view. Young
men visited young ladies in family parlors, accompanied them
to church, and escorted them to social functions. In fact, young
women insisted on being seen publicly with their beaux whenever possible as a means of staking claim to them. In all but the
most conservative villages and small towns, public intimacy—
holding hands, a male arm around a sweetheart's waist—was
quite acceptable.

Of course, young men could always preserve their girlfriends'
virtue by relieving their sexual urges with less virtuous women.
The world consisted, after all, of "good girls" and "bad girls."
One set of girls represented the ideals of romantic love, the
other set offered energetic and unadulterated sex. Common
wisdom assumed that boys and young men might obtain an
illicit education from the latter before marrying the former.
Social class played an important role in this division of labor.
Factory girls, shop girls, and hired girls offered neatly
stereotypical testing grounds for high-spirited middle-class
males. Prostitutes provided another release. Indeed, their profession proliferated to such a degree in the 1860s that police and
reformers had to confine it to certain districts of the community. They could not hope to suppress the evil—things had gone
too far for that—but they did intend to regulate it, limit the
spread of venereal disease, and save as many women as possible
from sin. Still, prostitution remained significant enough to cause
complaint. "Young men," charged an outraged matron,
"nightly spend their evenings, like dogs, smelling out all these
vile excrescences . . . in the full face of ladies and gentlemen
going and returning from church!" Even worse were young
men who spent "the early part of the evening in the society of
virtuous females, discoursing upon the charms of democratic

life, and the solace of home, and virtuous associations! and directly upon leaving, *cross the street and enter a house of ill fame."*

Yet, enough evidence exists, even about such a very private side of life, to suggest that "proper" people in Victorian America were not especially straightlaced. In fact, not a few observers; perhaps because of the sexual adventures of so many soldiers during the war, sensed a freer sexual atmosphere in most cities and towns. While much of this freedom involved "blatant masculine profligacy," young women also seemed to be less demure than in years past. "The fast girl is now the girl of fashion," lamented one woman in 1872. "In this exhausted age, the piquancy of sin" predominated. Certainly young people found ample evidence of free-and-easy life-styles splashed across the headlines of daily newspapers, as the press played up such spectacular sex scandals as the Beecher-Tilton trial and the McFarland-Richardson murder.

"Came up with Lizzie Green. I don't know how many kisses I had that evening, was almost smothered with the sweet things," exulted one lad about his evening out with a local girl. "I found the family as usual around the warm and crackling fire," reported another young man of a visit to his sweetheart's home. After spending the evening in parlor games, the young lady's family toddled off to bed, leaving the couple free "to talk and kiss and embrace and bathe in love." In both of these instances, men played the aggressor, but flirtatious young women sometimes encouraged the advances of reluctant suitors. One fellow wrote to his sweetheart following an evening of courtship, "We were too happy last night to part. You came very near persuading me to stay all night." Young ladies spoke of the need to "captivate young men [with] violent flirtations" and mused about whether a particular fellow "would be worth going after or not."

Sex and courtship became a game and the focus of much of life's meaning for young men and women. The battle of the sexes, as later generations would call it, flourished in the 1860s and 1870s. Young ladies used kisses or the promise of kisses to tame headstrong beaux. A young man might "forfeit the privilege" of "burning kisses" should he insist on smoking or chewing tobacco. "Don't you dare to say one word about the debt I owe you for in the way you calculate I *will never repay,*" teased another young lady. "I have been entirely too liberal in time past but I don't intend my kisses to diminish in value by their frequent repetition." Some girls prided themselves on their ability to flirt and win a man's "admiration." A Mississippi belle continued to flirt with former suitors even after becoming engaged, a not uncommon practice. "Talked to Mr. P nearly all the evening & dared even with Ruth and Jimmie looking on, to accept his arm for promenade," she boasted in her diary. "I took a walk with my tall victim," she added on a similar occasion, "& experienced a lofty satisfaction in convincing him I was the 'noble woman he believed me to be, not the flirt others called me!'"

Despite the openly sexual overtones of courtship, most young people seemed to regard fidelity as important to a lasting relationship, particularly after betrothal. Indeed, the ways in which they spoke of marriage suggest that sexual intercourse, at least, remained a privilege of the marriage bed. "I have bin true to my promise," an Indiana farmer away from home declared to his sweetheart. "I have not bin to see a girl since I have bin here neither do I expect [to] till I see you. I want you to do the same as I am doing." An equally devoted lass, not long before her marriage, confessed, "I have been looking over the past and can say that no ghost of a lover rises up to reproach me with infidelity." A midwesterner told his fiancée concerning their impending wedding night, "I look forward with much more pleasing anticipation when we may be united and enjoy all the pleasure of two loving souls joined in one and engulfed in each others arms and swim in a sea of pleasures." "I always want you to have a good time when you can," a trusting Michigan lad assured his fiancée. "You needn't think that I'm going to be jealous while I am away from you." "As to your having kissed me so much making me more willing or desirous to be kissed by others," asserted a young lady, "it is quite the contrary."

Not everyone approached marriage as a purely sexual adventure. Many people sought mates with similar intellectual interests, temperaments, and tastes. "Let us be more like one, let us communicate our ideas, our notions to each other," pleaded one young woman to her beau. "I want you to be as open & confiding *to me* as to any *one*, and I will be to *you.*" Love and affection counted for much in tying the marriage knot in the mid-nineteenth century. "[He] loves me tenderly, truly, and . . . I know now that I can place my hand in his and go with him thro life, be path smooth or stormy," one woman recorded in her diary. "We did not fall madly in love as I had always expected to," she confessed, "but have gradually 'grown into love.' " Most people also gave at least some attention to the man's ability to support a family. As more education and money were required to achieve this end, more couples delayed marriage. "I would rather live as a [bachelor] than to marry a lady who would expect a thousand luxuries and comforts that I could not furnish," one man told his sweetheart plainly. A declining birthrate as the nineteenth century progressed also indicates concern about financial responsibilities.

Whatever the basis for a marriage, certain formalities attended its consummation. Couples generally sought the permission of their parents, but this carried less weight than it had in earlier years. If a young man's sweetheart accepted his proposal, that was usually all that mattered. Elopements, as a result, were relatively few. One liberated young woman even became angry when her fiancé insisted on following tradition. "I knew that Pa's consent did not make one hair's difference to you," she berated him, "he knew that we would marry despite his consent, we both knew it was hypocritical asking & we are neither favorably impressed with *sham* courtesies, especially when they involve the observance of an old barbarous relic & recognize woman as property." What was more, fathers had become less important figures than mothers in marriage decisions. As mothers assumed wider responsibilities in advising and disciplining children, they more often became confidantes of their children, particularly of their daughters. So even though young women often married after informing their fathers of the decision, they still sought their mothers' advice about men and marriage.

This does not mean that Cupid could not, on occasion, inspire spontaneity. One man recalled how, on his seventeenth birthday, in 1867, he and some close friends were trying to think of a novel way to celebrate the event. Someone jokingly suggested that he and his sixteen-year-old sweetheart, Sophia, get married. "Sophia," the man recalled, "did not show any disposition to oppose," so the next day—the lateness of the hour prevented immediate action—he and Sophia marched off to the local justice of the peace. By that time, the marriage fever had spread. "Jack and Mary [two friends] stood up for us as witnesses," remembered the groom, "and we stood up for them, and so both couples were married. We went to a cheap restaurant and got a bite to eat as our wedding supper and then went to the theater. . . . Then I took my new bride to her home and I went over to my home." Neither set of parents had been informed of the nuptials, so "a sort of a hullabaloo" accompanied the announcement. But after the initial shock, no one objected to the match. "It was simply all right," the groom recalled, "and my wife came over to our house and lived with us. She was working and so was I. We paid board and saved whatever we could until finally we concluded to put up our own little nest."

The ritual of announcing betrothals changed during the era, becoming less formalized and more personal. By 1880, the word "betrothal" itself had become a quaint vestige of the past, in need of quotation marks when used in print. Whereas betrothals of the past had been announced in church, by the 1860s,

couples had begun to announce their "engagement" in local
newspapers and by writing letters to family and friends. Both
the prospective bride and groom joined in this chore. Likewise,
both wore engagement rings, a tradition that had begun in the
1840s. As one possessive bride-to-be explained when insisting
that her fiancé, like herself, should wear an engagement ring,
"You shall have my mark upon you." Both the rings and the
well-publicized engagement served to dramatize the couple's
commitment to each other.

The wedding ceremony itself grew more elaborate in the
1860s and 1870s. Whereas most couples had preferred simple
nuptials in the family parlor earlier in the century—frequently,
civil ceremonies presided over by a local judge or justice of the
peace—the Civil War era found more couples being married in
churches, at least partly to accommodate larger audiences.
Rather than inviting small numbers of relatives and close
friends as in the past, middle-class couples sent printed invitations to scores and hundreds of people. "I agree with you," a
sensible young lady wrote to her fiancé, "that our marriage be
simple and quick. I do not intend any parade whatever." Yet,
this same woman sent out a hundred engraved invitations.
What was more, beginning in the 1830s, brides who could afford
it began dressing for the grand occasion in flowing white gowns
and veils. Of course, the larger the affair, the more preparation
it required, including rehearsals. Multiple bridesmaids and
grooms joined the supporting cast in weddings that could not
possibly squeeze into any parlor. Sumptuous banqueting and
lively dancing followed the ceremony, usually at the bride's
home or a local hotel. If it was at the bride's home, her parents
prayed for good weather, so that most of the festivities could be
enjoyed outdoors.

Yet, it bears stressing that such lavish affairs were only beginning to gain popularity, initially among the middle classes of
town and city. Plenty of folks continued to "get hitched" the
old-fashioned way. "We came and stood outside the door, ready

for the signal from uncle Milton," reported one newly wed bride. "All marched solemnly into the kitchen. At a signal, the door opened, and stepping in, the ceremony was immediately begun." This young woman realized that a kitchen wedding ranked among the most humble possible scenarios, but it did not bother her. "Start not! ye fairy brides," she announced in her diary. "Beneath your veils and orange blossoms, in some home where wealth and fashion congregate, *your* vows are no truer, your heart no happier, than was this maiden's in the kitchen of a log cabin, in the wilderness of Nebraska."

The all-important post-wedding tour, or "honeymoon," had also changed from earlier days. Nearby cities and spas remained popular destinations for country folk, and growing numbers of people headed for New York and Niagara Falls. Yet these destinations had been popular before the war, too. What had really changed was the function of the wedding tour. In past days, friends and relatives had frequently accompanied newlyweds on their travels. In other instances, couples selected destinations, or at least planned their routes, with an eye toward visiting relatives. Honeymoons became more exclusive after the Civil War, less a family holiday and more a private celebration. Etiquette books suggested that newly married couples leave the church alone to enjoy "a honeymoon of repose, exempted from claims of society."

The average couple celebrated the birth of its first child eighteen months after the honeymoon. While most women were thrilled at the thought of producing a child, few relished the inconveniences of pregnancy. "You don't know how it is to realize," groaned one woman, "that from a condition of vigorous health I am suddenly to drop into illness." Despite their growing physical incapacity, many pregnant women, especially those lacking servants or nearby relatives, had to continue with their normal housekeeping chores. At the same time, once their delicate condition became visible, pregnant women were expected to stay out of public view as much as possible, although this was not so practical a tradition outside towns and cities. "I am allowed a seat where I can creep in and out easily and keep myself out of harm's way," explained a woman intent on attending a friend's party while seven months pregnant. "I am not a pretty figure for company," she admitted, "but I hope to manage so as not to be obnoxious."

Few women, however, failed to appreciate the miracle occurring within their bodies. A Californian, more articulate than many women who shared her feelings, described the sensation of her child's first movements within the womb. She had been attending church when the organ music suddenly made her feel "so strangely." "Its throbbing seemed to stifle me," she recalled, "and for the first time that pulse within me woke and throbbed so strong . . . it took away my breath." She fought off a swooning sensation but told no one what she had felt. "It seems absurd to talk so much about an experience common to every woman," she confessed to a friend, "but I think it one of the *strangest* feelings—that double pulse—that life within a life—I cannot get used to it." Plenty of women's and household magazines offered words of encouragement, too. "Do not fret; do not worry; do not be despondent," advised a journal in 1868. "Do not seek the shadows, but, as far as may be, keep yourself in the clear sunshine of the soul. . . . Breathe the atmosphere of refinement and peace, and in this time of seclusion . . . commune with your own heart and be still."

Under normal circumstances, the great event occurred in a bedroom. Not that some babies did not steal their first breath in the back of a prairie schooner, or at sea, or in some other equally inconvenient and unexpected spot; but very few mothers gave birth in hospitals. Public hospitals did not exist, except as charity wards for the indigent; and people who could afford the services of a private hospital preferred the security of their own homes to a strange medical facility. Then, too, most people regarded childbirth as a natural process that required no special medical environment or apparatus. Consequently, doctors, midwives, female relatives, or neighboring women—all of them possible overseers of the birthing process—rushed to the expectant mother's bedside when summoned. While most middle-class urban families relied on physicians to assist them by the 1870s, in less populous areas the entire process frequently proceeded without any professional medical attention. "Doctors were few and far between," explained a Minnesota woman. "My grandmother had all her babies without the help of a doctor and never had an anesthetic." Female relatives sometimes traveled long distances to help a sister, niece, or cousin during birthing, and sometimes stayed several months before and after the delivery to help with household chores and attend any necessary convalescence. As for neighbors who lent a helping hand, "A woman that was expecting had to take good care that she had plenty fixed to eat for her neighbors when they got there. There was no telling how long they was in for," warned one person. "There wasn't no paying these friends so you had to treat them good."

Expectant mothers without help at hand went it alone. One such woman lived with her husband and two small children in a four-room frame house on the Kansas prairie. On a bright summer day in 1873, her husband set off on an all-day trip to collect firewood. Naturally, the stork, being an undependable sort of bird, chose that moment to make his delivery. The wife found herself alone with the two children, one four years old, the other eighteen months, with the nearest neighbor three miles away and the nearest town sixteen miles distant. "So my brave mother," recalled one of the children in later years, "got the baby clothes together on a chair by the bed, water and scissors and what else was needed to take care of the baby; drew a bucket of fresh water from a sixty-foot well; made some bread-and-butter sandwiches; set out some milk for the babies." Her only serious problem came when, the delivery made, she tried to dress the new baby. She kept fainting. When her husband finally returned, "he found a very uncomfortable and thankful mother."

Being "natural" did not mean that childbirth could not be dangerous. "My darling wife went through the terrible ordeal bravely, and appears to be doing well tonight," a thankful Georgian recorded in his diary. He had good reason to be thankful, for death was no stranger to the birthing room, if not during the actual delivery, then in the week that followed. Even in so settled a state as Massachusetts the infant mortality rate hovered around 150 per 1,000 births throughout the 1860s and 1870s (compared with 19 per 1,000 in 1970). The vast majority of women survived childbirth, but few overcame fully their apprehension of the process. "Unfortunately, I have the prospect of adding again to the little members of my household," lamented one mother. "I am sincerely sorry for it." Fear became inbred early in a woman's life. Few girls reached adulthood without having witnessed at least one childbirth. In many families, adolescent girls learned to assist in the delivery as surely as they learned to cook, sew, and wash clothes. The spectacle caused such psychological fear in some girls that they shied away from sex altogether, or at least from consummation of the sex act.

Other couples used various contraceptive devices and techniques to reduce the chance of pregnancy. The whole notion of contraception caused an uproar in some circles. Many people, including many physicians, believed contraception interfered with the divine order and threatened home and family life. Those authorities who believed procreation to be the proper end of intercourse were particularly upset. Still, a variety of methods for avoiding conception existed. A woman's headache remained the most effective method; but even when both husband and wife wished to avoid impregnation, they could use approved "medical" devices, including diaphragms (called "vaginal tents"), douches (made from alum, pearlash, red rose leaves, carbolic acid, bicarbonate of soda, sulphate of zinc, potassium bitartrate, vinegar, lysol, or plain water), condoms ("a breast plate against pleasure and a cobweb against danger"), the "safe period" of a woman's ovulatory cycle, or any number of old wives' remedies. One popular superstition held that a woman could avoid conception by engaging in vigorous exercise, such as dancing or horseback riding, after intercourse. Another remedy suggested remaining passive during the sex act. Coitus interruptus (or *coup de piston,* as the French called it), perhaps the oldest and least complex method, was criticized for the physical and psychological trauma it supposedly inflicted on both men and women.

The difficulty with all these techniques was that people had to be aware of them, and evidence indicates that, because of the delicate nature of the subject, even educated people often knew nothing about contraception. One couple, who apparently had depended on the "safe period," grew desperate when, despite their precautions, the wife kept getting pregnant. They even gave thanks on one occasion when the woman miscarried. The only alternative seemed to be total abstinence, the unhappy husband advising his wife, "If you do not want children you will have to remain away from me, and hereafter when you come to me I shall know that you want another baby." Another woman, faced with a similar string of repeated pregnancies, wrote to a friend, "It is a delicate thing to speak of in a letter, but Mrs. Hague told me a sure way of limiting one's family—which is no injury to either father or mother." The new method, it turned out, had been recommended to Mrs. Hague (who had the *same* problem) by her physician. "Of course, I knew nothing about it practically and it sounds dreadful; but every way is dreadful except the one which it seems cannot be relied on [the "safe period"]." The new method involved using "shields of some kind." "These things are called condums [sic] and are made either of rubber or skin. They are to be had at first-class druggists." The whole idea sounded "perfectly revolting" to the woman, but, she emphasized once again, "one must face anything rather than the inevitable result of Nature's methods."

The problem of unwanted pregnancies could always be solved by abortion, but this solution, more popular than contraception before the Civil War, became less acceptable in the 1870s. The use of abortion, either with chemicals at home or at the hands of a professional abortionist, spread to all social classes in the 1850s and 1860s, not just as a means of destroying the fruits of "illicit" intercourse, but to benefit married couples of "higher repute." One historian has estimated that at mid-century one abortion was performed for every five to six live births. A long condemnatory article on the abortion trade appeared in the August 23, 1871, issue of the *New York Times,* and a respected physician complained in 1872 that "the luxury of an abortion is now within the reach of the serving girl." The physician knew of one abortionist who offered his services for a mere ten dollars, and accepted "his *pay in installments.*" Married couples usually desired abortions for one of two reasons: either to spare women the unwanted physical strain of pregnancy or to spare families the financial burden of another child. In any case, most Americans did not regard abortion as a moral issue, as they would in the twentieth century. Abortion seemed just another form of contraception. Most states, by the early 1860s, had laws restricting abortion, but they were intended to protect women from unqualified abortionists.

Divorce became an unpleasant but slowly spreading rite of passage for some married couples. The number of divorces remained small during the 1860s and 1870s—under 10,000 per year before 1868, only 15,000 in 1876, and this at a time when the nation included over fourteen million married couples. On the other hand, several trends in divorce cases suggest changing attitudes. For instance, divorces became easier to acquire after the Civil War, particularly in the South, where carpetbagger governments liberalized divorce laws. More significant than liberalized laws, however, were the many divorces sought by wives who had grown unhappy in their traditional, largely subordinate, roles as wives and housekeepers. Growing numbers of women found their expectations of marriage disappointed. They rebelled by seeking divorce. At the same time, wider employment opportunities allowed divorced women to support themselves more readily than in the past. Statistics show that unhappy wives initiated nearly two-thirds of all divorces granted in the late 1860s. Between 1872 and 1876, over 60 percent of divorces granted to women involved cruelty (physical and mental), desertion, drunkenness, or neglect by their husbands. Other evidence suggests that the majority of divorce cases occurred in the middle and working classes—among people, in other words, who would have been the most affected by the female population's growing independence.

Evidence of husbands seeking separations supports the assumption that changing attitudes by women proved an important factor in divorce. Over 80 percent of the men seeking divorce between 1872 and 1876 cited the failure of their wives to be submissive helpmates as the reason for separating. About 45 percent claimed their wives had deserted them; nearly 35 percent charged adultery (a claim, interestingly enough, made by only 14 percent of women seeking divorce). Less than 5 percent of the men claimed cruelty, but some of those cruelty cases involved physical cruelty. The descriptions of enraged wives wreaking havoc on their unobliging spouses would be humorous if the subject were not so grim. "Defendant is a powerful woman, weighing 190 pounds," read one court proceeding; "she struck plaintiff with a stove-lid and broke one of his ribs; on another occasion she knocked plaintiff down with a chair." More often, husbands divorced wives who had "acted in a unwife-like manner," such as refusing to wash their clothes, cook their meals, or bear them children.

Death, life's ultimate rite of passage, weighed heavily on nineteenth-century Americans. "I have made my will and divided off all my little things and don't mean to leave undone what I ought to do," one woman pregnant with her first child confided to a sister. "Sometimes I think I must be very frivolous not to keep a steady eye on death and eternity all the time." A people who had just borne the human cost of a civil war, whose infants and children died in large numbers (110,000 under the age of one in 1870; 203,000 under the age of five), and whose life expectancy at birth was under forty-five years knew how to mourn. Death could be brutally quick and uncomplicated. "On the 28th of August my little babe was born, a beautiful boy," one grieving mother recorded on September 25, 1861; "but he did not stay with us. God took him to his fold, this one pet lamb." Deadly plagues and illnesses joined with accidents and violence to threaten Americans with premature death. As incredible as it may seem to us, less than 10 percent of Americans in the 1870s who reached age fifteen had both parents and all of their siblings under age fifteen still living.

The importance of religion in daily life ensured that death held a prominent position. American churchmen for generations had painted in vivid oratory the contrasts between God's glorious kingdom and Satan's painful domain. Life on earth afforded a "battleground for the soul of man between the powers of heaven and hell." Hymns, poems, and novels furnished a standard "consolation literature" that assured Americans that, so long as one led a God-fearing life, death held no terrors. If London, in the early nineteenth century, could be described as a city much like hell, then heaven, by the 1860s, was being described as a place much like one's own home, the "home beyond the skies," as one poet put it. In heaven, the spirit of the deceased renewed old friendships, felt physically revived, pursued familiar occupations, and carried on with earthly life in all respects. Thus death signified, for all but religious skeptics, not an end to life but merely a transition to another form of life. "Death is a mood of life," confirmed one poet. "It is no whim by which life's Giver mocks a broken heart." Even a pronounced religious skeptic confessed over the bier of his brother,

"He who sleeps here, when dying, mistaking the approach of death for the return of health, whispered with his latest breath, 'I am better now.' Let us believe, in spite of doubts and dogmas, and tears and fears, that these dear words are true of all the countless dead." The converted, meanwhile, cast off all doubts and lifted their voices in joyous song:

> Oh then what raptured greetings
> On Canaan happy shore!
> What knitting severed friendships up,
> Where partings are no more!
> Then eyes with joy shall sparkle,
> That brimmed with tears of late,
> Orphans no longer fatherless,
> Nor widows desolate.

Deaths were announced in personal letters to friends, printed funeral invitations, and public notices in local newspapers. During most of the period, newspaper obituaries gave few details about the life of the deceased and said little about funeral arrangements. Rather, they concentrated on the loved one's preparation for death and the final days and hours. Like a good sermon, they were intended to provide inspirational messages for the living. "The fatal destroyer, consumption, had been at work for about six months," revealed a midwestern obituary in 1866. "Having some eight years ago united with the M.E. Church, and having lived a faithful member," the notice informed readers, "she met the change with joy. Glad to depart from earth to be with 'Jesus.' A few moments before dissolution took place (which was just as the sun was sinking in the west) she entreated her husband to prepare to meet her in Heaven. . . . The last sentence uttered was this, 'Who do I see? O I see him coming, coming to take me home.'" Obituaries for children were brief but particularly poignant. "Horace was an only son, the darling of the family," read one of these. "The little hat, the vacant chair, the toys of innocent childhood are there, but

he is gone. Silently they point to the grave—and then to
Heaven." By 1876, however, change had become evident. Obituaries became less inspirational and more informative. More
details appeared about the time and place of the funeral. Biographical sketches relating when and where the deceased had
been born, the number of surviving children and grandchil-
dren, lifetime achievements, and so on read like Horatio Alger
success stories. They celebrated life and family rather than
death and the hereafter, the new tone being inspired largely by
a growing tendency toward religious liberalism in the 1870s.

The funeral ceremony remained central to the rituals of
death. Neighbors generally helped a family "lay out" a corpse
by washing and clothing it. In fact, death in most places provided a shared community experience, a time to rally around
bereaved families by sending them food, offering sympathy,
helping with household chores, doing anything that might help
families ride out their time of grief. While on view in the parlor,
the corpse generally rested on a wooden board placed between
two chairs. In order to preserve the corpse for at least a day of
viewing, the family placed blocks of ice under the board with
smaller chunks arranged around the body. Very few families,
even in cities where undertakers took charge of the corpse,
embalmed bodies before the 1880s, unless they intended to
transport the body a long distance. Americans before that period judged embalming an "unnatural" and "revolting" practice. Cremation had never been very popular either.

Coffins, used to transport the corpse to the cemetery, were
simple affairs. On the frontier, some bodies were buried in
nothing more than a blanket or sack. Most everyone else settled
for a pine box lined with cloth. However, by the 1860s, and
more especially in the 1870s, prosperous city dwellers were
purchasing metal or fancy wood (rosewood or mahogany) "cas-
kets," to protect loved ones from worms. The very word *casket,*
implying a container for something precious, expressed the
value of its contents. Wooden coffins could be purchased from

local cabinetmakers or even be made by the family, but professional coffin/casket makers catered to more pretentious customers. Likewise, undertakers began to play a more prominent role in preparing the body for the funeral and making arrangements for burial, even though the use of funeral "homes" and funeral "parlors" was still a decade away. "Nothing in New York astonishes visitors from the country so much as the magnificent coffin-shops," insisted one observer as early as 1860. He saw coffins of "the latest style and pattern" on display, "set up on end in long rows and protected by long show-cases, with the lids removed to exhibit their rich satin linings." Some resourceful entrepreneurs even marketed "ice coffins" (more popularly known as "corpse coolers") to retard putrefaction.

Parlor and graveside services varied according to religious persuasion and the section of the country, but some common elements emerged. Most people decked their parlors with flowers, partly to mask any unpleasant odors emanating from the deceased. Once all the mourners had been given a chance to tiptoe into the parlor and comment on how natural and peaceful the deceased looked, everyone gathered around for the minister's requiem. This generally consisted of a Scripture reading, prayers, and a brief, glorious account of the loved one's life. Some religious denominations, most notably Catholics and Episcopalians, held a second, graveside service. Although the trappings of mourning were important and quite visible in some respects—a black wreath or ribbon hanging on the front door of the home, letters written to family members informing them of the tragedy on black-bordered stationery, pallbearers wearing black sashes—people attending the funeral, even members of the immediate family, seldom dressed in black. Rather than deepening the gloom of an already somber occasion, mourners preferred to dress "quietly" in Sunday clothes. Their attire, they believed, stressed the Victorian belief "that death is simply the passage from one life to another."

The final resting spot in life's journey had likewise changed from earlier days. Rustic "garden cemeteries," small churchyards, and private plots had been the rule before 1860; neatly manicured "lawn cemeteries" became the fashion thereafter. Both preferences reflected popular prejudices about landscaping in the respective eras. In the 1840s and 1850s, when Romanticism reigned and "scarcely a city of note" did not cherish "its rural cemetery," wildflowers, massive shade trees, and the rustic look epitomized peace and rest. But as the call went out for municipal parks with sweeping lawns to accommodate croquet and baseball, notions of tranquility shifted. People cherished order more than repose. Similarly, the growing size of headstones and monuments—which grew ever more popular with increasing middle-class prosperity—seemed out of place in a pastoral setting. Small towns also fancied that lawn cemeteries projected a more "urban" image and thus enhanced the importance of their communities.

Retirement did not rank as the significant milestone it does in modern America. People tended to work longer—far beyond what would be considered "retirement age"—because they had no incentive to stop working. Quite the opposite. Without Social Security, pensions, or worker's disability—all twentieth-century innovations—nineteenth-century Americans had to work as long as possible. Nearly 2 million of the nation's roughly 22.5 million gainfully employed workers over fifteen years of age were sixty and older. Dependency naturally increased with age, but studies suggest that significant drops in male employment in the 1860s and 1870s did not occur until after age seventy-five.

# 6

CAREERS AND OCCUPATIONS determined the principal patterns of adult lives, and large numbers of Americans experienced little trouble selecting that pattern. They had been born on farms and there they would stay. Nearly seven million Americans (53 percent of the laboring population in 1870) worked in agriculture. The two largest groups, roughly three million people each, were landowning farmers and hired hands. The neatness of the categories is somewhat misleading. People shifted constantly between one group and the other, as their fortunes rose and fell. Also, striking differences of wealth and holdings existed among the landowners. Yet the fact remains that attachment to the land and the hope of acquiring land loomed large in the ambitions of most Americans throughout the Civil War era. Towns may have been growing; more and more young people may have been attracted by the golden allure of the urban scene; but the nation would not soon desert the soil that had nurtured it for so long.

The money to buy land, livestock, tools, and all the other things required to work a farm seemed out of reach to many people. Between $500 and $750 was thought necessary to purchase and operate a twenty- to thirty-acre farm in most parts of the country. Many people acquired the needed capital by working for wages as farmhands or at jobs in town. Yet borrowing money was no longer so frowned upon by the 1860s as it had been a decade earlier. One farming journal asserted in 1863 that "among farmers the remark is often heard, 'that the best way to make money by farming is to buy and run in debt for land, and then go to work and pay for it.' " In a fairly typical Iowa county, nearly one-third of all land transactions in the 1860s involved mortgages. Renting a farm, although generally associated with postwar southern tenancy, also found favor among ambitious young men throughout the northern and western states. Farmers everywhere sometimes paid rent in kind, from a third to two-thirds of their crops. "Taking a farm to work on shares seems to be considered the next best thing to owning one," concluded a northern observer in the 1860s. "Hiring out by the day, month, or year, is accounted comparatively vulgar."

The size of the average farm in 1870 was 153 acres, but that average encompassed farmers in Wyoming, with an average holding of 25 acres of cultivated land, and California, where the average farm exceeded 480 acres. Arkansas came closest to the national norm, with 154 acres per farm, but its two million acres of cultivated land ranked well down the national list of total landholdings. Illinois, on the other hand, which led the nation with a total of over nineteen million acres of cultivated land statewide, had one of the lowest per-farm averages—just 128 acres. Even more substantial differences among farms and farmers derived from such factors as climate, quality of soil, types of crops, number of livestock, and size of work force. Consequently, the operation of a small family farm in Massachusetts had little in common with that of a tobacco farm in Virginia, a wheat farm in Minnesota, a cotton plantation in Mississippi, or a vineyard in California. The United States did not have a "typical" farm.

Henry K. Dey, who owned a 150-acre farm in Seneca County, New York, might be considered a typical northern farmer. Dey and nearly all his neighbors raised grains, mostly wheat but with some oats, barley, corn, and rye, as their chief cash crops. They supplemented grains with potatoes, apples, hay, butter, beef, pork, hides, and lumber. It was a good life. Despite fluctuations in the price of store-bought items, such as cloth, coffee, and tobacco, Dey and his neighbors lived comfortably. Part of Dey's profits paid the wages of a hired man and a hired girl. Quite often the daughter of a neighbor, the hired girl earned $1.25 per day plus room and board. She worked year-round, mostly indoors helping Mrs. Dey. If called on to perform outdoor chores, such as milking or helping with the harvest, she received additional compensation. She enjoyed a half day off every Saturday, which she used to visit her parents. The hired man helped Dey with rough, dirty outdoor work from April through November, the principal working season on the farm. For $75 plus board, he plowed, harrowed, harvested, split wood, hauled manure, and built fences. Dey also hired occasional help for special jobs, such as threshing wheat, drawing oats, and pitching hay. During harvest, Dey and his neighbors "exchanged" labor, which allowed them systematically to clear the fields of every farm in the community.

Dey and his hired hand worked fourteen- to fifteen-hour days. Caring for livestock—feeding the animals, cleaning stables, milking cows, turning cattle to pasture and bringing them back—occupied much of their time. Farmers with sons over the age of eight or nine turned over at least some of these chores to them, and most boys hated it. One midwesterner recalled, "I never rebelled at hard, clean work, like haying or harvest, but the slavery of being nurse to calves and scrub-boy to horses cankered my spirits." The legions of flies that accompanied the cows in summer made milking a "hated task," and winter milking, conducted in "narrow, ill-smelling stalls, close and filthy," was not much better. Woodcutting required long hours of work from men and boys alike, for the rapacious appetites of cooking and heating stoves knew no bounds. Even during the "slack" period of the year, from mid-November through March, threshing oats, slaughtering animals, cutting and hauling timber, splitting rails, replacing fences, hauling straw, shelling corn, cleaning seed, and repairing or constructing outbuildings, water troughs, and animal shelters kept farmers busy. Small wonder Dey concluded more than one day by telling his diary, "Don [sic] nothing but the chores today."

Some farmers had enough winter work to keep a hired man year-round. A midwestern hired hand thanked his good fortune in finding a full-time job, but he cursed the continual work. His employer, a prickly old fellow with restless habits, rose habitually at 3 A.M., summer and winter, and expected his hand to do the same. Early rising could be a formidable challenge on chilly winter mornings. The boss quickly stirred and sat beside his large kitchen hearth upon rising, "[b]ut for me up in the loft," lamented his hand, "getting up was a harder matter, and with the snow drifting through the chinks, the sensation was not tropical. Still, I had to crawl out, and then feed, water, clean, and harness the horses, though why this should be done at three o'clock in the morning I never could make out." His early morning chores required not much more than an hour's work, but the hand did not receive his breakfast until 7 A.M. In the interval, he sat hunched before the hearth. After breakfast, he went back outside to assist the farmer's daughter in milking the cows and feeding pigs and poultry. Daylight had broken by then, he reported, "and we could begin our regular work, wood-hauling, or whatever it might be."

Rainy weather might provide a rest, but that depended on the boss. A few hired hands insisted on written contracts with "wet and dry" clauses that stated whether they must work on inclement days. Some farmers avoided the problem by saving up indoor work or by operating a small workshop. Some commentators on rural life urged farmers to allow hands time for "self-improvement" (reading and writing) during bad weather. More realistic advisers suggested that they save "under cover fence-posts and rails to be fitted, gates, or portable fence to make, muck to be manipulated with manure, grain to thresh or clean, apples to be ground into cider or prepared for drying, and other jobs that can be attended to when work is impracticable."

The hardest work on any northern farm came during planting and harvesting months: April through October. Planting began for Henry Dey with plowing, rolling, pulling up stumps, burning refuse, and generally preparing the fields for sowing. Thereafter, seeds and young plants required devoted care and attention. June witnessed the annual hauling of manure, great wagonloads of it, tons of it, to be spread in a three- to five-day period. He harvested his earliest crops—hay and wheat—beginning in July. Dey owned both a mowing machine and a reaper, but some parts of his hay and wheat fields had to be cut with scythes. After cutting, the hay—all fifty to sixty tons of it—had to be raked and drawn to the barn. Wheat had to be shucked and stored. Barley and rye had to be mowed, usually by hand. Dey spent most of September threshing wheat. He could not afford to buy a mechanical thresher, so he rented one, and, with the help of his neighbors, finished threshing in a few days. He, in turn, made the rounds of neighboring farms to help thresh their wheat. Dey spent the remainder of September and all of October bringing in his vegetables—potatoes, corn, and beans mostly—threshing oats, husking corn, plowing up oats, corn, and wheat fields, planting next season's wheat crop, picking apples, making cider, and hauling his wheat to market. If he finished all this before November rains and snow swept across the land, he considered himself extremely lucky.

Grain farmers like Dey, with more than a few dozen acres to cultivate, found planting and harvesting machinery increasingly available and affordable after the Civil War. Beginning in the 1830s, when Cyrus McCormick patented his first harvester, a steady profusion of harvesters, reapers, threshers, rakes, harrows, mowers, seed drills, cultivators, and binders flooded the agricultural markets of the Midwest, the Northwest, and, to a lesser extent, the Northeast. The war years gave tremendous impetus to the development and use of farm machinery, as both demand for grain and a shortage of manpower soared. The number of mowing machines manufactured in northern factories between 1861 and 1864, for example, more than trebled, to seventy thousand. Machinery varied widely in price, depending on type and quality. Anyone who could afford to cultivate more than a hundred acres in 1870 could afford a cultivator (priced from $7 to $30), a seed drill ($65 to $80), and probably even a reaper ($155 to $255). Sometimes, a single well-to-do landowner would loan his thresher or self-raking reaper to neighbors in exchange for their labor. One Minnesota farmer who planted just eighty acres—seventy of wheat and ten of oats—owned both a reaper and a thresher. He paid $750 for the thresher, a debt that he paid off in just two years. Certainly, an intense rivalry existed among the salesmen of all this technology. They visited "the fields constantly during the season, advocating the merits of their different machines."

Even with the machinery, northern farm work required constant labor. A midwesterner described seeding, even with a horse-drawn harrow to cover the seeds, as "viciously hard work." The heels of his boots sank into the soft earth and became coated with mud. He felt like "a fly stuck in molasses," and the tendons of his heels ached with the strain. Machine threshing, whether "threshing from the shock" or threshing already cut wheat as it lay in piles in the barnyard, still required much bending and lifting. Just the thought of returning to the fields for another round of machine threshing depressed one farm boy. "The world always seemed a little darker at sunset on Sunday night than a Saturday night," he recalled. "The week ahead . . . seemed hopelessly long and profitless." When in the still-dark hours of Monday morning, he heard his father call, "Roll out, boys, roll out," he and his brothers responded "but feebly and gloomily."

However, cutting and binding wheat proved the toughest test of all. Wheat harvest came in the hottest and driest part of the summer. Small landowners waded through acres of golden wheat swinging their razor-edged cradle scythes back and forth in large sweeping arcs. On average, cutting, binding, and shucking wheat required twenty man-hours per acre, and that did not include the threshing, winnowing, and bagging. To save time and increase acreage, growing numbers of farmers acquired horse-drawn mechanical reapers to cut the wheat; some men even had self-raking reapers and harvesters, the latter being the very latest innovation, capable of cutting, raking, and bundling the grain ready for binding. Even machines, however, depended on the speed and skill of men to realize their potential value. To bind even five acres of wheat in a day required "blinding toil," "incessant and severe" labor. "Every motion must count," insisted one farmer's son. "No bands must break or slip, for at that precise moment a mountain of grain would be waiting for the band. . . . The motions of good binders were regular and graceful, and as certain as those of faultless machinery." Even so, a binder could rub his hands raw. Briers stuck in forearms and fingers, rust sores on the grain irritated the skin, hands became chapped, and fingertips split open from constant friction against the straw bands. Returning to work after dinner or a night of rest caused much groaning until a good sweat had lubricated the body and restored flexibility to fingers and hands. Only the invention of the self-binder, in the late 1870s, ended this summer torture.

Yet, truth be told, the majority of farmers in the Civil War era did not have to worry about mechanical reapers. They still turned the soil with a plow and seeded it by hand. Many of them continued to reap with a sickle and thresh with a flail. Certainly, pioneers worked virgin prairie land by traditional means. "It is difficult today," recalled one settler, "for us to realize what it meant to the first people of Kansas to settle on the broken prairie that had so recently been the homes of Indians, buffalo and other wild things. None of the settlers knew the rich possibilities of the untried fields. . . . Nor did they imagine the hard work, hardships and pests." "We prepared the soil for planting with a breaking plow," explained another homesteader, "and then used an ax or hatchet to make a hole in the sod, then dropped the seed and closed the hole with our heels. . . . Then next year we ran the sod cutter over this ground, harrowed it, and then seeded it with wheat." A family of German immigrants started life in Nebraska in even more primitive fashion. "Our first care was to prepare a sleeping place," reported the wife. After building a dugout for temporary shelter and constructing a sod house for their permanent home, the family planted its crops, "my husband with the blade," detailed the wife, "and I with the hoe. In the spring we purchased a yoke of oxen and a plow and sowed the grain. Thus the first year ended."

Yet, the postwar years brought change for small landowners, too. Introduction of the chilled-iron moldboard plow, in 1869, marked the most significant advance, particularly for farmers seeking to scour the tough sod and clinging loam of the prairies. Farmers everywhere raved about the "sulky" plow, also introduced in the 1860s, that allowed them to ride on a horse-drawn plow, rather than trudging along behind it. Farmers were getting smarter, too. Already in the late 1850s, prairie farmers recognized that they had used the soil shamefully. "It is true," confessed one of their band, "that us western farmers have been skimming God's heritage, taking the cream off, and leaving for parts unknown, until humanity has a heavy bill against us for wasting the vital energies of mother earth." Postwar farmers paid more attention to "scientific" agriculture. They began subscribing to farm journals, such as the *Prairie Farmer* and the *American Agriculturist,* to learn new ways of tilling, draining, and fertilizing their land. Crop rotation became more popular, as did nitrogen-packed artificial fertilizers. As one Illinois farmer put it, "To talk of manuring all our farms while they are so large is simply ridiculous." By 1880, North Central farmers alone were spending two million dollars annually on artificial fertilizers.

Small farmers without means to buy machinery found it impossible to cultivate more than a few dozen acres. One observer estimated that a single man could till crops and mow hay on no more than twenty to thirty acres. The methods and routines of these farmers differed little from the ones they had learned from their fathers and grandfathers.

> A lonely task it is to plough!
> All day the black and clinging soil
> Rolls like a ribbon from the mould-board's
> Glistening curve. All day the horses toil
> Battling with the flies—and strain
> Their creaking collars. All day
> The crickets jeer from wind-blown shocks of grain.

These verses, written by Hamlin Garland, who grew up on farms in Wisconsin and Iowa during the 1860s and 1870s, prove that not all poems about bucolic life need be romantic. Garland recalled little romance in plowing fields, haying, and picking corn. It took him seventy days as an eleven-year-old, working "all day, and every day but Sunday," to turn nearly 150 acres of corn stubble with a horse-drawn plow. Even though his father owned several machines to help harvest and thresh grain, no one had yet invented a mechanical corn picker. Men and boys walked the long rows of cornstalks picking individual ears and tossing them into a large wagon (holding fifty bushels) that traveled alongside them. Husking eighty to a hundred bushels, like binding wheat, produced "numb and swollen fingers, which almost refused to turn a button." To harrow the solidly packed soil of Iowa "was no light job" either, for dust blew so thickly on occasion that it stung the cheeks and produced "tears of rage and rebellion." "At such times," admitted Garland, "it seemed hard to be a prairie farmer's son."

Because nearly all farmers, regardless of region, acreage, or other crops, grew at least some corn, a description of the routine for planting and harvesting that quintessential American crop may help conjure up an image of the farmer at work. Planting began in spring. After plowing and harrowing the soil, farmers planted three or four seeds in "hills" about four feet apart. The seeds could be planted either by hand and hoe or with a small mechanical seeder. Farmers could space their hills precisely by drawing a sledge with four or five runners over the fields. This procedure marked the soil with grooves. By driving the sledge back across these grooves at a right angle, farmers could form hills at each clearly visible intersection. It sounds easy enough, "but nothing is easy when inexorably repeated for five hours at a stretch on a hot prairie field," insisted one farm girl familiar with the process. "The drills [that is, furrows] themselves produced a sense of giddiness from the chess-board like recurrence of the squares. At the end of a day's work, I began to be unable to drop the seeds steadily." She knew corn planting to be "deadly dogged work."

Corn required little care once it began to grow. A timely and skillful "cultivating"—digging up weeds and loosening the soil around the roots—was generally all the maintenance necessary. Cultivating could be done with a hoe, but many farmers had means to buy or hire a mechanical "cultivator." This elementary machine turned a potentially backbreaking chore into "rather pleasant work, not quite so heavy as ploughing." Corn ripened by September, but, unlike most crops, it did not have to be picked immediately. The ears, protected by their husks or shucks, could stand in the field for a long time without being damaged. When picking, or "husking," began, farmers would drive a wagon over one row. A hired hand walked along either side of the wagon, each man being responsible for husking three rows on his side. A third hand took the "down row"—that is, the row broken by the wagon—and assisted on either side as needed. Each hand carried a "shucking-peg" of wood or iron to tear open the husks and pluck out the ears, which he tossed into the wagon. When full, the wagon was driven to a corncrib and unloaded with a large scoop shovel. One farmer estimated, "The three of us could husk and unload about a hundred and twenty-five bushels a day, five waggons load."

One indication of how hard a man labors is the relief and joy he expresses when his job is finished. The first break most farmers enjoyed during planting and harvesting days, other than occasional swigs from the crockery water jugs they carried to the fields, was dinner. Most farmers already felt tired and hungry by 9:30 A.M.; by 11:00 A.M., their water jugs well-nigh drained, they were famished and ready to "peter out." "His stomach caved in and his knees trembled with weakness," testified one man on the condition of the average farmhand, "before the white flag fluttered from the chamber window, announcing dinner." Sometimes a dinner horn signaled mealtime, or a hired girl strolled across the fields to summon the men. With aching limbs and mouths like cotton, weary farmers trudged toward the house. They stopped first at the well. "No one can know how beautiful water is," insisted one hand, "till they have toiled thus in the harvest field, and have come at last to the spring or well, to lave a burning face, and worn, aching arms." Spirits suddenly soared. Men began to joke, shout, cuff each other, slosh water on themselves and their mates. After devouring a hearty meal, they then dozed in the cool breeze of a shade tree before returning to the fields. If the fields stood too far from the house, say two or more miles, men did not waste precious time traveling back and forth at dinnertime. Instead, they spread out a cold lunch and sprawled in whatever shade they could find to enjoy it. Occasionally, a hired girl carried a pitcher of cool milk to them from the house.

Farmers with extensive acres to harvest, whether by man or machine, often hired temporary hands; but obtaining extra laborers could be as exhausting as driving a plow. "The crying want of our farming districts is labor!" exclaimed a New Eng-

Union troops drilling in camp. *(Courtesy Minnesota Historical Society)*

A Civil War soldier had many daily duties. *(Courtesy Massachusetts Commandery, Military Order of the Loyal Legion and the U.S. Army Military History Institute)*

A proper parlor. *(Courtesy Ashfield Historical Society, Ashfield, Massachusetts)*

A dugout and sod house in Custer County, Nebraska. *(Courtesy Solomon D. Butcher Collection, Nebraska State Historical Society)*

This cabin near Humbolt, Kansas, built in 1856, typifies many a poor rural residence. *(Courtesy Kansas State Historical Society)*

An Idaho ranch house in 1872. W. H. Jackson photograph. *(Courtesy U.S. Geological Survey)*

Miner's cabin. *(Courtesy Colorado Historical Society)*

Main Street, Cheboygan, Michigan, 1875. *(Courtesy Burton Historical Collection, Detroit Public Library)*

Main Street, Iola, Kansas, 1871. *(Courtesy Kansas State Historical Society)*

Bridge Street, Helena, Montana, 1865. *(Courtesy Montana Historical Society)*

Five Points, a rugged district of New York City, ca. 1870. *(Courtesy Museum of the City of New York)*

A model American kitchen, 1874. *(Courtesy Library of Congress)*

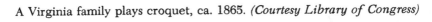

A Virginia family plays croquet, ca. 1865. *(Courtesy Library of Congress)*

Women's Central Relief Association at work in New York during the Civil War. *(Courtesy Museum of the City of New York)*

First Episcopal Church in Wichita, Kansas, 1869. *(Courtesy Kansas State Historical Society)*

This prohibition meeting at Bismarck Grove, Kansas, in 1878 looks like many an open-air camp meeting of the era. *(Courtesy Kansas State Historical Society)*

The very modern grade school of Columbus, Kansas, 1878. *(Courtesy Kansas State Historical Society)*

Western emigrants resting on the trail, 1860s. *(Courtesy Western History Department, Denver Public Library)*

Freedmen amid the ruins of Richmond, Virginia, 1865. *(Courtesy Library of Congress,*

Funeral at Woodland Park, Colorado. *(Courtesy Colorado Historical Society)*

A day at the plow, undated. *(Courtesy Library of Congress)*

Mechanized farming in the 1870s. *(Courtesy State Historical Society of Wisconsin)*

Cowboys around the chuck wagon. *(Courtesy Western History Collections, University of Oklahoma Library)*

Branding during a spring roundup. *(Courtesy Solomon D. Butcher Collection, Nebraska State Historical Society)*

Western miners, undated. *(Courtesy Special Collections Department, University of Nevada, Reno Library)*

Carpenters at work. *(Courtesy State Historical Society of Wisconsin)*

A blacksmith shop in Custer County, Nebraska. *(Courtesy Solomon D. Butcher Collection, Nebraska State Historical Society)*

Livery stable of C. N. Hogaboon, Broken Bow, Nebraska. *(Courtesy Solomon D. Butcher Collection, Nebraska State Historical Society)*

First steamer in De Père, Wisconsin, 1872. *(Courtesy State Historical Society of Wisconsin)*

Broadway looking north from Spring Street, New York City, 1867. *(Courtesy Museum of the City of New York)*

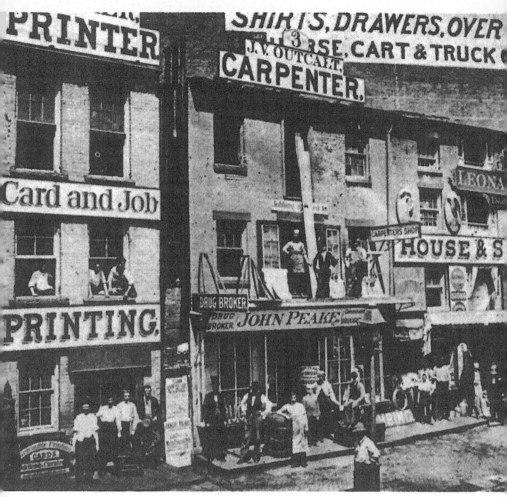

Parts of the laboring population on Hudson Street, New York City, ca. 1865. *(Courtesy New-York Historical Society)*

L. A. Fischer's general store, Oakley, Kansas, undated. *(Courtesy Kansas State Historical Society)*

Carrie Pratt's House of Pleasure, Holyoke, Massachusetts. *(Courtesy Ashfield Historical Society, Ashfield, Massachusetts)*

Vigilante justice in Nebraska, undated. *(Courtesy Solomon D. Butcher Collection, Nebraska State Historical Society)*

Ku Klux Klan in Alabama, 1869. *(Courtesy Rutherford B. Hayes Presidential Center)*

A Wisconsin baseball team in the 1870s. *(Courtesy State Historical Society of Wisconsin)*

Part of the scandalous cast of *The Black Crook. (Courtesy Harvard Theatre Collection, Harvard College Library)*

The circus comes to town in Michigan. *(Courtesy Burton Historical Collection, Detroit Public Library.)*

Machinery Hall (Corliss engine at center), Centennial Exposition, 1876. *(Courtesy Free Library of Philadelphia.)*

lander. "Machinery would seem to have usurped the place of human labor to some extent," he admitted, "but, as farming, in order to pay, requires the best cultivation of the soil, hand-labor is necessary. . . . During the haying season, men are rarely to be had at any price, and the high rate of wages puts it out of the reach of the ordinary farmer to hire a competent number of hands for the year or eight months." This disgruntled fellow had been reduced to hiring one hand full time and then trusting to luck "to catch some stray help when work pushes."

West of the Mississippi River, droves of seasonal, migratory hands worked their way northward from Missouri and Kansas through Iowa and Minnesota. They constituted "a rough-looking set of fellows, . . . able-bodied, hardy, of all shapes and sizes," who swept into a town like "a detachment of Goths and Vandals on a marauding expedition." In the years following the war, they arrived in Minnesota seeking three dollars a day (a dollar above the going rate) for their services. These were prosperous years for wheat farmers in Minnesota. The hands knew the farmers could afford high wages, and the farmers feared they had little choice but to hire them, unless they wanted to see their crops rot in the fields. Farmers tried to negotiate, but most of them paid the three dollars demanded. "He [the farmer] treats them [his new hands] very cordially now," reported one man after observing a successfully concluded negotiating session, "for he fears he may possibly lose them even yet, should more than three dollars be offered by some desperate fellow who has failed to secure any."

Seasonal, or day, workers led nomadic lives, and most people recognized "a distinct line" between these men and full-time hands. The latter, who might labor for years on the same farm, perhaps even marrying and building their own house on the boss's land, were generally respectable fellows. Like any good servant, they became "part of the family." Day laborers had a reputation for being hell raisers. While traveling, they carried their belongings—a change of clothes, a toilet kit, and "pictures of variety actresses"—in a satchel or carpetbag. They were frequently profane, reckless, licentious men, given to drink, gambling, and fisticuffs, and always "independent of bearing." Most of them were steady workers, but, having no responsibilities after a day's labor, they sought boisterous amusements. "They dressed well, in their own peculiar fashion," admitted one observer in Iowa, "and on Saturday night and Sunday spent their wages in mad revels" in nearby towns or at "roadhouses," or taverns. "When dressed in their best they were dashing fellows," continued this commentator. "They wore close-fitting, high-heeled boots of calfskin, dark trousers, with a silk handkerchief in the hip pocket, a colored shirt with gay armlets, and a vest, genteelly left unbuttoned. A showy watch-chain, a big signet-ring (useful in fighting) and a soft black hat completed a costume easy and not without grace."

Farm wives, asked to cook and wash for this sudden seasonal influx of men, found it a trying time, too. "For weeks and weeks, I might say months," complained one woman, "we have had workmen to cook for. First the plow boys, then the harvesters and the wheat stackers, and the end is not yet, for hay is at its height and the next week the threshers are coming." Washing dirt-caked, sweaty clothes for a half-dozen extra hands vastly increased her normal work load, and destroyed any semblance of accustomed routines. "I have been going all spring and summer like a well-regulated clock, am set running every morning at half-past four o'clock, and run all day, often until half-past eleven P.M." She concluded this desperate letter by asking, "Is it any wonder that I have become slightly demoralized?"

Some families employed temporary hired girls to help look after the temporary hired hands. Perhaps because they spent most of their time in the house, perhaps because they tended not to be so irritatingly boisterous, perhaps because, like full-time female help, they came largely from families in the neighborhood, most seasonal household workers were treated more like family members than were field hands. While always aware of their subordinate position, they often enjoyed an easy relationship in the household. This air of informality seemed to distinguish farm girls, both permanent and temporary, from "servants" in town and city. Rural inhabitants, employers and employees alike, seemed more embarrassed than townspeople by the servile implications of the word "servant." Consequently, rural employers rarely raised objections when farm girls insisted on being called "help," rather than "domestics" or "servants." Likewise, hired girls accomplished their multiple chores by working *with*, rather than *for*, their female employers, further diminishing the rural worker's image as a professional drudge.

Like her female employer, the hired girl divided her time between house and barnyard. She helped with cooking, baking, washing, ironing, and household cleaning, but she also fed chickens, milked cows, and hoed gardens. One Norwegian immigrant, working as a hired help in Wisconsin, called herself a "Handy-Andy." She not only labored in the house but, during harvest, raked hay in the fields. A Wisconsin farm boy, familiar with his region's tendency to hire strong Scandinavian women, verified that these hard-working immigrants "made excellent help." He described the girls hired by his father as "strong and buxom, used to hard work." A female help's first duties, however, remained centered on the house, and especially the kitchen. She had to rise before four o'clock, and could not retire until the supper dishes had been washed and put away. "The women work much harder than the men do," admitted an Illinois farmer. On the other hand, work often came in spurts—very hectic in the mornings and at mealtimes, but with the pace slackened in the afternoon. The hours twixt dinner and supper, even when spent working, might be used for doing "light chores," like sewing or peeling vegetables.

Farmers, if not their wives, operated differently in the South. Most obviously, many of their crops required different skills, techniques, and seasonal routines than those employed in the

North. Some things remained the same. Corn, for instance, occupied more acres than any other southern crop, and southern farmers planted and harvested corn much like farmers in Iowa or New York. Everybody grew some corn, for it served as the foundation of the southern diet for both man and beast. Southerners raised small amounts of oats and wheat, but other grains held less attraction, largely because of the region's humid climate. Southerners grew a variety of vegetables, fruits, and nuts. Yet, the Big Four of cotton, tobacco, rice, and sugar continued, as before the war, to form the backbone of the southern economy. Despite all their brave talk about crop diversification, southern farmers found it hard to break old habits and ways of life.

Cotton, naturally suited to the southern climate and soil, received even more attention after the war because of high demand and correspondingly high prices. An "epidemic cotton fever" struck southern farmers, large and small, so that nearly everyone grew at least a little cotton for market. "I tell you," declared a Georgian extolling the financial virtues of cotton, "it is the best friend the southern farmer has got now." Not that cotton grew by itself. "We don't have much spare time, and mighty little amusement," complained one planter in voicing the farmer's universal lament. "Cotton's a ticklish plant to raise. You've got to watch it mighty close." Preparation for a new crop began in January and February, when old stalks had to be pulled and the earth plowed and harrowed. These two months plus March also found farmers performing such "slack"-time chores as repairing fences and outbuildings, chopping wood, caring for livestock, and preparing their food crops for planting. Planting commenced in late March or early April, when piles of cottonseed were hauled by wagon from ginhouses to fields. Farmers sowed their seed by hand at an average of one ton per eight acres.

As soon as new stalks began to break through the soil—sometime in May—"scraping" commenced. "The hands weed every row carefully," explained one planter of the scraping routine, "and don't leave any weakly plants. That, and looking after the caterpillars keeps 'em busy till July." July to September constituted another "slack" period, although, as usual, farmers and hired hands (frequently tenant farmers or sharecroppers) enjoyed little spare time. The huge baskets used to harvest the cotton had to be mended, livestock always required attention, and budding cotton plants had to be checked daily for caterpillars, worms, excessive moisture, and "a hundred" other dangers. One often saw large bonfires in the fields during late summer and early autumn, intended to attract and destroy the moths that produced the feared cotton worm. Picking, ginning, and pressing began in early fall and lasted through December. Large planters hired scores of extra hands during picking season, and they expected the average hand to pick two hundred to three hundred pounds of cotton daily. Many of these extra hands came from nearby towns in hopes of supplementing depressed urban wages. "Frank gone to the country to pick cotton," reported a South Carolina woman, "and his po' hands all twis' up wid rheumatism, too. I don't see how he kin pick, but he said he had to go to make some money for us to pay de rent man."

The South's other three money crops required no less labor. "There is absolutely no rest on a large tobacco plantation," remarked one observer; "the last year's crop is rarely shipped to market before the seed must be sown for the next." As usual on any farm, early spring found tobacco farmers plowing, fertilizing, and harrowing. Whenever possible, they cleared "new ground," for no plant so exhausted the soil as tobacco. Nor did any other crop require as much tender loving care. Once the initial plowing had been completed, everything else had to be done by hand to avoid damaging the delicate plants. The area around the plants had to be kept free of all grass and weeds, a task accomplished only with a hoe. Then began a process of "topping," "priming," "suckering," and "worming." This routine involved, in order, pinching off the top bud of each plant, removing the lower leaves, removing every leaf bud that appeared after priming (so as to preserve the plant's sap and strength), and picking any parasites (mostly worms) from the maturing leaves. Of the four tasks, worming proved to be the most "tedious and unremitting." Then, as the plants began to ripen, each had to be cut with a short knife—a scythe or reaper would destroy it—and hung, head down, on scaffolds in the open air. The entire crop had to be safely stored, still hanging from the stem, in a tall, steep-roofed "tobacco barn" before the first frosts arrived. During winter months, leaves were smoked and "cured" before being divided into leaf for chewing and smoking (mostly in pipes; cigars and cigarette tobacco constituted only a third of domestic sales). Finally, tobacco was "prized," or packed, into hogsheads for delivery to market. So intense was the labor required that a typical tobacco farmer planted only two to six acres of tobacco, with a few additional acres of corn, other food crops, and some cotton.

The nature of their crops and their postwar financial condition meant that southern farmers enjoyed nowhere near the number of mechanical aids that eased the labors of northern farmers. Hay and wheat farmers came to rely on mowers, reapers, and harvesters, but crops like tobacco could easily be ruined by clumsy machinery. It would be a century beyond the Civil War before an effective tobacco harvester would be invented. Whereas cotton gins had proved to be indispensable since the 1790s, the technological difficulties of an effective cotton picker would not be solved until the twentieth century. Nor had anyone tackled the problems of mechanizing rice and sugar cultivation or harvesting. The cotton press, for compressing cotton into bales, remained the only other mechanical device in regular use, and even the majority of these machines were powered by men or horses. Only the largest plantations could afford hydraulic presses.

Besides the technological obstacles, several other facts of life kept southern agriculture in a rather primitive state. Most southern farmers simply could not afford machinery, even when it was available. The value of the average southern farm in 1870 was $1,456, lowest for any region of the country, and more than $1,000 below the national average. The South's postwar poverty prohibited even artificial fertilizers—which would have greatly enriched the region's exhausted, eroded soil—from being used in the amounts required. Then, too, the South's large surplus labor force limited the need to purchase existing machines and the incentive for developing new ones. The availability of so many black laborers at the lowest possible wages gave southern farmers an inexpensive alternative to labor-saving technology. Consequently, mules and plows, hoes and rakes remained the basic tools of southern farmers.

Bill Cook, a white farmer of western Georgia in the 1870s, may be taken as typical of the small southern landowner. Cook's assets included a wife, six children, twenty dollars' worth of tools, a mule, a milk cow, ten hogs, ten chickens, and a beehive. He owned 280 acres of land (about 50 acres below average in Georgia), but he cultivated only about 40 acres. The rest stood as unimproved woodland and pasture. Ten acres of corn produced fifty bushels; 20 acres of cotton yielded six bales; and the remaining acreage provided thirty bushels of cowpeas and sweet potatoes. His bees gave him twenty pounds of honey. After meeting his family's nutritional needs, Bill Cook earned about $300 annually.

Cook hired no hands to help work his farm, but larger landowners had several means of acquiring laborers. The most logical solution would have been to hire ex-slaves for cash wages, but it was not that easy. First of all, many blacks did not want to work for former masters, particularly not during the first year or so after emancipation. They wanted to "test" their freedom by leaving their slave homes and finding new places to live and work. Even then, many ex-slaves insisted on being their own bosses, not some white man's hired hand. "They appear to be willing to work," realized one white observer, "but are decisive in their expressions to work for no one but themselves." "They prefer to get a little patch where they can do as they choose," lamented a Tennessee planter. The average black man wanted to "set up for himself." Add to this predisposition the fact that most whites could not afford to pay cash wages anyway, and the labor problem became acute. At the same time, blacks found it difficult to acquire land and tools necessary to become independent farmers. Poor whites, the next most logical source of labor, remained aloof. They disdained to hire out "like niggers." Many had owned farms before the war, but either they lacked the means to work the land or they had lost their land for failure to pay taxes. These men, too, wanted to be independent farmers.

These doleful circumstances produced sharecropping and tenant farming. In sharecropping, blacks who wanted to be farmers struck a deal with "land poor" planters who lacked sufficient capital to hire laborers. Blacks agreed to work 20 to 40 acres of land (the average size of a family cotton farm) if the white landowner provided them with a house, tools, seed, and sometimes a mule. Profits from the resulting crops were to be divided equally between sharecropper and landowner. Tenant farming, more often involving poor whites than blacks, allowed families with a little cash, a few tools, but no land to reach similar arrangements. A landowner provided land, a house, and whatever tools or animals the tenant required. The tenant then used the profits from his crop to pay rent (usually a prearranged percentage of one-fourth to one-third) and to reimburse the landowner's initial outlay. The crop-lien system represented another variation of tenancy, in which farmers borrowed enough money from the landowner (sometimes a banker or merchant who held title to the land) to meet living and operating expenses while he planted and harvested his crop. A mortgage, or lien, was placed on his crop and any other chattel property he owned to ensure repayment of the loan plus rent.

These represented the most common means of acquiring non-wage farmhands in the South, but, as one observer commented, "the details of these variations in dealings of landlord and tenant are practically endless."

Clever and mutually beneficial as such arrangements appeared to be, they could produce unsatisfactory results. Share-cropping and tenancy became more than convenient ways to acquire hired hands; they also evolved into distinct social systems, just as had slavery. Conditions among sharecroppers and tenants varied considerably, depending on the usual agricultural factors of climate, soil, and crop; but equally important were the terms of the contracts and the men people worked for. Disastrous crop yields in much of the South during the first two years after the war placed most sharecroppers and tenants in debt, and many never escaped. Their drab, ramshackle cabins stood as testimony to the South's depressed economic future. Well into the twentieth century, one southerner testified, "All of our folks before us was tenant farmers and that's all we've ever been."

Of course, planting crops was not the only means of subsistence available to farmers in North or South. Livestock played a vital role in American agriculture. Fewer than twenty thousand people claimed to be stock raisers, herders, drovers, or dairymen in 1870, but nearly all farmers owned some livestock. The most interesting examples of the hidden value of livestock could be found in the southern backcountry, where "hillbillies" and "crackers" flourished. Thousands, perhaps tens of thousands, of southerners led isolated yet completely self-sufficient lives by raising a few acres of corn and a vegetable patch, hunting game, and letting their hogs and cattle run at large through the piney woods. Travelers through the South generally characterized these men of leisure as shiftless, lazy, and no-account. "He seems to fancy that he was born with his hands in his pockets, his back curved, and his slouch hat crowded over his eyes," remarked a northern sojourner in 1874, "and does his best to maintain this attitude forever." Yet, these apparent wastrels, by driving their hogs and cattle to market once a year, obtained all the cash they needed.

Southern hill folk were not the only people to appreciate the value of livestock. In the nation at large, American farmers produced more than twice as much corn as wheat, oats, and barley combined during the 1860s and 1870s. Much of that corn entered into the American diet, but a significant portion went to feed hundreds of thousands of head of livestock, particularly hogs and cattle. A midwestern farmer could easily use a dozen acres of corn just to feed his thousand hogs. So vast were the seas of hogs that every possible means of subsistence would be made available to them. "They run in the woods in vast droves," observed a visitor in Ohio. "They browse, root, and devour rattlesnakes. In the fall the woods are full of nuts. . . . On these the hogs revel and fatten." When corn ripened, farmers turned their hogs loose in portions of their fields. "They follow the cattle," continued this chronicler. "The corn is not gathered; that would be too much work; it is broken down and eaten by the cattle, and what they leave is gathered by the hogs."

Among professional stockmen, no laborer carved a more visible niche in American history and legend than the western "cowboy." Although ranchers had raised cattle and other livestock west of the Mississippi River before the Civil War, not until after Appomattox, with the coming of the railroad and massive western emigration, did the "cattle kingdom" become an important source of beef. By eastern standards, Texas longhorns, the earliest products of the industry, were embarrassingly small and scrawny, but, having been fed on the grassy plains of the public domain, they sold for considerably less than eastern cattle. With so many ex-Confederates fleeing to Texas after the war, a ready pool of laborers arrived at the precise moment drovers were required. Mexicans and blacks formed about a third of the cowboy population, but whatever their race, these rugged individualists tended to be young, vigorous, and illiterate.

The most distinctive feature of the cattle drover became his picturesque dress, adopted largely from the Mexicans and serving some very useful functions. His broad-brimmed hat protected his face and shaded his eyes from glaring sun. His brightly colored handkerchief, or "bandanna," when folded diagonally and knotted loosely around his neck, protected his throat from cold and wind; pulled over his nose and mouth, it filtered out dust. Leather gloves, seldom worn by farmers, protected a drover's hands from rope burn and weather. His broad, bullhide chaps, or "leggings" as they were first called, protected him from brush and briers and provided warmth in cold weather. His distinctive boots, tight-fitting with high heels and narrow soles, looked almost effeminate. Yet they announced to the world that here was a horseman, who felt "contempt for all human beings who walk."

The details of a cowboy's daily routine, as with farmers, varied, depending on when and where he worked. Almost universally, however, his life proved less glamorous than the one depicted by Hollywood in twentieth-century films. Cowboys spent most of their time in such dull occupations as range riding, herding, rescuing animals in distress, mending fences, repairing harnesses and buildings, and fighting brush fires. "The herding life was dreadfully monotonus," recalled one drover. "The romance of riding about all day soon wears off if one has six months of it at a stretch in all weathers, rain, blow, or shine, Sundays or weekends." And all for thirty dollars a month. Cowboys considered some chores downright undignified. One Texan spent three weeks doing nothing but gathering dried cattle manure—a common form of fuel on treeless plains—for fires. Other men had to pitch in with common farm chores, including milking cows and feeding chickens.

"It was not particularly easy work," declared one cowhand. The day began at 4 A.M., when he went out to clean, feed, and saddle his pony and milk a dozen cows before breakfast. By 7 A.M., the "long hot day" had begun in earnest. Many days he spent "seated in the saddle the whole time, twelve hours or more, checking the restless brutes from straying." The setting sun was his signal to herd the cattle together, either to run them back to the corral or to bed them down on the open prairie. "Then the same performances were gone through again," he sighed, "the milking and the picketing out, and after that came supper, by which time it was rather dark and late, and I was ready to go to bed to prepare for the next day's round."

Winter, as on midwestern farms, represented slack time on the range. Many cowboys, sometimes as much as two-thirds of an "outfit," would be laid off between November and March. Unemployed drovers usually took temporary jobs in nearby towns as bartenders, blacksmiths, and the like. Still, these could be critical times in cow country. Drovers remaining on the ranches had to monitor cattle as winter descended. Wearing clothing sometimes stiff with ice and cold, they rode the range looking for strays and prohibiting herds from lying on the ground for too long, lest the animals stiffen and become too cramped to rise. When snow fell, drovers moved the herds to areas where grass had not been completely buried, for cattle, unlike horses, lacked the instinct to paw away the snow and eat the grass beneath. Frequent rotation of "line riders" made winter months passable, however, and wolf hunts—necessary to protect helpless cattle—added a spark of excitement. When not on duty, cowboys spent winter in the "bunkhouse," a chronically untidy abode that smelled of dry cow dung, chewing tobacco, and woodsmoke. The time passed pleasantly enough. "We used to pile up the blazing logs, sing songs, and forget the weather outside," recalled one cowboy.

Springtime quickened the pace. A mere ten-hour or twelve-hour workday in winter became a sixteen-hour day in fair weather. First, new horses had to be "broken" or "gentled" for riding. The usual method called for a rider to mount a blindfolded horse. With the blindfold removed, the horse tried to shake off its unaccustomed burden by bucking and jumping. Breaking horses was hard, dangerous work, but most cowboys relished the challenge. Only one in a hundred horses could not be broken to the saddle, although many remained feisty enough to deliver a few token kicks whenever riders straddled their backs. Cowboys also relished this "bronc busting" because it marked an official end to dreary winter routines. With a new string of horses, cowboys began their spring "roundup" (from the Spanish *rodeo*), or "cow hunt," as it was originally termed. The roundup, which culminated in branding the new calves, allowed ranchers to locate strays, inventory herds, and identify new calves while they were still with their mothers. This was especially useful in regions where several ranchers herded their cattle in close proximity. In fact, roundups often turned into cooperative ventures, with crews from different outfits dividing a territory and driving cattle to a central spot on the open range. From these daily roundup chores of riding and roping, cowboys derived their favorite leisure activities of horse racing, bronc busting, steer wrestling, and bulldogging.

Immediately following the roundup came the "long drive" from Texas ranches to railheads in Missouri and Kansas. The heyday of the long drive lasted only about twenty years, from shortly after the Civil War to the mid-1880s. Yet, during that brief era, ten million cattle traveled a half-dozen established trails northward. The average herd numbered about 2,500 head and was tended by about a dozen men. The smallest herd worth driving numbered 500, and the largest recorded herd, driven north in 1869, had 15,000 steers. A drive started slowly, covering only a couple of miles a day until the "cows," as most drovers called cattle, became accustomed to the trail. Thereafter, a good outfit could move its herd at least ten to fifteen miles a day on the three-month journey.

Despite the apparently haphazard, chaotic, and random movement of a cattle drive, every cowboy had a particular function, and each day conformed to an established pattern. The foreman, who was familiar with the route, led the way. He knew the location of every watering hole, grazing area, river crossing, and hostile Indian encampment between Texas and central Kansas. The chuck wagon came next in column, followed by the herd. The most experienced drovers rode on either flank to prohibit straying and collisions with other herds. A "wrangler," leading the spare horses (usually two per man), rode to one side of the herd. The remainder of the outfit brought up the rear, where it swallowed the dust of hundreds of cattle and watched for stragglers. Life on the trail, as on the ranch, settled into a dull routine. Rising at dawn, cowhands pushed their herd until noon, when they paused for a cold dinner. The afternoon drive continued until they reached a watering place where their cows could "bed down." Supper was served up hot and in generous portions. Men not standing the first watch rolled up in blankets or buffalo robes to sleep soon after eating. They carried no tents or shelters other than a poncho, or "slicker."

Not that a drive lacked periodic excitement, or that sleeping in the open posed the biggest hardship. Consider some of the daily adventures of a diary-keeping cowboy in 1866:

> May 13th. Big Thunder Storm last night. Stampede lost 100 Beeves hunted all day found 50 all tired. Every thing discouraging.
>
> May 14th. Concluded to cross Brazos [River] swam our cattle and Horses built Raft and Rafted our provisions and blankets etc over Swam River with rope and then hauled wagon over lost Most of our Kitchen furniture such as camp Kettles Coffee Pots Cups Plates Canteens etc etc.
>
> May 31st. Swimming Cattle is the order We worked all day in the River and at dusk got the last Beefe over—and am now out of Texas—This day will long be remembered by men—There was one of our party Drowned to day (Mr. Carr) and several narrow escapes and I among the no.
>
> June 1st. Stampede last night among 6 droves and a general mix up and loss of Beeves. Hunt cattle again. Men all tired and want to leave. am in the Indian country am annoyed by them believe they scare the Cattle to get pay to collect them.

June 12th. Hard Rain and Wind Big stampede and here we are
among the Indians with 150 head of Cattle gone hunted all day
and the Rain pouring down with but poor success Dark days are
these to me Nothing but Bread and Coffee Hands all Growling
and Swearing

June 27th. My Back is Blistering badly from exposure while in the
River and I with two others are Suffering very much I was attacked by a Beefe in the River and had a narrow escape from
being hurt by Diving

One unanticipated result of these drives out of Texas was the
extension of the cattle kingdom northward to Kansas, Nebraska,
Colorado, and beyond. Much of the cattle from the drives of the
1860s went to stock new ranches on the northern plains. During
the 1870s, the size of herds in Kansas and Nebraska, much
nearer the railroad heads leading to markets in Chicago and the
East, grew from 500,000 to 2,500,000. Herds in Montana, Wyoming, and Colorado showed similar, if less spectacular, growth.
As these northern "spreads" grew, many Texas cowboys remained in the North at the conclusion of the summer drive to
work for higher northern wages. Then, the following spring,
they rode south again for the next roundup and long drive.
Somewhat unfairly, cowboys on the northern range received an
enduring nickname as a result of activities in northern shipping
yards. Yard workers, in order to move and direct cattle onto
railroad cars bound for eastern slaughterhouses, used prods to
jab the animals' flanks. By the late 1870s, northern cowboys had
become known as "cowpunchers."

# 7 WORKING IN TOWN:

## THE LABORERS

THE GROWING populations of towns and cities became one of the most visible changes in American life between 1860 and 1877. The change puzzled and worried some people. "The farmer is demonstrably better off than the worker of the city," insisted one observer in the 1870s. "He is more independent, has more command of his own time, fares better at table, lodges better, and gets a better return for his labor. What is the reason," he asked in bewilderment, "that the farmer's boy runs to the city the first chance he can get, and remains, if he can possibly find there the means of life?" The means of life provided the key, because growing numbers of farm boys, farm girls, and foreign immigrants found that city jobs and wages, when combined with city lights and amusements, offered an exciting new way of life. Critics of the trend complained, with some justification, that young people did not appreciate "the difference between living and getting a living." Yet the confidence and exuberance of youth ensured an ever-ready pool of willing hands for urban labor.

No single occupation remotely rivaled farm labor in numbers. The two largest groups of non-rural workers, domestic servants and common laborers, included just over one million workers each in 1870, only two-thirds the number of farmhands. The next two largest occupations, carpenters and shop owners, numbered about 350,000 each, but eight other occupations (out of 333 listed in census reports) included over 100,000 apiece. They were, in descending order, women in the "sewing trades," store clerks, textile mill workers, boot and shoe makers, railroad workers, blacksmiths, teachers, and draymen and hack drivers. In broader terms, about half of non-agricultural workers labored in mining, manufacturing, and construction. A description of conditions in a few of these occupations will suggest ways in which many unskilled and semi-skilled workers spent their working lives.

The world of artisans and craftsmen was disappearing by the 1870s. Mechanization did not extend much beyond the textile industry, and the evolution of other industries into more modern stages of development advanced unevenly and sporadically over the next several decades. Most workers still used hand tools. Yet many craftsmen found themselves competing against numbers as well as machines. Armies of "factory artisans," packed into shops and warehouses, divided old crafts into highly specialized yet unskilled steps. For example, less than a third of Cincinnati's work force labored in shops and manufactories with fifty or more people in 1850. By 1870, nearly half of the city's workers were so employed. Observers everywhere lamented the "virtual abandonment" of apprenticeships in the decade after the war. Instead of taking years to learn a craft, boys went directly to work as unskilled laborers. Only in smaller towns and villages did tailors, gunsmiths, millers, tanners, cigar makers, shoemakers, and similar artisans survive into the 1880s.

The shoe industry, which employed one of the nation's largest industrial work forces (171,000), produced one of the earliest large-scale encounters of American craftsmen with machine competition. "Work has been scattered," reported one analyst, "but new machinery coming into use—pegging and stitching machines, one of them doing the work of ten, twenty, or thirty men and these set up in factories—soon will have only factory shoes." Shoemakers had to "adjust," he warned, or "follow the business to places where the factories are located." Some shoe-makers adjusted by becoming semi-merchants: they purchased supplies of ready-made shoes to sell in their shops while continuing to do custom work and make repairs. Others failed to adjust. One shoemaker, in 1868, kept a "shop for making and repairing boots." By 1876, he had been reduced to doing "a little cobbling," and shortly after that he found work in a shirt factory.

Shoemakers who chose to join the future entered a very different world. One New England shoe factory, a three-story, red-brick model of efficiency, swarmed with men, women, and children engaged in a bewildering array of tasks. At seven each morning, an engineer ignited a powerful steam engine, which, in turn, gave motion to innumerable gears, belts, and pistons. The whirring, moaning, and rattling produced by these mechanized parts formed the background for an additional discordant jumble of sounds and motions, as hands set to work and the factory came to life. Despite the fact that only a portion of the workers operated machines, the impression of mechanical precision engendered by the swarm of activity and division of labor gave the scene a look and feel of technological efficiency. "The arrangements of this building are perfect in their way," insisted one observer. "It is a complete beehive of industry; everything is systemized, everything economized, and each part made to act in concert with every other part. There is no clashing or jarring, and the harmony that prevails speaks volumes for the master mind that planned and controls its operation." The pounding and vibrating continued until 6 P.M., when the factory shut down.

Shoe production began on the ground floor with workers cutting leather by hand and sorting it according to size. Transported on a small cart to an elevator, the sorted leather arrived on the third floor, where stitchers (using sewing machines), pasters, liners, and buttonhole sewers fashioned the top portion of boots and shoes. Placed back on the elevator, these "uppers" then descended to the second floor, where platoons of operatives matched uppers and soles before returning the bound, or "pegged," sets once again to the third floor so that other workers could shape, button, heel, and pack the finished products. This last journey down the production line betrayed the still-incomplete mechanization of the trade. For while uppers and soles could be stitched together by machines at a ratio of eighty to one over hand stitching, machines had not yet been developed to complete the processes of the finishing line. Altogether, thirty-five to forty specific steps were necessary to produce a factory-made shoe. Still, speed of production soared. If one compares production statistics of 1855 and 1875, the factory system, in the latter year, required two thousand fewer workers to manufacture seven million more shoes. "Of course, the system is yet in its infancy," reported a New Englander in 1863, "but the wheels of revolution are moving rapidly. . . . Operatives are pouring in as fast as room can be made for them, buildings for 'shoe factories' are going up in every direction, the hum of machinery is heard on every hand, old things are passing away, and all things are becoming new."

Workers, however, found the new world monotonous and exhausting. Some of them, accustomed to the relaxed atmosphere of the shop, where workers took turns reading aloud or chattered back and forth about the day's news, felt constricted and oppressed. "In the factory there is no chance to read," explained one man, "and the noise and hum of machinery prevent general conversation, even when the rules and discipline do not positively forbid it." One man who worked ten hours a day, six days a week, complained that he grew "fretful and nervous" as the day wore on. Operators who stood or sat nine to ten hours a day, "most of the time in the same posture, the same motion being necessary every four or five minutes through the day," complained of cramps and stiffness. To reduce stress and allow a little freedom, two or three workers would sometimes "club together" and hire a boy or girl (age eight and up) to help them. Most shoemakers earned $600 to $800 a year, "which sum," complained one worker, "would only give a small family a hand-to-mouth subsistence." Only a few skilled mechanics earned as much as $1,200. Far from receiving paid vacations, shoemakers—and this would be true of most unskilled and semi-skilled workers—were lucky to have a full working year. Seasonal slowdowns and layoffs plagued nearly every industry. Many shoemakers blamed layoffs on overproduction spawned by introduction of the new factory system. "Since that time," explained a Massachusetts shoemaker in 1871, "there has never been a year of steady work. At first a month only would be lost; now it has got so that we lose over four months' time every year."

Tens of thousands of cigar makers experienced a similar threat. A wartime tax that benefited large producers soon pushed cigar making out of small shops, where individual craftsmen had purchased the tobacco, made the cigars, and sold them to customers, into factory production. "Any kind of an old loft served as a cigar shop," complained one worker in describing the new system. "If there were enough windows, we had sufficient light for our work; if not, it was apparently no concern of the management." Fifty workers shared a single toilet and sink for washing. Workers supplied their own tools (a cutting board and knife) and sat at worktables seldom designed for comfort. Boys, known as "strippers," drew the leaves from their heavy stems and supplied them in "pads" of fifty to the cigar makers, who shaped, rolled, and wrapped the leaves as of old. Hours were long, the work tedious, and workers performed their tasks "more or less mechanically."

Then, in the late 1860s, came the hated "molds," small presses used to shape cigars in the "mold and filler system." The molds allowed even unskilled workers to become "cigar makers." The resulting product was clearly inferior to the hand-wrapped variety, but the volume of production and low labor costs persuaded most manufacturers to scrap factory production in favor of "tenement" work. "The manufacturers bought or rented a block of tenements," explained one disgruntled worker, "and subrented the apartments to [unskilled] cigar-makers who with their families lived and worked in three or four rooms." Cigar makers bought their supplies from the manufacturer, furnished their own tools, and received "a small wage for completed work sometimes in script or in supplies from the company store on the ground floor." It was a return to the old putting-out system, organized along the lines of a company town. It was also a "degrading" system, insisted one worker, that "killed craft skill and demoralized the industry."

If farm boys led the migration to towns and cities, farm girls did more to define the changing work environment. The changes began, like so many alterations in everyday life, during the war. Some 300,000 women who might never have entered the job market secured employment during the war. With so many men in the army, and with increased production needs in industry, female labor was in demand. Some new occupations, such as nursing, seemed particularly suited to female skills. Many previously male-dominated jobs, like clerical work and teaching, showed that women could excel outside their natural "sphere." What began as a wartime emergency became a permanent revolution. By 1870, nearly two million women had filled hundreds of occupations, from old standbys like domestic service and sewing, to less feminine pursuits as teamsters, bridge keepers, and undertakers. One book, published in 1868, described over five hundred employments "adapted to women." The following year, the *New York Times* declared, "Women's field of labor in this part of the country has been very greatly enlarged during the past eight or ten years, and it is annually extending to embrace occupations, trades and professions heretofore considered as closed to them."

Domestic service claimed half of all female workers, the majority of women working in towns, and, in the 1870s, 8 percent of the nation's entire labor force. Life in service offered some benefits. The average "maid-of-all-work" received about two dollars a week plus room and board (closer to three dollars outside the South). Servants on large staffs could earn more or less than that, depending on their skills. Good cooks, for example, commanded as high as ten dollars a week, while lowly scullery maids often settled for a dollar. On the other hand, a servant's workday seemed endless. Even when not actually laboring more than eight or ten hours a day, servants remained "on call," regardless of the day or hour. Where single servants worked without comrades, life could be quite lonely. Moreover, many workers regarded service as a degrading occupation, not far removed from feudalism and slavery. Their whole lives, not just their working hours, contended these unhappy folk, were controlled by "masters" and "mistresses." "Many who try this kind of labor become discouraged, and prefer the greater freedom and independence of the shop-girl," concluded one observer. Women working in factories, even when paid lower wages, rejoiced that they occupied "a higher place in the social scale" than that accorded domestics.

What made matters worse was the fact that servants, while integral parts of a household, were usually excluded from the family circle. Servants became, in the language of a popular, sympathetic description of their plight, "strangers within the gates." They slept in attics or back bedrooms, relaxed in the kitchen, entered the house through rear entrances, and spent most of their time secluded in work areas. Families too often regarded servants as "aliens" and "sphinxes," unknown and unknowable. Immigrant domestics (roughly a third of all servants), often so different in race, dress, religion, customs, and language from middle-class Americans, made employers apprehensive and suspicious. Similar problems arose when lower-class Americans were employed, and black Americans, most often serving in the South, frequently had to live outside the house entirely. Not a few families—probably more than tradition allows—offered good homes to their domestic workers.

One servant, for example, rejoiced to find herself "treated more like a daughter than a hired girl." Yet an undeniable stigma attached itself to the occupation.

Unfortunately, most alternative jobs left intelligent, competitive women feeling discouraged, frustrated, and unfulfilled. Most professions remained largely closed to women. Only 5 of the nation's 40,736 lawyers, 67 of 43,874 clergymen, and 525 of 62,383 physicians were women in 1870. Wages presented an even more pressing grievance. Few women earned as much as men working in the same occupations. Most employers believed that woman's proper place was in the home, so women who wanted to work had to do so on management's terms. Then, too, male employers believed in the physical and intellectual inferiority of women, which made it unnatural to pay men and women the same wages. Meanwhile, wages remained low in traditionally female employments because of the glut of women seeking such jobs.

The "sewing trades," second only to domestic service for female employment, provided work for nearly 200,000 seamstresses, tailoresses, and shirt, cuff, and collar makers. Varied circumstances characterized the sewing trades. Women who operated their own shops often enjoyed quite respectable positions, but only the very best independent seamstresses earned comfortable livings, and the number of new milliner and dressmaking shops opening each year usually equaled the number that failed. Most sewing women were paid by "the piece," working either in their homes or in large mass-producing warehouses. A typical urban piece worker sewed "for a miserable pittance," making cotton shirts for six cents each, flannel shirts for a dollar a dozen, and men's overalls for sixty-two cents a dozen. In order to meet expenses of rent (one dollar a week for a sparsely furnished tenement room), fuel (three cents for a bundle of kindling; fifteen cents a pail for coal), and food (mostly bread and potatoes), she had to average at least twelve hours' work every day. Then, too, home workers sometimes lost part of their earnings to unscrupulous employers who refused full payment for alleged flaws in workmanship. "If she owns a sewing machine, and very few do," observed one man of New York's needlewomen, "she can earn more than one who sews by hand, but constant work at the machine means a speedy breaking down of health and a lingering death, or a transfer to the charity hospital." Desperate to increase productivity, some women succumbed to advertisements that declared, "Sewing machines for sale and paid for in work." They put down a few dollars on a sixty-five-dollar machine. The salesman promised to furnish enough work to pay off the balance in a few months. Sometimes the arrangement worked. Other times, salesmen stopped providing work and repossessed the machine when it was nearly paid for.

Working in sewing lofts—not yet referred to as "sweat shops"—was only marginally better. The usual sewing girl reported to work at 7 A.M. and stitched until noon, when she enjoyed "a brief intermission" of about thirty minutes before resuming work until 6 P.M. Women paid by the piece, rather than a weekly wage, frequently took work home to sew for another two to four hours after supper. "You may see them in the morning," reported an observer of New York's needlewomen, "thinly clad, weary and anxious, going in crowds to their work. They have few holidays except on Sunday, and but few pleasures at any time." Most shops were unhealthy places to work. Some of them lacked sufficient ventilation in summer and provided inadequate heat in winter. "The work rooms . . . are almost always up three or four flights of stairs," revealed a commentator on conditions in New England, "and are filled with women as closely as they can sit at their work. They have no means of ventilation except by the windows, which are frequently on but one side of the room. . . . Fully one-half of these rooms are without water-closets or water for drinking." Skilled custom workers earned as high as fifteen dollars a week, but few qualified for such work. Most needlewomen earned in the range

of two to six dollars, but it must be remembered that their jobs
were seasonal, and few women worked more than six months
of the year.

The nation's textile mills, 60 percent of their employees
being female, offered an alternative to needlework in some
parts of the country. "Women are more orderly, more easily
governed, and more cleanly than men," explained one observer
of the preference for female mill workers in 1868. "They are
more attentive, as a general thing, where the labor requires
only looking after, creating no fatigue, except that which arises
from close attention." They also worked for less. Women generally operated power looms and other machines that reduced
the need for laborers. In 1870, for instance, the woolens industry introduced a new machine, the "slasher," to size yarn. This
innovation replaced well-paid female dressers who had previously performed the task. Increasingly efficient power looms
reduced the number of women in cotton mills and required
more labor of the workers who remained. Instead of tending
four looms with six hundred picks per minute, each operative
supervised six to eight looms with an output as high as fifteen
hundred picks per minute.

The quality of life in textile mills had declined, too. Some
mills, such as those at Lawrence, Massachusetts, retained many
of the advantages associated with mills of the 1830s and 1840s,
when workers had enjoyed good wages, labored in clean, pleasant factories, and resided in comfortable dormitories. But such
vestiges of the old system were rapidly disappearing. Mill girls
of the 1870s often worked shorter hours than they had a decade
earlier, but they performed more work for lower wages. Far
from enjoying the pleasant, healthy surroundings of earlier
days, mill workers found themselves "always on the jump,"
with "no time to improve themselves." Temperatures in cotton
mills, most of them still in New England, ranged between seventy and eighty degrees during most of the year, as high as
ninety degrees in summer. Woolens mills were only slightly less

warm. Operatives in a Rhode Island cotton mill worked sixty-nine hours a week (twelve hours Monday through Friday, nine hours on Saturday), and earned $4 to $5 a week. A New Haven mill paid an average of $2.30 for a sixty-six-hour week, but provided free board, valued at $1.25. Typically, about half the hands were immigrants; native-born New Englanders, who had once contributed the bulk of mill needs, took better-paying and less strenuous jobs outside the mills. Meanwhile, a Georgia mill paid seventy white women fifty cents to one dollar per ten-hour day to operate its 136 looms.

Tens of thousands of children also worked at menial jobs in town and city. They did not match the number of children aged ten to sixteen who hired out to work on farms, nor did they match the even larger proportion of children who would join the labor force in the 1890s. Yet the growing use of children in urban employment was no illusion. They worked alongside their elders in factories, mines, shops, and on the streets. Most labored because their families needed the extra income. Employers, recognizing the situation, paid bottom dollar. The largest number of children (109,503) worked as domestic servants, with unspecified "laborers" running a distant second (32,159). Most public concern, however, developed over the 75,643 children who worked in factories, mills, and mines, and that number does not include children *under* age ten. The number does not even fully account for all child laborers over ten, for employers often lied about the number of children they employed. "A majority of employers," insisted an investigator of child labor in New York City, "were found to be either afraid or ashamed to acknowledge that they employ children." One man, when asked the age of his youngest "hands," proudly asserted, "We have none younger than eleven or twelve." Other employers tried to justify their use of children by insisting that they employed only immigrants, who did form a large portion of the urban child labor force.

In New York, the city with the largest number of wage-earning children, tykes as young as five performed simple manual chores in the cigar, clothing, hat, shoe, paper box, artificial flower, and feather trades. "What kind of work is stripping feathers?" one woman asked a fatherless ten-year-old working girl. "Why, like that in your hat," she responded. "That is what they are like when we have finished them; but we girls work at them before they are dyed. I make about three dollars a week, and my sister—she is only six years old—she does not make as much; sometimes a dollar a week, sometimes more." Most children worked the same hours and under the same physical conditions as adults. For children who operated machines, this meant facing the same dangers. The most numerous injuries to factory children occurred on "twister machines" in twine manufactories, where children—mostly girls—lost one or two joints of their fingers with alarming frequency. "A few girls," confessed the owner of one such factory, "have had their fingers *hurt* in these machines; but it is always in cases where they forgot or neglected their work to talk or play. The twisters are not more dangerous than other machines at which children work." In another part of the same factory, ten boys, age twelve and thirteen, manned a machine for "hackling" flax. "They were mounted upon a platform to enable them to reach and change the clamps which held the flax," related an observer. "This monster machine . . . requires to be fed at either end continuously, and it works with the regularity and remorselessness of fate." All ten boys worked "for dear life" trying to keep pace with the terrible machinery.

New England's textile mills also employed large numbers of children. New England states required children to attend school at least fourteen weeks every year, but many parents who complied with this minimal requirement placed their children in factories the remainder of the year. Because the law specified no particular time of the year for children to be in class, some mill owners employed a corps of children year-round by dividing them into shifts to be educated whenever a slack period struck the industry. More enlightened employers operated "half-time" schools, which permitted children to work half a day and attend class half a day.

Most working children in northern cities came from poor white and immigrant families, but in the South they tended to be black. In slavery, black children had accompanied their parents to plantation fields, worked as domestic servants, and taken numerous odd jobs in town and country. In freedom, most blacks—adults and children—found themselves restricted largely to those same unskilled, ill-paid jobs. In 1870, Atlanta blacks held over three-fourths of their city's unskilled jobs. While whites took comparatively well-paid jobs in cotton mills, blacks marched off to work in flour mills and tobacco factories. Even when working at the same jobs, blacks received lower wages than whites. In 1870, white hands at the Atlanta Rolling Mill earned three dollars a day while blacks received one dollar. As common laborers, blacks found themselves relegated to undesirable and dangerous tasks, such as digging wells and laying sewers. "In this city it is the negroes who do the hard work," observed a man in Nashville. "They handle goods on the levee and at the railroad; drive drays and hacks; lay gas pipes; and work on new buildings." An English traveler in the South summarized the situation when he identified the Negro as "a natural-born Cockney."

A glimpse of the routine of a Richmond, Virginia, chewing tobacco factory gives some idea of how thousands of black urbanites—men, women, and children—spent their working days. After first steaming the tobacco to make it pliable, workers hauled it into the "stemming room," where women and children stripped the tobacco leaves of their stems and tied them in bundles. Stemmers were paid by weight—so much per pound of tobacco according to current market prices. Workers then hung the leaves on sticks in a "drying room." When "bone dry," the bundles destined for chewing were dipped into troughs filled with a boiling mixture of syrup and licorice. After drying in the sun, the medicated leaves were sprinkled with rum and delivered to the "twist room," where "lumpers" and "twisters" shaped the tobacco. Lumpers and twisters, the industry's most skilled workers, earned twelve to fifteen dollars a week, although each man usually paid one to two dollars of his wages to a boy who assisted him. The completed twists, having been inspected by a white overseer, were packed into wooden boxes by the twisters' assistants and carried to the "press room." There, men operating long rows of hydraulic presses flattened the twists into commercial "plugs." Other hands packed the plugs into tins and placed the tins into shipping crates. Draymen hauled the completed product to ship wharves and railroad depots. The manufacture of smoking tobacco represented "a much less intricate and troublesome process," but it, too, offered a livelihood to large numbers of blacks in the upper South. In Richmond, for example, the manufacture of tobacco products ranked as the city's "principal industry" by the 1870s.

Desperate people of all ages and both sexes eked out an existence as street vendors. Every town had them. Some vendors operated from permanent stands; others roamed the streets carrying their wares in baskets, bags, or carts. They sold watches, jewelry, newspapers, fruit, tobacco, toys, candy, nuts, flowers, small pets (mostly dogs, cats, and birds), oysters, balloons, anything and everything. Foreign immigrants seemed to dominate the trade in northern cities, while blacks held sway in the South, but anyone down on his luck could make a few cents a day by taking to the streets. After the war, many ex-soldiers, most of them lame or blind, were reduced to selling newspapers and shoelaces. "Little girls are numerous among the street vendors," reported a New Yorker. "They sell matches, tooth-picks, cigars, newspapers, songs and flowers."

Despite the inroads made by women and children, men remained the main source of manual and industrial labor. For instance, no women labored among the nation's more than

150,000 miners. Whether hunting coal, lead, copper, gold, or silver, this hearty breed used similar equipment and followed similar routines. "Hard-rock" miners of the postwar West's spectacularly productive "bonanza" mines generally worked one of three eight-hour shifts, beginning at 7 A.M., 3 P.M., and 11 P.M., six (sometimes seven) days a week. Hours varied, depending on the size and productivity of the mine. Wages varied, too, anywhere from $1.50 to $5 a day. Small mines, some no larger than "glorified prospect holes," employed fewer than a half-dozen men, while vast subterranean "extractories" employed hundreds of workers. The smaller the mine, the more likely the miners were to use hand tools, such as hammers, picks, and shovels. Large mining companies, like large farms, became increasingly mechanized during the 1860s and 1870s.

The average miner's day began well before he actually started work. When working the 7 A.M. shift—and miners usually changed shifts every few weeks—he had to be in the mine and at his station by that time, not merely arrived at the mouth of the shaft. Depending on how far he lived from the mine, this usually forced him to rise at least an hour earlier in order to eat, dress, and walk to the mine. His apparel was rugged: "rough circular jackets or ragged coats stained and smeared with clay, loose woolen shirts, blue duck overalls wrinkled and dirty, heavy shapeless brogans, and coarse felt hats." If entering a horizontal shaft, he might ride to his station in an ore car; if a vertical shaft, he descended in a crank-operated bucket or cage (although mechanized mines had steam winches by 1860). Each man carried his own lunch pail, an allotment of candles (usually three), a candle holder or lantern, and a box of matches. Safety hats and glasses were unheard of.

From the moment he entered the shaft, a miner earned every dollar of his day's pay. Descent in the ore bucket, as it swayed precariously from side to side in the dark shaft, set the tone for a dangerous and physically demanding job. "Three hundred feet or so of that," admitted a miner, "when the hoist was working jerkily with an occasional back slip, engraves itself on one's memory." The cage set down at a "work station," which, lighted by kerosene lanterns, served as repository for tools, equipment, and water barrels. From their stations, miners entered on foot the maze of drifts, crosscuts, tunnels, and horizontal shafts where they spent the day drilling, blasting, and shoveling rock. Additionally, they had much "dead work"—roughly equivalent to the farmer's "slack time"—that involved shoring up underground works, removing accumulated waste rock, and exploring new veins of minerals. Novice workers generally drew the least skilled and most arduous of these tasks, particularly "mucking" (shoveling rock) and "tramming" (pushing heavily laden ore cars from the interior to ore buckets at each station). Experienced miners used hand drills or, by 1872, a compressed-air drill to break off ore from rock, and they assumed responsibility for loading and detonating the black powder and "giant powder" (dynamite) charges used in blasting. "Has to be handled carefully," explained one veteran miner in a marvelous understatement of blasting precautions. "Tamping is done very nicely—not too much—or cap explodes and one is likely to go flying out of the shaft."

Sometimes, as with cave-ins ("caves" to the miners), nature contributed to the danger. Even a small cave could easily kill a dozen men. One cave in Nevada's Comstock ledge killed "only" four men. They found two of the bodies. One of them, volunteered a witness, had been "much distorted" in the accident. As for the second victim, "His bowels were crushed out of the lower part of his belly—& he was turned black and blue & stunk very badly." On another occasion in the same region, a two-hundred-foot shaft, supported by timbers, collapsed totally. Miraculously, all one hundred men who had been belowground at the time escaped through adjoining shafts. However, even survivors often suffered loss of limbs or other permanent disabilities. One cave-in victim staggered out of a mine with a smashed shoulder. "Removed all the upper part of arm bone from shoulder socket down," recorded the surgeon's assistant, "some dozen or more pieces of it—down half way to elbow."

Discomfort accentuated the danger. Most mines were poorly ventilated, which did little to rid their shafts of accumulated dust or the smells of powder smoke and human waste. A few mining companies introduced air-compressor blowers in 1865. Temperatures varied widely from mine to mine, but they tended toward extremes. Low-altitude mines, often as deep as a half mile, recorded temperatures of 110 degrees. One miner, in 1873, reported an underground pool of water "so hot that eggs could readily be cooked in it." Such mines often used the "double-gang" system, in which two men did the work of one on a thirty- to sixty-minute rotation. While one man worked, his partner rested at the station and drank large quantities of ice water. At the other extreme, miners left fires burning overnight in high-altitude mines so that the rock would be sufficiently thawed for the next day's drilling.

The dangers and discomforts were nearly as great for the eighty thousand men who sweated and strained in the nation's burgeoning iron and steel industries. In terms of manpower and investment, it is probably more proper to speak of the iron industry, for not until the 1880s did the United States develop a significant steel industry. Wrought iron remained the nation's principal "heavy industry" through the 1870s, and most early steel mills produced both metals. The average ironworker earned $524 in 1869, the highest wage of any American industrial worker, but the figure reflected an extremely broad salary range that varied according to geography and skill. Unskilled workers earned no more than the usual $1.50 per day for common laborers, whereas "aristocrats" in the industry—skilled men like "puddlers"—received three or four times these wages and worked shorter days (ten hours instead of twelve). The average working year for all ironworkers lasted about ten months.

Noise, heat, and manual labor characterized work in America's wrought-iron mills, for the "fatal weakness" of the industry remained its resistance to mechanization. The typical iron-works consisted of smelting furnaces, puddling furnaces, and rolling mills. All three processes relied essentially on manual labor. At the largest mills, hundreds of sooty-faced men initiated production by shoveling tons of iron ore from boats and barges. Once wheeled into the mills on railcars, raw ore had to be smelted in blast furnaces to create an alloy of iron and carbon called pig iron. Scores of brawny men, "bedewed by perspiration . . . , nude to their waists, their feet incased in hobnailed shoes," labored frantically for several hours to feed the smallest furnace. From the blast furnace, pig iron was transferred to puddling furnaces, where "puddlers" supervised the most vital stage of iron manufacture. These men, the most skilled in the plant, stirred and agitated small batches of molten pig iron and cinder with the end of a long pole until the purified metal crystallized into balls. On average, each puddler, his "strong hands turning, thrusting, pulling, and piling the molten . . . iron in ways innumerable amid the the heat, the smoke, and the short-lived splendor of a thousand red-hot metallic sparks," produced a ton of iron ingots every day. The crystallized metal, hauled from the furnace in iron buggies, was then rolled into plate or bars, depending on its intended use. Both rolling and puddling required highly skilled workmen who were frequently wooed from England with high-paying, five-year contracts.

Unloading ore, feeding furnaces, puddling, and rolling required heavy labor, usually performed under intense heat. Noxious, often poisonous, fumes enveloped many workers. Transportation of huge quantities of ore and the constant presence of roaring furnaces and molten metal produced almost daily instances of workers being burned or maimed. Temperatures in the mill, particularly in the vicinity of the furnaces, easily topped a hundred degrees. In puddling, the weight of the molten metal required that the work be done in stints. Each puddler, in fact, hired a small crew of men (from his own wages) to assist him. "An exceedingly hard and laborious job," confessed one mill manager. "They were constantly in a cloud of moist vapor of high temperature, which of itself was . . . debilitating." One furnace worker described his day as "working aside of hell ahead of time." Commenting on the strength required to shovel ore and transfer molten iron, another worker concluded, "Gorilla men are what we need."

The nation's 142,000 blacksmiths knew something about iron and steel, too. In an age when most transportation still depended on horses, no community could function without at least one blacksmith. Horses pulled farm wagons and family buggies. They hauled heavy freight to and from factories, warehouses, depots, and wharves. Many stores owned single-horse delivery wagons (often with business advertisements printed on the sides), and all sorts of delivery services—such as ice and coal—used wagons and carts. Hotels used hacks to transport patrons, and public transportation, including cabs and streetcars, relied on horsepower. Blacksmiths had to keep this necessary motive power well shod. Transportation companies hired their own full-time blacksmiths, but most smiths worked independently. In addition to shoeing horses, mules, and oxen, they repaired wagons and, in agricultural towns, sharpened plows and other farming implements. Some men operated a livery stable in conjunction with their smithy. Small towns sometimes offered good blacksmiths free town lots as incentive for them to settle in the community. During the 1870s, smiths earned in the range of $2.50 to $3 a day. These wages ranked below those earned by skilled craftsmen, such as carpenters, masons, and plumbers ($2.80 to $3.80), but above the pay of teamsters ($2), boilermakers ($2.50), and day laborers.

The construction trades provided a living wage for hundreds of thousands of workers, despite frequent periods of inactivity between jobs and disruption of work by inclement weather. "Depression and dullness in trade contributes to lower the morale of labor somewhat," asserted one workman, "but not to the extent of serious or permanent injury." Carpenters, the most numerous construction workers, averaged only $1.60 for a ten-hour day in 1860; by 1870, they earned close to $2.90. Frequently working outdoors, carpenters enjoyed a healthier environment than miners and factory hands. Still, every job has its perils. "Broken bones, cuts, bruises, etc., are the common accidents of the trade," shrugged one workman, "and carpenters are also liable to receive bad colds from working on a roof one day and on the next in a close, heated room, or in a damp cellar or basement." When accidents did occur, few employers accepted responsibility. "Pay never goes on after an accident," pointed out the same carpenter, somewhat bitterly; "but if we break anything while at work this is taken from our wages." Carpenters, it is true, were responsible for purchasing and maintaining their own tools, but, after an initial outlay of $150 to $200 for hammers, saws, chisels, files, planes, and such, maintenance and replacement costs rarely exceeded $25 a year.

Carpentry was one of the largest remaining occupations to require a lengthy apprenticeship, generally four years. Apprenticeships supposedly helped to maintain standards and to control the number of workmen in the occupation, but experienced carpenters protested that employers increasingly ignored the traditional insistence on apprenticeships. Old-timers complained about working alongside men who, even if paid lower wages than journeymen, did not "know the plan of a house from hen's tracks." They also fumed about handling twice their normal work load in order to compensate for the ignorance of novices. "Where there are so many at work that have never served an apprenticeship," verified a New Englander in 1871, "it becomes harder for those that have, as they must do their own work and show others how to do theirs." Many men became disgusted with the pretense of maintaining standards. "The rule as to apprentices," admitted a master carpenter, "is to get as much out of them and in return teach as little as possible." The declining standards could be blamed at least partly on balloon-frame housing and newly patented lathes and other mechanical tools that reduced the need for skilled workers.

Hundreds of thousands of additional men manned the country's vast transportation network. All sorts of dray, hack, stage, cab, coach, and omnibus drivers spent their days fighting city traffic. Most drivers, regardless of whether they delivered goods, hauled freight, or transported people, worked twelve-hour days, six days a week. They generally followed a casual, if dull, routine. Passenger carriers most often complained about the perils and frustrations of being a "driver." Cabdrivers, who drove one- and two-passenger hacks, generally voiced the fewest complaints, but city stage drivers could fairly pull out their hair after a day's combat with traffic and the public. Nearly all drivers were jostled and shaken as they traversed city streets. Paved streets—where they existed—remained primitive. Mining towns, cattle towns, farm towns, and small towns generally had no pavement at all, only dusty thoroughfares or muddy quagmires, depending on the weather. Most large towns and cities used macadam to pave low-rent districts, while cobblestone paved main arteries. Cobblestone, however, proved difficult to clean, raised a nerve-racking din, and shook a person's whole body. New York City first replaced its cobblestone streets with more durable and comfortable granite blocks in 1869, and other cities slowly followed suit, despite the high cost of granite. Western towns, when convenient, used wooden blocks of pine or spruce. Brick pavement, an idea imported from Europe, first appeared in the 1870s in some West Virginia and Illinois towns. Asphalt, another European invention, did not become popular until the 1880s.

Stage, or omnibus, drivers operated one of the most basic forms of mass transportation in towns and cities. Everyone grumbled about the omnibus. The heavy, ill-ventilated, twelve-passenger vehicles, with twin unpadded benches, lurched and vibrated over city streets at a snail's pace (three to four miles per hour). Passengers likened the ordeal to "modern martyrdom." Drivers complained about being exposed to all sorts of weather, from blazing sun to blinding snow, as they sat atop their vehicles. They complained about the paltry wages paid by stage companies that expected them to serve as both driver and conductor for a percentage of their total fares. They complained about passengers who, when stepping up through the vehicle's rear entrance and thrusting their ten-cent fares through a hole in the roof behind the driver's seat, expected change for a five-dollar bill. Passengers called the drivers surly. They also called them "Jehu," after the reckless Biblical charioteer, even though most stage drivers ranked among a city's safest professional drivers.

Horse-drawn trolleys—"horsecars"—served as the other major source of urban transportation. Weary omnibus-tossed commuters hailed the horsecars, introduced in the 1850s, as the "improvement of the age." They were larger than an omnibus, carrying thirty to forty passengers, and, as they glided along their steel rails, horsecars traveled at twice the speed, for half the price, and with appreciably more comfort. And horsecar lines employed lots of people. One Boston line, operating 108 cars, required 470 employees, including 108 drivers and conductors, plus carpenters, mechanics, painters, blacksmiths, watchmen, harness makers, trackmen, hostlers, switchmen, over two dozen categories in all. Drivers, who earned $1.75 a day for their twelve to fifteen hours, reported for duty at 6:40 A.M. Except for an hour at dinner, they drove their teams all day on a route that varied from forty-five minutes to two hours. "The best class of drivers are green men who come in from the farm, and have no trade," admitted the company superintendent. "Never having had much money, $12.25 per week seems a good deal to them." Conductors, on the other hand, required some degree of education, as they were responsible for keeping accounts on their routes. "We have as conductors and drivers," reported one superintendent, "broken-down merchants, ministers, and lawyers, and men from all professions and walks of life." None of the men had contracts. They worked on a daily basis and were paid once a week. In conjunction with omnibuses and commuter trains, already stretching into the suburbs of cities like New York, Philadelphia, and Chicago at the start of the war, horsecars facilitated transportation within the city, permitted the outward expansion of cities, and enabled suburbanites to keep city jobs.

After the Civil War, railroads became the dominant form of long-distance travel. They replaced stagecoaches, which, even west of the Mississippi, soon served only for local transportation. Trains were simply faster, cheaper, and more convenient. A stage journey from Saint Louis to San Francisco cost $200 and lasted three weeks. Coach "springs" were nothing more than leather straps. Leather curtains covering open windows did little to shield passengers from clouds of choking dust and torrents of driving rain. Stage companies sold meals of bacon, beans, bread, and coffee for $1.50 at their "home stations"— spaced approximately every fifty miles along the line—but many passengers preferred to carry at least part of their provisions. Passengers slept (or tried to sleep) most nights in the moving coach, which might be occupied by as many as nine people. Bathing and shaving facilities did not exist. A train trip from Philadelphia to San Francisco, on the other hand, cost $140 and lasted barely one week. Most "cars," as Americans dubbed their railroad carriages, were brightly painted with twenty rows of cushioned seats on either side of a carpeted middle aisle. Each seat accommodated two people. A heat stove stood at one end of each car; a vat of iced drinking water (with a public dipper) rested at the other end. Some cars had ventilation systems that allowed cool air to pass through in summer and warm air in winter. A "train boy," ranging in age from eight to eighteen, passed down the aisle about once an hour selling candy, nuts, fruit, newspapers, and magazines.

By the 1870s, train travel had become positively luxurious. In 1865, George M. Pullman introduced his "palace" sleeping car, which offered travelers polished black walnut woodwork, thick carpeting, gas chandeliers, and French plate mirrors. A "hotel car" (combination sleeper and diner) followed in 1867, a dining car in 1868, and a "drawing-room" car (later dubbed a "parlor car") in 1875. Nearly every train had a smoking car for the pleasure of male passengers (smoking being forbidden by law and courtesy in passenger cars). A ladies' car allowed women traveling alone to avoid mixed—and occasionally annoying—company. Pullman's dining car provided tables and chairs arranged for four and offered a menu that included wine and pheasant. Prices were high, but some people preferred this arrangement to packing their own food, buying snacks from the train boy, or joining the chaotic rush for beefsteak and pastry at station restaurants during a twenty-minute stop. The hotel car provided private cabins (complete with cushioned sofa and chairs) and a small kitchen. One traveler exclaimed, "It is like a little traveling hotel."

The tens of thousands of workers needed to operate this elaborate and extensive system formed one of the most closely regulated and strictly organized industries in the country. By the mid-1870s, most state legislatures in the Northeast and Midwest had passed laws making employers liable for deaths and injuries caused by negligence, carelessness, or drunkenness on their lines. As a result, nearly every company gave their employees handbooks, some of them up to a hundred pages long, to specify the precise duties of each worker and to establish standards of proper behavior. Most roads insisted that workers carry their manuals with them at all times while on the job.

Thus engine men knew that they were responsible for maintaining and operating their locomotives, and that they should assist mechanics in machine shops when not on a run. Firemen worked under the absolute authority of their engineers, and were responsible for keeping boilers fired, all "working joints" properly oiled, and the signal cords for bells and whistles free of obstructions. Conductors collected and recorded fares, attended to the comfort of passengers, maintained the appearance of coaches, and generally saw to the smooth operation of the train. Brakemen, who worked under the immediate supervision of the conductor, attended the brakes of two to five cars, made sure all stoves and lights in their assigned cars functioned properly, assisted passengers with carry-on baggage, helped load and unload baggage cars, collected articles left in passenger cars, and swept and cleaned cars between runs. Station agents followed specific regulations in selling and receiving tickets, maintaining company buildings, and supervising switchmen and porters. Everyone else, from dispatchers and baggagemasters to road repairmen and mechanics, followed similarly clear and concise regulations governing their particular jobs. Wages within this myriad of occupations averaged $3.50 (engine men and mechanics) to $1.50 (unskilled hands) per day.

Finally, something should be said about labor unions. Town laborers of the Civil War era launched what may be regarded as the modern labor movement. Most labor unions organized on behalf of particular occupations—shoemakers, miners, carpenters—but others, such as the Colored National Labor Union and Knights of Labor, embraced a variety of occupations and levels of skill. They varied in geographic scope, most unions being organized for the benefit of local workers, but with thirty national trade unions being formed between 1860 and 1880. Most unions also divided along sexual and racial lines, and many ethnic groups formed their own organizations. Some unions concerned themselves with broad social and economic reforms. Others, mainly unions of skilled workers, attacked specific grievances, such as hours, wages, health and safety conditions. Nearly all appreciated the social and fraternal benefits of organization. Most informed estimates put the number of union members at 300,000 by the early 1870s, but one may assume that only ten in every hundred members paid their dues regularly, attended meetings, or participated in union activities.

Economic inflation and deteriorating conditions of labor caused unions to spread rapidly after 1862. At least one union formed every week in places like New York and Philadelphia during the war. Many unions remained quite small, embracing perhaps a dozen members in a single shop; and the attrition rate among fledgling unions became fearful.

Labor unions held regular weekly or monthly meetings. Small organizations met in rented space above saloons, stores, and livery stables. Established unions often built their own halls, where they held social functions as well as business meetings, initiations, and lectures. Most unions charged modest dues, usually an initiation fee of a dollar plus twenty-five to fifty cents per month. During strikes, unions tried to provide members with small stipends, and during layoffs they operated soup kitchens or distributed food and clothing. Workers in particularly dangerous occupations could also acquire insurance for job-related accidents. The Gold Hill Miners' Union, on the Comstock Lode, provided ten-dollar weekly payments to victims of sickness or accident and did what it could to provide medicine, nursing care, and transportation to nearby doctors. The union's records also show that a "visiting committee" regularly called on convalescent members to check on their condition. In 1868, for instance, records show Mr. Lyons "very weak but improving very fast," Mr. Fitzpatrick "doing well but not able to work," Mr. Duffey "improving very slowly [and] will not be able to work for some time," and Mr. Collins "not doing very well—the small bone of leg is broken, and he needs attention."

Early unions often organized as secret societies, so that employers could not retaliate against members. "A great deal of bitterness was evinced against trade union organization," recalled one labor leader of the 1870s, "and men were blacklisted to an extent hardly ever equalled." One local leader of the Machinists and Blacksmiths Union would never forget the Saturday evening when, just before quitting time, the master mechanic in his shop informed him that he need not report to work on Monday. "You are the president of the union and it is thought best to dismiss you in order to head off trouble" was the explanation he received. Even the Noble Order of the Knights of Labor, the era's largest general union, was founded as a secret fraternity in 1869 by Philadelphia garment workers whose earlier union had been shattered by employers. Members never wrote and rarely even spoke the name of their order. Rather, they referred to the "Noble and Holy Order of * * * * *," known to those few outsiders aware of its existence as "the society of the five stars."

Unions of the era sometimes differed from modern unions in their methods of protest. Street parades followed any vote to strike. Hundreds, sometimes thousands, of workers might join the procession to sing protest songs and carry banners emblazoned with defiant slogans. Strikers posted bills throughout the town listing their grievances (usually wages or hours) and identifying those employers who still opposed them. "Pickets" positioned themselves outside hostile shops, factories, or stores to encourage boycotts (although that term had not yet been coined), incite other workers to join the protest, and dissuade nonunion members from seeking employment there. Yet strikes could be extremely haphazard, often called on the spur of the moment. The vast majority were limited to a single workplace or even part of a workplace. Workers in other trades or industries rarely staged "sympathy" strikes. When the Workingmen's Benevolent Association, a union of Pennsylvania coal miners, declared a strike in July 1868 over wage reductions, members had to march from mine to mine in order to stop work and urge other mine workers—carpenters, mechanics, and so on—to join them. In mines outside their immediate vicinity, they found complete indifference.

The Knights of Saint Crispin, representing the nation's shoemakers, became one of the first effective national unions and, except for its large membership and cooperation with female workers in the trade (it forged direct links with the independent Daughters of Saint Crispin), was fairly typical of the era's unionization movement. Organized at Milwaukee in 1867, the Knights grew to embrace over 320 lodges with 50,000 members by 1871. Masonic-like rituals and structure shaped its origins. Its chief initial object was to protect skilled journeymen from the competition of unskilled factory hands, but the factory workers themselves soon took control of the union and used it as a means of improving working conditions. A typical "Crispin," known to history only as "S," had been a shoemaker for over thirty years before the pressure of competition forced him to seek work in a Lynn, Massachusetts, shoe factory in 1865. He struggled to make a living. Three of his children joined him in the factory, while his wife stayed at home to care for the younger children and stitch baseballs for piece wages. After work, "S" devoted much of his time to the union. He visited the Crispin lodge one to two nights every week from 7:30 to 10:00. In fair weather, he and his mates might meet outdoors immediately after work to roll tenpins or play baseball. On Saturday nights, he and his wife likely attended the union's weekly dance. "S" valued not only the fellowship of the lodge but the union's stand against dictatorial manufacturers. "But for the Crispin order," he insisted, "shoemakers would to-day have been virtually beggars."

# 8 WORKING IN TOWN:

## SHOPKEEPERS AND PROFESSIONALS

⁂ _____

JOINING factory workers, miners, and laborers in the nation's towns and cities were shopkeepers, professional people, and other white-collar workers who operated along Main Street. From all outward appearances, these people stood apart from both industrial and agricultural workers, an appearance that, in cities and large towns, generally proved accurate. Yet shop-keepers and professionals in the nation's many small towns and villages remained an integral part of the surrounding country-side. Their occupations, while non-agricultural as well as non-industrial, still depended on the rural economy. In turn, not a few farmers and ranchers took second jobs as shopkeepers, law-yers, salesmen, newspaper editors, and bartenders in town. This interdependence of town and country, quite aside from the numbers of farmers, is what made Civil War–era America so overwhelmingly "rural."

Proprietors of general merchandise stores filled prominent roles on Main Street. Besides selling the widest possible selec-tion of groceries, dry goods, and hardware, they usually oper-ated the local post office, served as a font for town gossip, offered a haven for local wags and philosophers, and provided a meeting place for clubs and fraternal groups. It was, in the words of one shopkeeper, "a clustering point for all of village life." Its inevitable potbellied stove drew cold-weather customers like a magnet. Its broad shaded porch invited passersby to sit and chat in fair weather. The man who presided over such an establishment naturally had to be something more than a mere merchant. He ranked as a public figure, a celebrity. Everyone knew him; everyone had to trust him. He even set the style for architecture and civic boosterism along Main Street by adding a substantial-looking false front to his single-story building. Even shopkeepers with genuine second stories squared them off to add breadth and height to their storefronts. The facades fooled no one, but they did announce a spirit of unabashed confidence in the future. They also served as clearly visible billboards where proprietors blazoned their business titles and listed their specialties in wares and services. As a town grew, and its general store faced competition from a variety of specialized meat markets, hardware stores, milliner shops, and ice-cream parlors, inhabitants still referred to it as *the* store.

The interior of a country store looked as crowded and cluttered as a Victorian parlor. Shelf upon shelf of tobacco jars, kitchen wares, crockery, bolts of cloth, bottles of whiskey, ready-made clothing, canned goods, laundry soaps, patent medicines, school slates, meal and flour, hats, and scores and scores of other items lined the two side walls. Shopkeepers often tried to keep groceries and canned goods on one side and dry goods on the other, but nearly as often order receded against the tide of plenty. Some wall space accommodated various-sized drawers to hold small items like socks, suspenders, spools of thread, stationery, and fish hooks. Separating customers from the walls of shelves and drawers, two long counters ran the length of the store, which tended to be narrow and deep, rather than broad and shallow. Display cases for buttons, needles, ribbons, corset stays, pencils, pipes, rings, dollar watches, scissors, and thimbles occupied space on the counters. At least one case held toilet articles, including hair tonic, pomade, shaving soap, razors, talcum powder, camphor, and perfume. Jars of assorted candies also lined the counters, and some portion, usually in the rear, inevitably provided hungry customers with an array of cheese, sausage, sardines, crackers, and essential seasonings. A mingled odor of vinegar, cheese, coffee, leather, kerosene, and peppermint permeated all.

Because most merchandise arrived in bulk, numerous barrels, bins, and kegs lined the back wall of the store and stood at intervals along the counters. Barrel items most frequently included groceries, like rice, sugar, vinegar, crackers, lard, salt, coffee, and pickles, and hardware, such as nails, horseshoes, and ax heads. Overhead, dangling from hooks and rafters, harnesses, baskets, hats, buckets, and chamber pots greeted customers. Piled here and there, wherever space allowed, they found rope, wagon wheels, farm tools, brooms, mops, feed sacks, even plows. In fair weather, many of these items lined the front porch. Near the rear of the store, within convenient range of the lunch counter, sat a large potbellied stove, with an assortment of old wooden chairs and empty crates encircling it. In cold or wet weather, local men with time on their hands sat around the stove whittling, chewing tobacco (oftentimes spitting on the floor), munching pickles or crackers, and thrashing out the major issues of the day, everything from politics and religion to farm prices and baseball.

The storekeeper and his clerk (usually male) followed no rigid routine. They operated six days a week, usually from 6 A.M. to 6 P.M., although earlier openings and later closings were not uncommon if townspeople demanded them. Nearly all storekeepers opened early on Saturday, their only genuinely hectic day, to accommodate the waves of farmers who traveled into town to pick up mail and do weekly shopping. Some storekeepers relied heavily on mail-order houses to supply their customers' needs, especially dry goods, but few merchants could escape the army of traveling salesmen (known popularly as "drummers" or "runners") that infested the countryside. Drummers, representing wholesale merchants and manufacturers in nearby cities and the Northeast, hauled their trunks of samples from town to town in the hinterland. They seemed to specialize most often in dry goods, hardware, and patent medicines, but few articles of merchandise went unpeddled. One observer in Georgia found the state "full of 'runners' from Louisville and Cincinnati. They represented all branches of trade, and pretty generally reported that they were getting many orders." Most drummers, in addition to selling stock, also kept an "ear to the ground," always on the alert for likely areas to establish new retail stores that would specialize in their company's "line." Moreover, they were always willing to give storekeepers advice on pricing, credit policies, displays, bookkeeping, and advertising.

Every town and village had at least a few citizens permanently in arrears to the store. They all had good excuses. One might be a widow with five children, another a farmer down on his luck. Debtors generally stopped by once a week seeking soft looks and gentle words from the shopkeeper, each "hoping to bask a little longer in the sunshine of his confidence." Other customers, affluent enough to pay cash, sought full value for their dollar. They carefully eyed the scale as the shopkeeper poured out the proper measure of coffee or sugar. Some people questioned his weights and grumbled about his prices. The most audacious reminded him of their generous patronage and insisted on discounts. Reflecting on the habits of a crusty matron who regularly made such demands, one clerk acknowledged, "I wonder if that good woman . . . knows how she is tempting me to stilt my prices up for her especial benefit?"

More often, high degrees of understanding and trust prevailed between small-town shopkeepers and their customers. Few items in a general store had prices marked on them, and shopkeepers rarely mentioned prices in published advertisements or placards. "Low prices" and "Good goods at fair bargains" were about as far as they went. "We consider it humbug to advertise prices," one man stated bluntly; "we will do that at our counter, and will always sell goods and sell cheap!" Likewise, shopkeepers universally sold on credit to local people who requested it. They also adopted the farmer's view that monthly bills impugned a man's honesty. Farmers expected a year's credit, the balance to be paid when they sold their crops.

Cities and large towns offered a far wider variety of stores, shops, and services, and most shopkeepers specialized. One store sold fabrics, another boots and shoes, another groceries, another baked goods, another meat, another fish, another china and crockery, another hats, another jewelry, and so on. Even rough mining and cow towns sponsored bustling business districts where dozens of clerks and shopkeepers earned their living. Virginia City, Nevada, by the early 1860s, had over 200 more or less substantial wood-frame buildings and over 150 businesses. Besides 25 saloons (the most numerous business ventures), inhabitants enjoyed the services of 10 livery stables, 10 laundries, 9 restaurants, 9 bakeries, 8 lawyers, 7 boarding-houses, 7 shoemakers, 7 blacksmiths, 6 physicians, 5 lumber-yards, 4 cigar stores, 4 butchers, 3 drugstores, 3 watchmakers, 2 fruit markets, 2 barbers, 2 stationery shops, 2 express offices, 2 assayers, and a surveyor, dentist, gunsmith, saddler, tailor, dressmaker, theater, music hall, and post office. The town eventually added a bank, as did most thriving communities, to lend an air of commercial and financial stability. The nation had 3,776 banks by 1870 (almost equally divided between private banks and state or national banks). Private banks most often served small communities that could not meet the high capital requirements to secure a state or national bank. Consequently, even a rural state like Iowa had 200 private banks (compared to 75 national ones) in 1875.

Employees in small shops and stores worked long hours, often under tedious conditions. In Abilene, Kansas, for instance, they derived most of their exercise from swatting flies. "In dog days the men sweat profusely while figuring in their little stores or offices," recalled one resident. "Between sales or trades you behold them idling there, longing for something to occur.

. . . Godsends in the way of news were a dogfight, a swearing quarrel between two residents, the broken limb of a neighbor tumbling off a new roof." Still, most employers expected their clerks to keep busy. If not waiting on customers, they were to inventory stock, shelve new merchandise, dust counters, clean windows, sweep the walk, and generally tidy up. If they had done all that, and it was a particularly slow day, clerks took boxes off shelves, opened them, rearranged the contents, and replaced them on the shelves. No matter how slow the day, no matter how little genuine work they had to do, employees had to appear "closely occupied" and "give the impression that much business is transacted in the establishment." Most city shops remained open from 7 A.M. to 10 P.M., and in some locales handled their heaviest traffic after 5 P.M. Still, hours often depended on local custom, the economy, and individual employers. So did wages. Even in cities, where workers presumably received the highest wages, shop girls contented themselves with $2.50 to $4 weekly, and they earned that amount only after an apprenticeship of several weeks at one dollar.

Some innovative entrepreneurs decided that city dwellers, always in a hurry, never with enough time, would be attracted to large, convenient stores that offered a myriad of goods under one roof. Consequently, increasing numbers of cities had their own version of the country stores (without the groceries): department stores. This new mode of retailing emerged in the late 1850s, when economic expansion and the expectations of urban life transformed familiar dry goods stores into emporiums that sold ready-made clothing and a wide assortment of other nonperishable goods. But if the concept of convenience linked the two styles of retailing, no one could mistake the size, luxury, and efficiency of a department store for its country cousin.

The first department store, A. T. Stewart's, in New York City, remained a model for decades to come. Constructed between 1859 and 1862 on the block bounded by Broadway, Fourth Avenue, Ninth Street, and Tenth Street (about twenty acres),

Stewart's five-story emporium, with its cast-iron facade, rows of plate-glass display windows, and hydraulic passenger elevators, gave New Yorkers a strikingly modern piece of architecture that rapidly became the norm (with the addition of steel-frame construction) for commercial buildings after the war. Inside Stewart's, a mammoth rotunda, extending from the ground floor to the roof, inspired a sense of grandeur equaled by few cathedrals. The four upper floors, flooded with "ample light" from dozens of windows implanted in the outer walls, were open on the rotunda side, allowing customers to peer over the railings and inspect the swarming masses below. "All kinds of people come here," concluded one customer, "from the poor woman whose scanty garb tells too plainly the story of her poverty, to the wife of the millionaire whose purchases amount to a small fortune, and all classes can be suited." Besides the huge windows, numerous gas jets provided light. Customers gained access to all public floors either by way of two grand staircases or on one of three "handsome elevators." Eight enormous boilers, located in the cellar, powered ten steam engines, which, in turn, provided power for the elevators, gave steam heat in winter, and kept hot water flowing to the fifth-floor laundry.

Such a store, patronized by 15,000 customers each day (50,000 during the Christmas season), required hundreds of workers (1,709 to be exact), with extra seasonal help pushing the number to 2,200. While men dominated in managerial and sales positions through the 1870s, women gained early footholds in department stores like Stewart's. Over half of the regular employees were women. Most of them labored as seamstresses, laundresses, and janitors, but growing numbers of women worked behind counters. Created primarily for a female clientele, department stores placed heavy emphasis on women's clothing and household goods. It made sense, then, for women, well versed in the likes and dislikes of their sex, to serve female customers. The stores also emphasized courtesy, graciousness, and ease in serving customers. While many male clerks could claim these attributes, they tended, more often than not, to be overly formal, even aloof. Female clerks already waited on customers in stores selling dry goods, women's clothing, and other "fancy" goods, not to mention numerous family-owned groceries, tobacconists, and other specialty shops. Besides, most people believed that young men should pursue manly occupations, not waste their "health, strength, and talents selling gloves, tape, and dress goods."

Stewart's, like most department stores, opened at 7 A.M. and closed at 7 P.M. "Door boys," about age twelve, opened the heavy plate-glass doors for customers. In stormy weather, the boys offered to take charge of customers' umbrellas. Some thirty male ushers scattered throughout the store directed customers to the department they sought, and over three hundred eager salesmen and saleswomen stood ready to serve them. None of the salespeople accepted cash payments for purchases. Instead, when making a sale, they summoned one of two hundred "cash boys" to carry the payment and a sales memorandum to one of nine male cashiers. Each cashier sat in a little wooden booth enclosed with latticework. He collected the money and returned the cash boy with any change due and a copy of the sales slip. Cash boys, who also worked as door boys, errand runners, and performers of "sundry other useful acts," earned three to eight dollars a week. Female clerks received about the same wages as the boys; male clerks earned six to twelve dollars. Only the largest stores gave paid vacations to employees (up to eight weeks in some cases), but many stores did force workers to take six- to eight-week unpaid vacations during slow summer months. Employees enjoyed a thirty-minute dinner break, and one-half of them alternately went home each day at 6 P.M. Stewart's enforced a strict dress code. In fact, one observer found general discipline to be "very rigid, . . . enforced by a system of fines and other penalties." Store detectives inspected employees as they went home to make certain no one carried away "any of the property of the house."

But if the clean, efficient environment of the department store made it a more cheerful place to work in than a warehouse or a factory, that did not mean employees worked without complaint. Discipline and regimentation rubbed some people the wrong way. Salesclerks complained about being forced to stand for ten hours every working day. Female clerks in a Saint Louis store became so infuriated that they demanded high-backed chairs to sit on when not serving customers. When the store owner rejected their demand, they went on strike, picketed the store, and handed out leaflets to inform customers of their grievances. One Saint Louis labor agitator even penned a song to broadcast their stand:

> My neighbors and myself have met,
> And talked the matter o'er;
> And we've resolved and firmly too,
> To patronize no more
> Those barbarous establishments
> Not one of them in town—
> That keep the girls upon their feet,
> And let them ne'er sit down.

Several weeks later, the store owner gave in to the clerks' demand.

If not more numerous than shopkeepers, physicians did rank as the most numerous, respected, and important "professional" people in town. Widespread sickness and a shortage of doctors placed a heavy burden on the medical profession. Besides the usual colds, fevers, accidents, and internal disorders, mid-nineteenth-century Americans were subject to epidemics of deadly diseases, including cholera, smallpox, typhoid, and diphtheria. In 1870, the nation could rely on over 62,000 physicians to battle these villains, far above the number of clergymen (44,000), lawyers (41,000), or bankers (11,000). Villages and hamlets of a hundred people generally had at least one doctor; small towns of a thousand people might have four or five. Still, Americans complained of a shortage, partly because a disproportionate number of physicians practiced in cities, partly because in rural areas, where people lived miles from town, it took so long to contact local doctors and have them respond.

Other conditions also made people think a shortage existed. A resident of western Illinois encouraged a nearby physician to relocate in his town. The town, insisted this supplicant, was prosperous and growing. Indeed, he admitted, it already had five physicians. Unfortunately, all five men were Republicans, while the majority of citizens were Democrats. "If you come here you can commence all the democratic practice besides some of the other," swore the recruiter. "I can insure your introduction into many of the best families here. . . . You will [find] a set of public men here that will do what they can for you."

Apparent shortages certainly could not be explained by any difficulty in claiming the title "doctor." Although the nation had 110 medical schools that were producing approximately 2,000 new physicians every year by 1870, entrance requirements and course work remained ridiculously easy until the mid-1870s. Few schools required more than a high school diploma, and many schools expected a good deal less, sometimes only the ability to read and write English. The standard medical curriculum could be completed in a year or less, and few schools offered any laboratory or clinical work. One graduate of the University of Louisville's medical department felt so ill prepared after two months in practice that he took down his shingle. His Waterloo, he later revealed, had been an incurable case of diabetes. "I was overwhelmed," he acknowledged in recalling his patient's death, "with the conviction that I was unfit to take the grave responsibility of the life and health and happiness of those who might be willing to place themselves under my care." Three years later, in 1872, he entered a New York medical school for postgraduate training. By that time, some reform-minded schools had established two- or three-year curricula, insisted on more rigid entrance requirements, and demanded tougher final examinations.

A large, if declining, number of budding physicians received their training through apprenticeships. This had been the standard means of entering most professions before the war. In addition to paying a monetary settlement of $100 to $250, the novice swept his preceptor's office, kept his accounts, chopped wood, ran errands, "read medicine" (mostly biology, anatomy, chemistry, physiology, and pharmacy), accompanied the master on house calls, and observed how his master lanced boils, set fractures, and amputated limbs. In time, the apprentice attempted uncomplicated medical procedures and learned to mix drugs, dress wounds, prepare plasters, and administer bloodlettings, or "bleedings." Three years was thought sufficient for this training, after which the apprentice was turned loose to practice his new art. "They are honest, conscientious, hard-working men," insisted one doctor of his apprentice-trained colleagues in 1875, "who are inclined to place great weight on their experience, and to be rather contemptuous of what they call 'book learning and theories.' " The system declined as the number of medical schools multiplied and as more states required medical school certification for physicians.

Whatever his training, the average doctor worked long days. Irregular hours, broken rest, and the hardships of travel wore down the physician's health. Most small-town doctors had numerous rural patients whom they visited by buggy or on horseback; but in wet weather, when roads and fields turned into quagmires, many of them insisted on walking cross-country the five or six miles required. There were life-threatening dangers, too. Wolves, mountain lions, and bears still frequented some regions, and outlaws were not above holding up a doctor along the road. Most physicians accepted the danger and plowed ahead. When friends begged one female doctor in Indiana to carry a weapon on night visitations, the spunky little woman replied, "For an ordinary criminal? I should be ashamed of myself if I could not outwit three or four of them." Yet most country doctors went prepared for any emergency, with a shovel, ax, wire cutters, lantern, and rifle stashed beneath the seats of their buggies.

City doctors relied more heavily on "office practice" than did small-town doctors. Even the most successful city practitioner held generous daily office hours, even on Sundays. Yet most of their callers were transients and first-time patients, for the vast majority of middle-class patients received doctors in their homes. John Burke, a typical New York physician, left a detailed record of his daily activities for 1866. On a normal day, Dr. Burke rose at 7 A.M., received his early office patients, read the morning newspaper, and, if he had time, ate a hurried breakfast in order to begin house calls by 8:30. He visited a local dispensary between noon and 1 P.M. More house calls followed until 3 P.M., when he returned to his office to receive patients until 5 P.M. He ate supper and took a nap between 5 P.M. and 7 P.M., then returned to his office to see patients until 8:30. He made one final round of three to five house calls before returning home at about 11 P.M. After an hour spent reading, he went to bed. As for variety, one "not . . . very busy" day in December found Dr. Burke treating two cases of scarlatina, seven of bronchitis, four of typhoid, one of pneumonia, two of tuberculosis, one of dysentery, one of vomiting and diarrhea, one sore throat, one scalding, one hip injury, one threatened miscarriage, and one remittent fever.

All physicians, by modern standards, worked with primitive tools (mostly scalpels, forceps, and probes) and had little knowledge of what caused diseases or how to prevent their spread. Such basic medical tools as thermometers and stethoscopes did not find general acceptance until after 1880. Doctors wore no surgical gowns or masks when operating. They remained dressed in suits, although "the more fastidious" deigned to turn up their cuffs. Unwise surgical procedures, especially bloodletting, endangered patients' lives. Actually, opposition to bloodletting intensified during the 1860s. Nonetheless, many physicians continued to advocate use of the lancet during "earlier and gravescent stages" of acute diseases and fevers. They insisted that bloodletting released contaminated blood from the body, so, while bleeding may have temporarily weakened patients, it also purged them of "impurities." One leading advocate, in the 1870s, prescribed general bleeding as "at once the most speedy and the most efficient means of relief." Insofar as rural doctors lagged behind in the latest medical theories, it is likely that bloodletting continued in small towns and the countryside to a wider extent than in cities.

Both urban and country doctors mixed most of their own drugs and prescriptions, although, here again, controversy brewed. Some drugs of long standing, including arsenic, calomel, and tartar emetic, drew opposition in the 1860s and 1870s. Doctors also had to contend with increasing numbers of patent medicines, sold in both general stores and pharmacist shops. Some doctors, hoping to limit the use of patent medicines, arranged with pharmacists to send them patients in return for a share of prescription sales. Other doctors solved the problem of competition by operating their own drugstores, a business that sometimes garnered larger profits than their medical practices. Another form of competition came from home remedies, for many rural doctors prescribed such concoctions as wahoo root tea for rheumatism, ginger tea for chills, and sulphur and molasses for ague and scrofula.

Only a few big-city doctors got rich from medical practice. Most doctors charged one to two dollars for office visits and a like amount plus fifty cents per mile for house calls. The price of medicine, surgery, or any treatment would be extra. Many doctors, however, charged far below these levels, sometimes as low as twenty-five cents for an office consultation and fifty cents for a house call. Most rural doctors, regardless of their fees, also accepted payment in kind, be it a calf, bushel of corn, jug of cider, or pound of butter. One doctor, having visited a farm twenty-three miles from town to remove a tumor from a woman's shoulder, received a barrel of apple brandy. He sold half the brandy for twenty dollars. Very few doctors, even in cities, kept very accurate accounts of their professional services. The majority of doctors knew their patients as neighbors, not just as recipients of their skill and knowledge. They knew all about Nate Jenkins—how many bushels of corn he sold last year, what losses he sustained in the recent drought, what domestic difficulties he faced, his general physical, financial, and spiritual condition. The smaller the community, the stronger the sense of family. "A country doctor," testified one man, "isn't necessarily more humane than the city's practitioner, but he's likely to be more human. . . . [T]he country doctor's approach is as friend or neighbor as well as physician."

If, as someone once observed, newspapers are the characteristic literature of America, then journalists were indispensable to the daily life of any community. The number of newspapers and periodicals suggests the demand. Nearly eight hundred daily, triweekly, and semiweekly papers kept Americans abreast of current events in 1870, and over five thousand additional weekly, monthly, and quarterly papers, magazines, and journals specialized in such diverse areas as politics, religion, commerce, agriculture, labor, charities, literature, and sports. Still, few journalists could be called "professional." Certainly, few of them fit the image of the crusading reformer who used a free press to attack corruption and chicanery. Typically, their papers were modest affairs, usually four eight-column pages. Many editors combined their newspaper chores with other occupations. Lawyers frequently published local sheets, a sideline that not only provided a little extra revenue but allowed them to advertise prominently. "If legal assistance is desired," read the lawyer-edited *Neosho Valley Register,* in Kansas, "call at the *Register* office." The editor of the Omaha *Arrow* not only practiced law, he also operated a blacksmith shop, sold insurance, and ran a general store. One prairie newspaper regretfully informed its readers that the senior editor had been "so busy gathering corn, fighting prairie fires, building winter quarters for his livestock, etc. that we have had nearly nothing from his pencil for this number." Finally, some editors supplemented their incomes by printing Christmas cards, wedding invitations, and business circulars.

The internal workings of a newspaper office varied as widely as the operations of different-size farms and shops. A small-town editor might operate his paper single-handedly, gathering news, setting type, soliciting advertisers, selling subscriptions, perhaps even delivering the paper. He usually operated from a small, cluttered, one-room office, occupied primarily by a rolltop desk (piled high with correspondence, drafts of articles and editorials, subscription lists, and ledger books) and a hand-powered printing press. When possible, he hired an adolescent boy to serve as apprentice, run errands, set type, and—despite the odds—keep the office clean and orderly. A metropolitan daily, on the other hand, might be housed in a three- or four-story building with dozens of offices, several conference rooms, and a mammoth printing plant. The staff of a big-city newspaper could number several hundred reporters, office workers, and machinsts. As many as a dozen editors, all supervised by an editor-in-chief, supervised this small army. Large papers frequently received stories from free-lance or special correspondents, particularly for national and foreign news. Most local news came from salaried reporters who worked regular "beats" at the law courts, city hall, sporting events, social soirees, and so on.

Most editors serving outside big cities tried to avoid controversy, largely because they served several masters and wanted to offend none. Few of them dared disregard community opinion or the feelings of advertisers. Editorial "puffs" and "plugs" for local products and businesses were common. Likewise, editors endorsed ideas, causes, and sentiments, such as education, religion, economic growth, and civic improvements, that pleased their readers. Support for the reigning political party was mandatory where one party dominated; elsewhere each party had its own organ. In fact, many newspapers, whether in New York or Neosho, were little more than political sheets dedicated to reporting party activities, urging voters to cast a straight ticket at elections, and condemning all who opposed their party. Such support usually received its reward in the form of operating funds from county, state, or even national headquarters. "My negotiations with Fenton and Schell have been very important," rejoiced one editor after conferring with party leaders prior to the 1872 presidential campaign, "and the latter . . . has positively promised 'material aid' for The Republican [his newspaper] during the Canvass. Would have given me some at once, but is just organizing his Committee . . . and had not yet levied supplies." If an editor's party won local elections, printing contracts became another source of revenue. Similarly, editors vied for contracts to publish tax lists, land sales, and other legal notices. Contracts sometimes resulted from party connections; other times they came from local developers and speculators who wanted to draw attention to the community. This partly explains the phenomenal growth of country weeklies in the postwar era. The editor of the *Pioneer Press*, in Algona, Iowa, for example, launched a newspaper in order to advertise his own real estate office and obtain revenue from nearby counties for printing their tax rolls.

While doctors and good newspaper editors always seemed to be in short supply, people seldom complained about a dearth of lawyers. As in medicine, educational requirements for the bar were not very high. A couple of years spent "reading law" with a judge or practicing attorney provided a reasonably bright lad with sufficient knowledge to pass state bar examinations. Law schools existed (thirty-one of them in 1870), but the training they provided resembled the informality of the medical schools.

A spirit of reform appeared in the 1870s, but it proceeded much more slowly than in medicine. The vast majority of lawyers still acquired their education as apprentices. The results could be very uneven. A Massachusetts-trained lawyer who had moved to Kansas expressed shock at the low quality of his western-trained colleagues. "My success is not so much attributable to superior personal merit," he admitted to his father, "as to the want of ability among the practitioners generally. A more ignorant, detestable set of adle-headed numbskulls and blackguards I have seldom met."

Few lawyers limited themselves to the bar. Many lawyers were also budding politicians who used their knowledge of the law to secure positions of influence in local affairs. As with other professionals, such as doctors and editors, lawyers received tremendous benefits from belonging to the "right" party. Similarly, they frequently acquired influence and gained the trust of residents by functioning as local land agents. Whereas criminal trials occasionally brightened the legal life of a town, few lawyers could have survived without the paperwork and litigation provided by land purchases, transfers, mortgages, sales, and claim jumping. Collecting debts may have been a lawyer's next most important source of income.

A growing contingent of workers enjoyed a semi-professional status by serving on public payrolls as postmen, police officers, fire fighters, office clerks, and the like. Many of these occupations had not existed a generation earlier, at least not in the form they achieved during the Civil War era; yet they became increasingly numerous and necessary to the smooth functioning of town and city life after the war. Some of the jobs, such as fire fighting, required manual labor; but most citizens ranked these workers a cut above most workers in mining, construction, transportation, and manufacturing.

Towns with fifty thousand or more inhabitants required letter carriers, or "postmen," after 1865, when such towns began enjoying the luxury of free mail delivery. New York City operated the largest postal system, with over seven hundred employees at its main office and fourteen "stations." For eight hundred to one thousand dollars a year, postmen sorted and delivered local mail, starting at 6:30 A.M., six days a week. "They are obliged to perform their duties regardless of weather," observed one admiring citizen, "and are subjected to an exposure which is very trying to them." Unlike modern letter carriers, however, they also had to contend with shifting political winds. All postal workers, from postmasters to carriers, received their jobs through political patronage. From 1 to 2 percent of every postal worker's salary was deducted "for party expenses," and workers were expected to donate at least five dollars to the party in every local and state election. "A new Postmaster may remove any or all of them," marveled one observer, "to make way for his political friends, and any refusal on their part to submit to the orders or extortions of their party-managers is sure to result in a dismissal."

Methods of local law enforcement varied from region to region and town to town. Small western and southern towns relied on local sheriffs to round up evildoers. More populous places had turned to organized police forces by the 1870s. A large city force could number, as it did in New York, close to three thousand men, including officers, sergeants, patrolmen, and detectives. Most cities were divided into districts or precincts with a captain "held to strict accountability for the preservation of the peace and good order" of his area. Each patrolman (nearly 2,100 of them in New York) walked a particular "beat," where he was expected "to exercise the utmost vigilance to prevent the occurrence of any crime." The standard police uniform consisted of dark-colored frock coat and trousers (usually navy blue), badge, and glazed cap. Each man carried a hard wooden baton and revolver. They worked alternately on five different shifts, or "tours," with one-third of the men on duty during the day and two-thirds at night. While the police moved swiftly in cases of murder, robbery, and assault, they

spent most of their time apprehending people involved in mis-
demeanors, such as petty theft, picking pockets, cruelty to animals, interference with telegraph wires, staging prize fights and
cock fights, destruction of property, disorderly conduct, and
public drunkenness. The average patrolman received $1,200
annually.

All cities established professional fire-fighting departments in
the Civil War era, a move intended to improve on the efficiency
and stem the rowdiness of older volunteer fire companies. Cincinnati acted first, in the mid-1850s. In New York, nearly six
hundred officers and men, formed into scores of companies
scattered through the city, served the needs of the nation's most
populous urban area. Each New York company contained a
dozen men, including foreman, assistant foreman, engineer,
stoker, driver, and seven fire fighters. Each company operated
its own house, with engine room, stables, and living quarters.
Most companies were steam-engine companies, but the city
also sponsored four old hand-pump companies, twelve hook-
and-ladder companies, and a powerful floating engine to extinguish fires on piers and sailing vessels. Only physically fit and
morally upright men could qualify for the fire fighter's very
respectable $1,000 annual salary (slightly higher for officers).

Much daily activity centered on the care of horses (including
feeding, exercising, and grooming), equipage, and equipment,
but the fire fighter's principal job was to fight fires. "As soon as
the sharp strokes of the gong give the signal of danger," reported one New Yorker, "every man springs to his post. The
horses are attached in a few seconds [fifteen seconds during the
day, sixty seconds at night], the fire is lighted in the furnace, and
the steamer and hose carriage start for the scene of action." The
foreman ran ahead to clear the way. The engine, carrying
driver, stoker, and chief engineer, followed close behind but
could not pass the foreman: "Fast driving is seriously punished,
and racing is absolutely prohibited." Upon reaching the confla-
gration, fire fighters, who had followed the engine on foot,

linked their engine to the nearest hydrant and, under direction of the engineer, drowned the flames. In most instances, squads of policemen assisted by roping off streets and redirecting traffic in the surrounding area.

Clerical work provided many new job opportunities for women. Employment of female office workers began as an experiment during the war, when the United States government and some private businessmen hired female clerks, copyists, and bookkeepers to fill a wartime manpower shortage. Women who proved competent in their new roles gained permanent jobs. A reorganization of office work also helped them by creating more jobs. Correspondence and other paperwork mushroomed in government and business during and after the war. Large numbers of specialized file clerks, shipping clerks, billing clerks, and other clerical workers had to assist the traditional office staff of copyists, bookkeepers, general clerks, and messengers. What was more, women seemed better suited then men for two skilled jobs—stenographer and typist—created by the newly invented typewriter. Last, but far from least, women in all positions worked more cheaply than men. One New York merchant replaced his $1,800-a-year male bookkeeper with an equally competent woman for $500. "Some of the females are doing more and better work for $900 per annum than many male clerks who were paid double that amount," confirmed a Washington bureaucrat in 1869.

Something more might be said about typewriters. The new machine facilitated rather than caused the emerging dominance of women in clerical work, and its eventual impact could not have been imagined in 1876. Typewriters caught on slowly in the business community. Early machines were slow, expensive (about $125), and undependable. Moreover, many people considered it rude for a firm to type its correspondence. Still, many government, legal, and business offices were employing "type girls" by the mid-1870s. In 1875, one national advertisement recommended typewriters as appropriate Christmas gifts for "poor, deserving" young women seeking a good living as copyists or corresponding clerks. "No invention has opened for women so broad and easy an avenue to profitable and suitable employment. . . . More girls are now earning from $10 to $20 per week with the 'Type-Writer,' and we can at once secure good situations for one hundred expert writers on it."

With or without typewriters, educated women—the sort required for clerical work—preferred the new occupations to sewing, teaching, and domestic service. Office work was clean and quiet, and it spared young ladies from working alongside members of the lower classes. Not surprisingly, the vast majority of early office workers were native-born, middle-class white women with at least a high school education. Many were daughters, widows, and wives of doctors, lawyers, clergymen, and other professionals. They sought work most often in order to supplement family incomes, although in some cases they needed to support themselves. One wife, in her mid-twenties, applied for work in a federal office after the war because her ne'er-do-well husband failed to support her after being discharged from the army. "Warm-hearted, social, and easily influenced he proved too susceptible to the temptations and many allurements of camp life," she grieved, "and like many of our brave and noble soldiers yielded to the demon intemperance, rendering him unfit, for society, and too soon unworthy of a wife's care, forgiveness, or endurance." Such women found the average salary of $900 per year paid to federal clerks very appealing, especially when comparing it with other jobs— teachers earned $400 to $800 a year—in the District of Columbia.

Women office workers naturally faced stiff opposition as they entered a male-dominated world. One engraving, published in an 1875 issue of *Harper's Bazar* depicted an office "taken over by ladies." The scene is total chaos. Female clerks, some with quill pens tucked behind their ears and sitting on desks, preen themselves in mirrors, arrange their hair, study the latest fashions (in *Harper's Bazar* of course), decorate hats, play practical jokes, use ledger books as building blocks, stare out the window, do everything except an honest day's work. Concerned citizens also worried about the moral implications of men and women working in close physical proximity, a familiar situation for men and women who worked in factories, but a new experience for the middle classes. Female office workers heard themselves called strumpets. Married women, especially, drew criticism. Public speculation about their adulterous affairs was rivaled only by accusations that they had, at the very least, deserted their "natural" responsibilities as mothers and housekeepers.

Of course, every community had genuine members of the world's oldest "profession." "Is it any wonder that so many . . . working women and girls . . . glide into sin, with the hope of bettering their hard lot?" asked a concerned observer of females in the sewing trades. Many people found the link between prostitution and the sewing trades a natural one, for the most wretched and desperate sewing women sometimes supplemented legitimate incomes by selling their bodies. Additionally, many madams, having to explain why so many young ladies frequented their lodgings, listed their occupation as "dressmaker." So notorious did this association become that newspapers used "plain sewing" as a euphemism for prostitution. Actually, prostitutes fell into various categories and lived under varied circumstances. The least fortunate of them survived as streetwalkers or worked in the "back rooms" of saloons, dance halls, and "cigar stores." "In front of the dirty little shanties, a beggarly display of cigars and fruits is made," commented an observer in a midwestern town, "while behind in a sitting room containing some gay furniture and a wheezy organ, or jingling piano is found, while several asthmatic painted females are preparing to sing or play cards." Cowboys and soldiers found "fallen women" ready to greet them at "hog ranches." Authorities charged the owners of one ranch/brothel near Fort Laramie with "keeping a common, ill-governed and disorderly house to the encouragement of idleness, drinking, and fornication." Prostitutes generally regarded city brothels as the safest and most remunerative places to work.

The brothels of Minneapolis typified those in most towns of the nation. Like workplaces in any business, brothels, or "parlor houses" as they became known, varied in size, comfort, and convenience. The lowest class of establishment was ill kept and sparsely furnished. Houses in the middle range, with genuine parlors in which to entertain guests, could be as tastefully appointed as any minister's house. At the other extreme, grand bordellos, with large, stately rooms and elegant furniture, sponsored inmates who were "beautiful, accomplished, [and] captivating in dress and manner." Most Minneapolis brothels fell into the middle range. Inmates were young and mobile. They ranged in age from sixteen to thirty, with a median of twenty-two years. The vast majority were unmarried, although married women occasionally sought employment, either on their own initiative or through the coercion of husbands. The average house employed six women. Prostitutes seldom stayed more than a few years in a single brothel, and tenure of only a few months was not uncommon. Some madams insisted on high turnover rates in order to reduce emotional involvement between girls and customers, maintain a constant supply of "fresh faces," and minimize possible friction on the brothel's staff. Sometimes girls moved to another house in the same city; more often they traveled to new towns. Brothel wages in Minneapolis are hard to determine. Customers probably paid a flat fee plus whatever tips they thought suitable. In some places, inmates received a percentage of the flat rate; elsewhere they worked for tips alone. In any case, Minneapolis police raided city brothels at monthly intervals, at which time madams paid fines of fifteen to one hundred dollars, depending on the number of employees. Each girl paid a fine of ten dollars.

Only a few Minneapolis prostitutes seem to have been seduced, abducted, or otherwise physically forced into the profession, although, like many details of the trade, this is largely supposition. Most women entered prostitution after failing to make a living at other, low-paying jobs. Some, beginning as domestic servants in houses of ill fame, were attracted to less virtuous occupations by the nice clothes and "easy living" of the women they served. Most, however, used the occupation as an expedient and left it as soon as possible. Nature determined the length of time most women worked. Every passing year detracted a little more from their sexual appeal and, consequently, from their value. Physical wear and tear counted for something, too. Most prostitutes drank, many heavily. Not a few used drugs, mostly opium, morphine, and laudanum. Occasionally, prostitutes died of drug overdoses, as well as from abortions and, quite frequently, suicide. Sadistic customers sometimes abused them, and the possibility of contracting venereal disease was an ever-present danger. Women who survived the ordeals of their profession sometimes married and settled down into respectable lives. Most simply acquired other work.

In sum, Americans earned their living in numerous ways. Subtle shifts and new trends could be detected in their choice of occupations. Though still the majority, farmers did not hold such a large proportional share of the total work force by the late 1870s as they had in 1860. Mining, manufacturing, construction, and transportation had made impressive inroads among laborers. Proportionately larger numbers of women joined the work force, and not just poor women who had to work to help support their families. Educated, middle-class women appeared more frequently in shops and offices. Former craftsmen left their independent shops to become industrial craftsmen in factories. Their growing numbers and discontent with the new system transformed many industries and spawned a more vigorous trade union movement. In the professions, formal training was more often required, and white-collar jobs became more numerous as the demand for clerks, managers, and shopkeepers kept pace with the growth of urbanization and industrialization. If not yet at center stage, a recognizably modern American work force was at least standing in the wings by 1876.

# 9      DAILY WOES

WHILE Americans of the Civil War era would agree that their most constant complaints and gripes focused on their bosses, wages, and other conditions associated with their working lives, other perils, pressures, and pitfalls also confounded them. Sicknesses and epidemics, Indians and outlaws, natural disasters and man-made catastrophes topped a list of daily woes that plagued physicians and miners, farmers and shopkeepers alike. Most of these obstacles to happiness defied human efforts to control or abolish them. They became aspects of daily life that people endured as best they could.

Nature produced a large share of the trouble. Each season brought new dangers for people who, still bound closely to the earth, trusted their lives and livelihoods to a beneficent nature. In spring, floods could destroy young crops and sod houses. In summer, droughts and hot winds could wither promising harvests. In autumn, prairie fires, often man made but with nature providing the tinderbox, could sweep ferociously across the plains to destroy crops, homes, and whole towns. In winter, blizzards and subfreezing temperatures could kill livestock and people. Winter's only blessing was as a respite from the insects that wreaked havoc during most of the rest of the year.

"A terrible storm and cloudburst came upon us and we lost almost everything, except the cows and an old team in the pasture," recalled one homesteader. Farmers had a love/hate relationship with rain. Too little courted disaster; too much endangered property and lives as well as crops. "The creek was up to the house and [rain] still pouring down," insisted one woman. "When we opened the door to get out, the water came up to our necks. We had to struggle to get out and I can't tell to this day how we ever made it but the Lord must have been with us." The family—man, wife, and baby daughter—reached a haven on high ground. When the storm subsided and the waters receded, they found their house "full of rubbish," with furniture upended and an inch of mud covering floors and carpets. "Our cow barn and ponies were swept away," added the woman, "also our stock of millet. Practically everything we had was gone or ruined: machinery, wagons and nice garden." They found the ponies sixteen miles downstream.

The other extreme, drought, could linger for months at a time, the record for the era being sixteen months in the prairie states. "Night after night we could see the lightening flash all around the horizon," recalled a Kansan, "but it was only heat and not the forerunner of rain. By and by, hope failed the stoutest heart." People without sufficient stores to withstand long periods of drought left the land. Those who remained required several years to recover, and they lived ever after with fearful memories of their experience. "The leaves on the trees shriveled and dried up, and every living thing was seeking shelter from the hot rays of the sun," testified one farmer's daughter. "The earth opened in great cracks several inches across and two feet deep. We used to play these were earthquake crevices and scores of imaginery people met an untimely end." A rather dark game for children.

Drought also set the stage for devastating fires. "There ain't nothing worse than fire on the prairie," reported a Nebraskan, yet rural Americans could take but few preventive measures. Settlers made firebreaks in some areas by plowing two furrows about ten yards apart and burning (on a calm day) the grass between. Very little could be done to extinguish head fires in open country, but they could be contained by beating less ferocious side fires with animal skins or damp garments until the wind died, the rains came, or the fire consumed itself. "A rush was made for the stables to cut the horses loose," recalled one farmer of his battle against a prairie fire. He and his hands finally hurled enough water on the flames to save the house, but a large straw stack, nearly all the hay, large stores of wheat, and the cattle corral went up in smoke. Even to conquer a fire produced a mingled sense of exhaustion, relief, and despair. "Your throat is full of ashes and you can hardly breathe for the choking of the fluff in the air," explained one woman. "If you call to your nearest pal on the back firing line the chances are that he or she has moved away, and may be half a mile distant. You may feel as if you were the last survivor in a horrible world of cinders and blackness."

Fire also threatened towns and cities with disaster. Even densely populated cities made little effort to regulate building construction before the 1870s, and still-primitive fire-fighting equipment provided scant help against monster conflagrations. Every house, shop, office, theater, and church was a potential tinderbox. A carelessly tossed match, a bolt of lightning, a smoldering cigar butt, a kerosene lamp, any source of fire could send a neighborhood up in flames. Smaller towns had fire gongs to summon volunteer firemen or the general citizenry to man pumps and buckets. "There could be no mistaking that direful sound," insisted one woman. At "9 o'clock the fire bells rang & all hands rushed," recorded a volunteer fireman. "Engines were on the ground very promptly, as usual—fire spread to buildings on each side, but it was soon subdued & extinguished." Not all fire fighters were so swift or so effective. Fire swept through Boston's business section in 1872 and destroyed hundreds of structures, even brick and granite ones. The fire spread by leaping from one roof to the next along the town's narrow streets. In Virginia City, fire destroyed two thousand buildings, inflicted ten million dollars' worth of property damage, and left thousands homeless in 1875.

Chicago survived the most spectacular and devastating fire of the century. Whether or not Mrs. O'Leary's cow really started the blaze is uncertain. We do know that the fire probably started in a small wooden barn on DeKoven Street on a Sunday night in early October 1871. The fire, driven by strong winds, swept through squalid shanties and lumberyards before racing toward the central business district. The inferno destroyed over 17,000 buildings—houses, banks, offices, shops, theaters, hotels, the courthouse, even the water works—and left 150,000 people homeless. "Rozet's losses are fearful," one survivor reported of her husband's totally destroyed real estate office, "& his insurance not worth more than 10 cts on the dollar." Even more devastating, she continued, the fire had consumed their "beautiful home & every thing in it." Yet, she concluded optimistically, "we are well and Rozet has all his pluck and fortitude to help him." More poignant were the numerous "Personals" that appeared in newspapers for days after the fire, as people tried to locate friends and relatives: "Henry Schneider, baby, in blue poland waist, red skirt, has white hair. Lost."

The Chicago fire sparked serious consideration of reform. "Newspapers . . . dwell on the probability that like disaster or worse may befall us any windy winter night," reported a concerned New Yorker. "One need only . . . contemplate Drexel's immense banking house on the corner of Wall and Broad, now culminating in a vast mansard roof and towers all lath and pinewood and quite out of effective engine range. . . . Such structures are scattered throughout the city like so many sporadic powder magazines." City officials responded by passing stiffer building codes. Builders responded by using safer construction materials. Concrete, all but unknown in the United States just after the Civil War, came into wider use. Plate glass reduced the need for much wood construction. The Bessemer process produced fireproof steel to replace wrought iron. By the late 1870s, even asbestos had been discovered.

No amount of American know-how or ingenuity seemed capable of controlling another plague of nature. Insects, particularly flies and mosquitoes, could drive people and animals crazy, but for sheer destructive force, nothing matched the grasshopper. Incredible swarms of large grasshoppers, or locusts, blotted out western and midwestern skies in some summers. One such year, 1874, old-timers of the Central Plains and Southwest remembered as "the grasshopper year." "They came gradually like a fall of snow," recalled one Kansan. "At first they came down so slowly that the fowls could clear them up, but presently they began to fall in earnest, and then nothing could check them." "Grasshoppers by the millions in a solid mass filled the sky," reported another combatant. They ate everything in their path, not just crops but weeds, tree leaves, clothing, harness, wooden handles on tools, and weather-beaten boards on houses and fences. When they settled on railroad tracks, mighty locomotives ground to a halt, as the mashed bodies of thousands of insects made the tracks so slick that engines could acquire no traction. In houses, they terrified pets and children as they ate their way through clothing, curtains, and uncovered food.

Settlers tried every conceivable way of combating the two-week reign of terror, but to no avail. They set bonfires in orchards, fields, and gardens to ward off the scavengers and cremate them. "Along the fence they were piled a foot deep or more, a moving, struggling mass," recalled one settler in describing his mode of attack. "Jake [the hired hand] began to dig a trench outside the fence about two feet deep and the width of the shovel." They raked grasshoppers into the trench and set it ablaze. Soon, however, the fire was "covered and smothered" by new waves of locusts. "Think of it," marveled this witness, "grasshoppers putting out a fire." Other farmers tied burlap sacks, blankets, and old quilts around plants, only to see the cloth eaten through and the plants devoured. People beat and flailed with shovels, tree branches, gunny sacks, anything that might flatten or disable the hordes. Nothing, save time, helped. "It was enough to make a man's heart ache," admitted one victim, "to stand and see every bit of vegetation destroyed as it was, and at the same time to be utterly powerless to prevent it."

Grasshoppers left their mark on more than just the devastated landscape. Everything reeked of the taste and odor of insects. Water from wells, streams, rivers, and ponds, turned brown by their excrement, became totally unfit to drink. Hogs and poultry, bloated to bursting after feasting on the invaders, tasted so strongly of grasshoppers as to be inedible. What was more, the insects had deposited their eggs in the soil before departing. The next several years, therefore, brought a continuation, albeit on a lesser scale, of the terror. "Our crops were just coming up so that the fields looked green in the slanting sunset, when the grasshoppers came," cried one woman following a relatively mild infestation, "and in a few short hours destroyed the work of weeks, and about all the hopes we had. Of course others have suffered, but this has just about used us up."

Genuine blizzards—of snow and ice rather than locusts— held further perils. Like summer insects, winter storms often struck without warning. One day in late fall or early spring, farmers went barefoot to the fields. The next morning, they awoke to darkened skies and snowdrifts. Winter blizzards, recalled a midwesterner, "came with a mighty blast, sweeping with almost the strength of a cyclone, taking the life of stock and sometimes human beings." Wind and snow penetrated every crack and crevice of house and barn. People caught without adequate supplies could freeze to death trying to secure food. Many families weathered the storm by living for several days on bread and snow water. Animals suffered, too. Cattle on the open range often froze to death. Even enclosed livestock could die of suffocation and exposure in their stalls. Other animals died of starvation because farmers could not get from house to barn, perhaps only fifty yards away. Small farmers sometimes herded calves, colts, chickens, and pigs into the house, where people and animals huddled together in front of fireplaces and around stoves.

A blizzard might rage for two or three days before people could start digging out. As they emerged from their houses, farming folk saw nothing but white tundra in all directions. Six-foot piles of snow completely submerged chicken coops, rail fences, and wood piles. "Communication with the outside world would be completely cut off," insisted one woman, "until two or three hundred men could dig an opening through the snow." Even when the snow stopped, bitter cold produced hardships. "The poor cattle and other stock suffer a great deal from the cold," explained one farmhand. "Cows are often seen with their ears and tails frozen off, and dogs and cats the same, while the combs and feet of poultry get rather badly used up, too."

Town and city folk did not suffer from the fickleness of nature nearly so much as farmers and ranchers, but they may have been more exposed than country folk to the dangers of illness and epidemics. The close contact of town and city dwellers, particularly residents of tightly packed tenements, invited the rapid spread of contagious diseases. Likewise, the filth of city slums offered breeding grounds for infectious diseases, such as cholera and typhoid. Given the period's primitive medical knowledge of inoculation and sanitation, occasional disasters became inevitable. Typhoid, smallpox, scarlet fever, typhus fever, and cholera seldom remained idle in the nation's cities.

Cholera ranked as the most feared killer, the nineteenth-century equivalent of medieval plague. The last national epidemic struck in 1866, but a severe regional outbreak swept through the Mississippi River valley in 1873, and cholera remained a formidable local threat. Dirt and filth entering the digestive tract caused cholera. Unwashed hands, unwashed or uncooked vegetables, and sewage-contaminated water most often proved the source. Consider the sanitary conditions of some cities. Garbage accumulated in areas of New York and Philadelphia until streets became impassable. City sewers emptied directly into rivers that supplied drinking water. Only a few cities provided regular garbage collection, and many people continued to toss "house slop," not infrequently mixed with urine and feces, into city streets. Tenement privies in New York were often "mere wells, extending from the upper floors to the cellars, and provided with an opening and seat on each floor, but with no provision for water." One New Yorker referred angrily to the city's slums as "foul," "disgraceful," "filthy as pigsties and even less wholesome." He attributed the cholera epidemic of 1866, in which nearly six hundred citizens died, to God's judgment on a community that could create and permit such cesspools to exist. Most cities established boards of health to deal with these problems in the late 1860s, but progress in finding remedies proceeded slowly.

People who survived a cholera epidemic seldom forgot it. Early symptoms included acute diarrhea, spasmodic vomiting, and painful cramps. Resulting dehydration gave a bluish, pinched appearance to the sufferer's face; extremities turned cold and dark, and the skin of hands and feet became drawn and puckered. Death came swiftly, in a matter of hours, a day at most. Even the first symptoms appeared without warning. "To see individuals well in the morning & buried before night," marveled one survivor, "retiring apparently well & dead in the morning is something which is appalling to the boldest heart."

Cholera was not the only killer. In Philadelphia, nearly 800 people fell to typhoid fever and nearly 350 to typhus in 1865. Whereas the cholera epidemic killed 900 citizens of the Quaker City in 1866, scarlet fever took 1,755 lives in 1869 and 1870, and it left hundreds more deaf, crippled, or mentally enfeebled. Two thousand Philadelphians died from a smallpox epidemic in 1870. Other cities, including Chicago, Boston, Baltimore, and Washington, suffered similar casualties from the same agents of the Grim Reaper. Southern cities, having fewer cold spells to kill vermin and deaden the stench of accumulated garbage and feces, faced additional perils. New Orleans, one of the nation's least healthy cities, had soil "saturated . . . with the oozings of foul privy vaults, and the infiltrations of accumulations on the surface of the streets and in the rear of houses." Charleston and Mobile offered the same unhappy spectacle. Memphis, with a population of 40,000, suffered three fearful epidemics in 1873: yellow fever, smallpox, and cholera. One-fourth of the city's population succumbed to the combined attacks, and many thousands, black and white, died. "The deaths grew daily more numerous," claimed one witness; "funerals blocked the way. . . . Tens of thousands of people fled; other thousands not daring to sleep in the plague-smitten town, left Memphis nightly, to return in the day."

This is not to say that rural folk escaped the ravages of cholera, malaria, smallpox, or typhoid. Although not packed into unhealthy tenements, rural residents living in sod houses, relying on outdoor privies, and eating something less than a balanced diet remained highly susceptible to illnesses of all sorts. "As is usual in new countries where much land is newly broken," recalled a western settler, "there was a great deal of sickness of a malarial nature. Few families escaped the ague and fever." An Indiana doctor recalled, "An unbalanced ration of fat pork, too much fruit and exposure to the heat of August days caused indigestion that went hand in hand with the malaria carrying mosquito, brought intermittent fevers, cholera morbus among adults, and cholera infantum among children, and filled the cabins and even the homes of prosperous people with sickness."

Besides the ravages of nature, people suffered the violence of men. In cities, the desperate and mean-spirited preyed on the timid and unsuspecting. Gambling dens, saloons, dance halls, and cat houses catered to men and women of questionable virtue. In rural and frontier regions, Indians and desperadoes

threatened life and property. Many people insisted that violence and crime increased markedly after the war, and statistics
bear them out. Barely 19,000 people resided in American pris-
ons in 1860. By 1870, the number had leaped to nearly 33,000.
Approximately half of the latter number represented native-
born whites; the other half was evenly divided between blacks
and immigrants.

People living on the frontier and in crowded cities had long
since accustomed themselves to random violence, but the war
seemed to make violence less shocking, if no less acceptable, to
a broader portion of the population. During the war, many
parts of the country had witnessed intimidation of civilians
whose wartime sympathies conflicted with those of their neighbors. In Missouri, Kansas, and Nebraska, gangs of thugs known
variously as Jayhawkers, Red Legs, and bushwhackers used the
war as an excuse to steal horses, confiscate property, and otherwise terrorize farmers and townspeople they identified as
"rebel sympathizers." Meanwhile, crowds of Copperheads and
Butternuts—southern sympathizers living in the North—organized violent public demonstrations against the war and attacked small groups of Union soldiers in southern Iowa, Illinois,
and Indiana. Likewise, Unionists living in Confederate strong-
holds of Kentucky, Tennessee, and Virginia felt the ire of their
neighbors. Men in both sections of the country were drafted
and forced to serve in armies whose causes they thoroughly
detested.

The nation's most famous "family feuds," virtually unknown
before the war, developed from animosities engendered by the
war years. The mountain feuds of Kentucky, Virginia, and West
Virginia, best known for the Hatfield-McCoy feud of 1873–88,
spawned the most violent and long-lasting battles. This could be
accounted for both by the intense Union/Confederate rivalries
that developed in the region and by the isolation, poverty, and
minimal education of mountain communities. Add to this a
dearth of regular law enforcement, and it became inevitable

that mountain families, like the Scottish clans from which so many had descended, would take the law into their own hands. Central Texas also witnessed a host of bitter postwar feuds, some of them, like the Sutton-Taylor feud of 1869–77, equaling the Hatfields and McCoys in violence, longevity, and bitterness. Southwestern conflicts grew from a combination of divided wartime loyalties, Reconstruction animosities, rapid growth of the postwar cattle industry, and instability produced by Indian wars with Comanches and Kiowas.

One vivid episode suggests the response of wartime civilians caught in these circumstances. "Last week one of the neighbor boys came galloping up to the door in breathless haste and informed us the 'bushwhackers' were almost upon us," a Nebraska farm woman reported to her diary. Her family immediately buried all its money in the yard and hid a trunk containing all its best clothing under a nearby bridge. Then they made ready for the impending attack by gathering together "all the implements of warfare on the premises, comprising axes, shovels, hatchets, and clubs." The men armed themselves with guns. "Each female was to battle with the weapons of defense assigned to her. In case they came to close quarters, . . . Nan [was to] use the ax or hatchet, and Addie the clubs, while to me was given the box of red pepper to throw into their eyes." All gave thanks when the bushwhackers, on this occasion, failed to appear.

Wartime draft riots rocked northern communities from Massachusetts to Wisconsin. Insurgent Copperheads instigated many of these violent demonstrations, but poor citizens, angered by unfair laws that exempted draftees who could procure a substitute or pay a commutation fee, seldom needed encouragement. The New York City draft riots of July 1863, the only disturbances to get completely out of hand, grew from latent hostility against the squalid condition of tenement neighborhoods and the economic injustice of the commutation system. The Democratic/Copperhead press whipped up this animosity still further by telling draftees that they were being sent to free southern blacks who would come north to take already scarce jobs. The riots, which lasted four days, began when an angry mob of about five hundred people, including many immigrants, armed with clubs, sticks, stones, brickbats, and swords, stormed the conscription office at Third Avenue and Forty-sixth Street. After sending a small coterie of military guards fleeing down side streets, rioters proceeded to destroy the government's conscription records. "Elated with success," reported the unsympathetic *New York Times*, "the mob . . . next formed themselves into marauding parties, and paraded through the neighboring streets, looking more like so many infuriated demons, than men being more or less intoxicated, dirty and half clothed." Hundreds of people died in several days of continuing riots, and nineteen men went to prison.

The South witnessed fewer wartime riots, but those that did occur reflected the desperate nature of daily life. "Something very sad has just happened in Richmond—something that makes me ashamed of all my jeremiads over the loss of the petty comforts and conveniences of life," a middle-class woman confided to a friend in April 1863. The sad event was a "bread riot" in the Confederate capital. The weekly family food bill in Richmond had soared from $6.65 in 1861 to $68.25 by 1863. "We are starving," proclaimed one woman. "As soon as enough of us get together we are going to the bakeries and each of us will take a loaf of bread. This is little enough for the government to give us after it has taken our men." Once the rioting started, all sorts of lowlifes and thugs took advantage of the situation to loot shops of clothing, jewelry, and anything else that took their fancy. One merchant reported losses of $13,000. Order could be restored only by President Jefferson Davis's threatening to have troops fire upon the rioters.

Anticipation of violence forced many southern families to flee their homes during the war. As Yankee armies approached Confederate neighborhoods, people scurried to hide or pack their valuables, grab whatever necessities—blankets, clothing, food—they could carry or load into a wagon, board up their houses (for all the good it did), and strike out for safer havens. Children frequently added a touch of pathetic humor to the crisis. Terrible tales of two-headed, fire-beathing Yankees had produced in them a mortal fear of the Union hordes. "As soon as they heard the Yankees were coming," testified one mother, "they would jump up and get under the bed, or run out of the house. In fact they would have no idea of what they ought to do to preserve themselves." Neither did some adults. They became little more than gypsies as they wandered from place to place, doing what they could to stay out of harm's way. "Another perch for Noah's duck! Where will I be in a week or two from this?" expresses one woman's lighthearted assessment of her plight. "The life we are leading now is a miserable, frightened one," recorded a less sanguine belle, "living in constant dread of great danger, not knowing what form it may take, and utterly helpless to protect ourselves."

Violence and intimidation continued after the war. In some former Confederate states, previously outnumbered Unionists sought revenge. "When I went home," recalled a Tennessee soldier, "the people who had been in the Union army were so bitter that I had to leave home. I went first to Ga. Then to Texas and stayed until the bitter feeling had passed away to some extent." Another man told of whippings and murders by Unionist bushwhackers. "It was very unsafe," he claimed; "nearly all the Rebels in our neighborhood had to leave for protection." A Missourian who found himself "in Danger of being shot from the Brush at any time" fled the state. Other die-hard Rebels responded in kind rather than fleeing. A federal occupation officer described one South Carolina town as being "inhabited by thieves, murderers, and disloyal men, who promenade the street with six shooters in their belts and Bowie knives thrust in their boots." The officer had never seen "so wild and lawless a country."

Some graduates of wartime rowdiness went on to postwar careers in crime. The Jayhawking James brothers and Younger brothers are probably the most famous examples. Neither the James nor Younger families could settle down to farming in their demoralized and impoverished region of postwar Missouri. They turned, instead, to robbing banks and trains—two new forms of criminal activity—and achieved reputations as heroes among ex-Confederates and Grange-minded farmers. Jesse James, in particular, became an American Robin Hood, celebrated in legend and popular song. The 1870s marked the heyday of such western desperadoes and gunslingers. Every western sheriff and federal marshal had the names and descriptions of thousands of men wanted for murder, arson, robbery, horse stealing, cattle rustling, claim jumping, and similar crimes. Most of these outlaws were drifters, cowboys, or other ordinary fellows gone wrong.

Even some lawmen had dubious reputations. James Butler Hickok, better known as Wild Bill, drifted west from Illinois in the 1850s. He soon earned a reputation as a rowdy character with some prowess as a "pistoleer." As a federal marshal in Hays, Fort Riley, and Abilene, Kansas, he became one law officer with whom few outlaws wished to tangle. "Wild Bill was one of the finest-looking men you ever saw on horseback and always a perfect gentleman as far as we were concerned," insisted a female resident of Abilene. "He always shot to kill but . . . he never killed anyone that did not deserve killing."

A lot of problems in western towns involved cowboys out on a spree. "Shooting up the town," usually on Saturday nights or at the end of a long drive, became a "ritual" in cattle country. "When they took a notion to shoot up a town," recalled a settler, "it was well for the residents to stay inside to avoid being hit by stray bullets. As a usual thing there was no loss of life; however, I remember once . . . a dining-room girl looked out the door to see how many were in town, and was shot." On the other hand, despite an occasional stray bullet, cowboys generally confined their violence and roughhousing to members of their own fraternity. "Our houses stood between the jaws of Texas street," pointed out one Abilene resident, "and no cowboy ever entered the yard nor paid the slightest heed there to members of our household. Crazily drunk, they raced past, filling the air with shots and curses, while our doors stood always open or unlocked." Murder, too, remained fairly well restricted to cowboys, gamblers, lawmen, and, in some districts, miners. "Crimes of passion," barroom quarrels, political arguments, and personal feuds accounted for most of the killings. "At 5 PM a duel was fought between 'Boss Fox' and 'Handsome Charley,' " reported one westerner. "[D]istance 10 paces—six shooters—fire and advance, firing as often as they could—fired six shots each and were satisfied—Charley not hit—Boss shot across the breast—flesh wound . . . no arrests made—no loss to community if both had got killed."

And not all the rabble-rousers were men. Martha Jane Canary, an unlikely name for the woman who became known as Calamity Jane, was big, coarse, strong, vulgar, lewd, and promiscuous. She wore men's clothing, chewed tobacco, could outcuss a mule driver (one of her own occasional occupations), and outdrink a soldier. She went through a string of lovers and bore at least one (illegitimate) child. She earned the name "Calamity" because of her sudden flares of violent temper and the premature, sudden, and mysterious deaths of several of her paramours. Jane's chief rival as *femme fatale* of the West was Belle Starr, proclaimed the "bandit queen" by New York's *Police Gazette*. Like the James and Younger boys, Belle grew up in that cauldron known as Missouri. After participating in several holdups in her own state, she fled to Dallas, where law-abiding citizens stood with mouths gaping as she sashayed down the street in a clinging black velvet dress with a six-shooter strapped to each hip.

Townspeople, east and west, commented on the perceptible decline in law and order after the war. While farmers could leave plows and tools standing in the field all weekend, residents of the larger towns began locking their doors at night. An Illinois town of just 7,500 people became alarmed by the number of vagrants, many of them ex-soldiers, who drifted through the community frightening residents with their appearance and contributing to the livelihoods of local prostitutes and saloonkeepers. "This city and county are tolerably well filled up with a lot of worthless scoundrels," snorted the local newspaper. When a series of "startling robberies" struck the community in the spring of 1865, the editor barked, "These lawless manifestations are alarming, and no citizen can feel safe until the 'city fathers' take energetic steps to ferret out the perpetrators of these acts of robbery." The town hired additional policemen, even a few "secret police," to investigate the reign of terror. Policemen began carrying large billy clubs "got up in city style." Some people subsequently complained about excessive use of force and indiscriminate vice raids by law officers, but consensus generally supported occasional excesses to ensure an "orderly and quiet town."

Communities with too few law officers, too many corrupt judges, or other impediments to reliable law enforcement sometimes took matters into their own hands. "Every morning from one to three or four dead men were picked up back of the dance halls and saloons," reported a citizen of one mining town. "No one was ever arrested or any effort ever made to find the guilty parties. Miners going back and forth to work were held up and robbed day and night, not one or two but dozens of them. It grew from bad to worse until the leading business men decided that the only salvation for decent people was to organize a vigilance committee." Vigilance committees patrolled neighborhoods, tracked down wrongdoers, and, when necessary, administered justice. A resident of Abilene, Kansas, recalled how the town awoke one morning to find the dead body of a local man lying along the railroad tracks. Nothing unusual about that, but when investigation turned up the dead man's clothes and money in the possession of another local citizen, townspeople reacted. "[They] forthwith took this man to the creek a little northeast of our house and hung him to a beam of the old mill," recalled a woman. "The school was on the south side and the next morning . . . the school children came running past our house, all excited. They were going to see the man who was hanging in the mill. They seemed to think it quite a lark and swung him back and forth by his toes."

Elsewhere, vigilantes formed "courts" to expedite local justice. For instance, if an extensive network of horse thieves, including local farmers, businessmen, and city officials, began operating in a town or territory, honest citizens found it impossible to arrest, much less convict, the culprits. Such "rings" were fairly commonplace in the Civil War era. Indeed, the problem became so widespread that a distinctive anti–horse-thief movement, consisting of thousands of local societies, clubs, and associations, sprang up from New England to the Rio Grande. Unlike genuine vigilantes, most of these groups, after apprehending gang members, turned the outlaws over to reliable legal authorities. But not always. In the spring of 1870, after a gang operating between Winfield and Wichita, Kansas, had driven 250 stolen mules into Texas, outraged citizens struck back. Known and trusted residents formed secretly to operate as detectives and soon identified many gang members. They shot and killed two outlaws in a raid on the gang's headquarters, and "Judge Lynch" sentenced seven other rustlers to hanging. The horse stealing ended abruptly, and many men on a published list of remaining gang members silently left the region.

Probably no more telling incidents of western violence and vigilance could be found than in the region's sporadic homesteader-cattleman "wars." The fiercest of these wars came in the 1880s, but as early as 1871 lines were being drawn. Farming and ranching did not flourish together. In the early postwar days, when western settlement remained sparse and cattle ranchers were relatively isolated, little friction developed. However, as ranchers and farmers began competing for land

and water rights, and as massive cattle drives tramped through cultivated territory, tempers flared. Farmers put up fences, stampeded herds, "rustled" cattle, and tried to intimidate drovers by waving six-shooters under their noses. Cowboys retaliated by scaring off potential "nesters" with stories of hostile Indian, droughts, and barren soil. If that failed, ranchers, like farmers, resorted to intimidation and violence.

A fairly typical encounter occurred in Rice County, Kansas. Many cattle had died in the winter of 1871–72. The survivors, many on the verge of death, huddled together along streams to keep warm. Local homesteaders preyed ruthlessly on the animals, killing and skinning them. Ranchers sent an ultimatum to the farmers, warning that the next man caught skinning an animal would be shot on the spot. The farmers, not to be outdone, warned that if any settler met harm, the cattle's grazing lands would be torched. A standoff ensued. Each side had the other at a disadvantage. An uneasy truce continued.

The rancher-farmer duel met its match in the cattleman–sheep-herder wars. The principal cause of this conflict lay in the contrary eating habits of cattle and sheep. Sheep eat grass close to the nub, far closer than any self-respecting steer would eat it. Consequently, when too many sheep grazed in one area for very long, they stripped the grasslands clean. Cattlemen also complained that sheep fouled drinking holes and left such an offensive odor in the grass that cattle would not graze where sheep had eaten. Moreover, the cattlemen had arrived on the prairies first. Not until the 1870s did the sheep industry begin to shift from eastern states to the plains. Cattlemen, believing they had prior claims to the grasslands, resented the encroachment of sheep herders as much as they did the nesters. "A sheepman is lower down than a thief," drawled one Texan in offering the consensus among cattle ranchers, "just too low down for any use."

The tactics employed by both sides paralleled those of the rancher-farmer feuds. Cattlemen initially warned off encroaching sheepmen. Sheepmen ignored the warning. Establishment of a "dead line" followed. Sometimes by mutual agreement, more often as an edict by cattlemen, this imaginary line ran through the contested lands: sheep on one side, cattle on the other. If sheepmen ignored the line, as they often did, a "range war" ensued. Cattlemen were usually the aggressors, but both sides employed violence to intimidate their foes. Poison became an effective agent against livestock. Poisoning water holes and spreading grain or bran laced with saltpeter (deadly to sheep but not to cattle), blue vitriol, or strychnine through grazing areas became accepted methods. Dynamite tossed into corraled livestock could be effective, as was "rim-rocking"—driving livestock over cliffs. Most often, though, guns, knives, and clubs served the purpose against man and beast. In order of frequency, contestants used guns to shoot each other (cartridges were too expensive to kill large numbers of livestock), knives to slit the throats of cattle, and clubs to pound hapless sheep senseless.

It is hard to generalize about the "Indian menace." Indian wars raged west of the Mississippi River all through the 1860s and 1870s. Reports of bloody attacks on homesteaders and wagon trains occurred regularly. Yet many settlers voiced no complaints at all about frequently congenial Indian neighbors, and many others grumbled about their irrepressible curiosity rather than their violence. "Although there are Indians to be seen here," reported a settler in Nebraska, "they are very peaceable and are much more afraid of the whites than the whites are of them. In fact the white people do not fear them at all." That might have been something of an exaggeration. Many women, even when knowing they had little cause to fear the Indians, never grew accustomed to their presence. "In our frontier experience," recalled one woman, "the thing that continually harrowed the feelings of myself and my mother was the fearful dread of Indians." Aware that no hostile Indian resided in their region of Kansas, mother and daughter still had nightmares of "the horrible tales of Indian depredations further west." "As a child I had three gripping fears," claimed another woman, "—starvation, Indians, and ghosts." The fact that this woman never met a hostile Indian made little difference in her attitude: "Long after I had outgrown the fear of not having enough to eat, and the fear of a ghostly hand being laid upon my shoulder from behind, I still had horrible dreams of trying to hide from Indians."

Consider the nonviolent encounters of the following two women. "One day three squaws rode up, jumped off their horses and came right into the house," marveled one farm wife. "They did not speak to me or act as if they saw me, but proceeded to investigate the room. They went all around looking at everything and when they came to my dish cupboard, . . . they pulled back the curtain and looked at the dishes, pointing laughingly and jabbering." Going into the bedroom, the squaws gawked at the long, high bed "with its pieced quilt and pillows with white cases." Content with their inspection, they turned and departed as silently as they had arrived. "Mother never could quite conquer her fear of the Indians but she became more or less accustomed to their appearance," reported another woman. "She was always startled when an Indian face would suddenly and noiselessly appear at the window or door, and although she soon learned that they meant no harm but were only curious to see into the room, she never could conquer the sudden fear that gripped the heart."

If all this makes the Indian seem like some sort of natural obstacle in the path of western settlement, it is because most white settlers—not to mention their government—viewed Indian tribes in precisely that way. Their ignorance of Indian culture and their assumption that United States claims to the "national domain" superseded ancient Indian claims to those same lands reflected a mindless arrogance that permeated white relations with the Indians. Even so sympathetic an observer of the Indian's plight as John Wesley Powell took, by modern standards, an embarrassingly condescending view of the situation. In 1874, Powell acknowledged the need to place "these unfortunate people" on reservations in order to provide "relief of the white people from their petty depredations" and to eliminate "the demoralizing influences accompanying the presence of savages in civilized communities."

City dwellers did not worry about Indians, but they did have to combat a remarkable variety of dishonest and dangerous characters. "Crime was never so bold, so frequent, and so safe as it is this winter," wailed a New Yorker in 1870. "We breathe an atmosphere of highway robbery, burglary, and murder. Few criminals are caught, and fewer punished." An estimated thirty thousand "professional thieves" operated in New York in 1871, and police records show an average of seventy-two thousand arrests per year during the 1860s. Yet even such large numbers do not adequately suggest the city's crime problem. "The reports and estimates of the Police Commissioners are notoriously incomplete and unreliable," pointed out one contemporary. "They show a large number of arrests, but they deal mainly with the class known as 'casuals,' persons who merely dabble in crime." Clever crooks escaped arrest, and the professional ones were highly specialized. Police departments, for example, recognized at least six distinct categories of thieves, and one of these, burglars, could be subdivided still more precisely. The underworld had its own language, too. In fact, some police departments issued manuals to their officers with a glossary to inform them that *bag of nails* meant "all in confusion," *balram* was money, *barking irons* were pistols, a *Benjamin* was a coat, and *bingo* was liquor.

Pickpockets (*buggers* in street lingo) posed the most widespread threat to the average citizen. Streetcars displayed signs warning, "Beware of Pick-Pockets!" "These wretches work in gangs of two, or three or four," reported one observer. "They make their way into crowded cars, and rarely leave them without bringing away something of value." Horsecars, ferryboats, theaters, any crowded place where people expected occasional jostling and pushing became favorite haunts for light-fingered villains. Many women, with their deft, delicate touch, excelled at picking pockets, as well as at shoplifting. "Others are boys," cautioned an observer. "These are usually termed 'kids,' and are very dangerous, as people are not inclined to suspect them. They work in gangs of three or four, and, pushing against their victim, seize what they can, and make off."

The city "rough" also threatened respectable people. "He is familiar with crime of all kinds, for he was born in the slums and has never known anything better," explained one city dweller. "They are the patrons and supporters of dog and rat pits, and every brutal sport. Their boon companions are the keepers of the low-class bar rooms and dance houses, prize fighters, thieves, and fallen women." Roughs generally stayed in their own depressed part of the city, watching for opportunities to "fall upon some unoffending and helpless person" whom they would first rob and then, frequently out of sheer maliciousness, "beat . . . to a jelly." However, gangs of roughs sometimes invaded peaceable parts of town, where they infested parks and areas of public entertainment. On some occasions they seemed content to leer at young ladies or jostle old men. Other times they acted more boldly. "They fall upon the unoffending pleasure-seekers, beat the men unmercifully, maltreat, insult, and sometimes outrage the women, rob all parties who have valuables to be taken, and then make their escape." Indeed, declared one disgusted citizen, "The Rough does not hesitate to commit murder. . . . He is capable of any crime. He is a sort of human hyena who lives only to prey upon the better portions of the community."

An increasing threat of town and city violence emanated from the fledgling trade union movement. Frustrated workers, unable to win concessions on wages and working conditions through negotiations and peaceful strikes, turned to more active protest. Few strikes of the Civil War era led to violence. Not until the "great strike year" of 1877 did large numbers of

industrial workers, pushed to desperation by the decade's economic depression, boldly declare themselves engaged in a
power struggle with employers. Still, as employers attempted
to disrupt unionization efforts through blacklisting, lockouts,
espionage, and legal prosecution, and as they continued to antagonize workers by resisting reforms, labor began to strike
back. When mill workers near Boise, Idaho, went several weeks
without wages, they seized the superintendent, barricaded the
mill, and refused to work until they were paid. Ten years later,
in 1876, western miners, seeking two months' back wages, kidnapped the superintendent of the Golden Chariot Mine. They
held him for three weeks, until the company's headquarters, in
San Francisco, relented and paid up. "It is useless to talk to men
who are starving for bread," declared a local editor sympathetic
to the strike. Employers who abused workers and ignored their
rights had to expect "revenge of some sort."

Sometimes fear of impending violence led town officials and
police to foment trouble. One labor leader recalled a protest
march in New York City during the depression year of 1874.
The police department had issued the marchers a permit, but
the night before the demonstration, the city park commissioner
insisted that the permit be revoked in order to preserve "public
peace." Next morning, mounted policemen began to disperse
protesters before the march could begin. "Without a word of
warning," reported a marcher, "they swept down on the defenseless workers, striking down the standard-bearer and using
their clubs right and left indiscriminately on the heads of all
they could reach." Most workers fled the scene, but a few halted
to regroup. The police pursued, "riding them down and attacking men, women, and children." "I was caught in the crowd on
the street," recalled a participant, "and barely saved my head
from being cracked by jumping down a cellarway. The attacks
of the police kept up all day long—whenever the police saw a
group of poorly dressed persons standing or moving together."

Prejudice and violence added to the daily woes of racial and
ethnic minorities, particularly blacks. Even whites who disap-

proved of slavery frequently balked at giving full political and social rights to blacks. The treatment of black soldiers, relegation of most blacks to menial jobs, and legal segregation of the races in schools, theaters, and other public places betrayed underlying notions of racial inferiority. "The truth is," summarized an Englishman visiting the United States during the Civil War, "the negroes, slave or free, are a race apart, in both North and South." Not even black tradesmen, merchants, and professionals entirely escaped verbal abuse. When J. W. Allston, pastor of Philadelphia's Colored Episcopal Church, attempted to ride a city horsecar, the white driver ordered him off. The Reverend Allston politely refused to disembark. The driver refused to continue until he did so. A crowd gathered around the stalled streetcar. Five more streetcars became strung out behind it. A policeman, summoned to escort Allston away, charged the minister with "assault and battery and inciting to riot."

This confrontation ended peaceably enough, but many others did not. In New York's wartime draft riots, many blacks suffered injury and death. With so many whites believing that northern blacks would take the jobs of conscripted whites and that freed southern slaves would soon swarm northward, blacks became as much targets of the mob as government conscription officers. "It seemed to be an understood thing throughout the City," reported one newspaper, "that the negroes would be attacked wherever found, whether they offered provocation or not." When blacks committed crimes against whites, punishment could be swift and severe, especially in cases of violent crimes, like murder or rape.

Seventy-eight race-related riots occurred in the South between 1865 and 1876. Nearly 44 percent of those riots took place in the volatile election years of 1868, 1872, and 1876. Additionally, southerners lynched over four hundred blacks between 1868 and 1871, and untold thousands of blacks suffered injury. Southern whites justified their actions by insisting upon the need to control an intellectually inferior race. Social upheaval and racial conflict would result, they said, without proper restraints on "uppity blacks." Once blacks gained admission to white churches, theaters, hotels, railroad cars, and concert halls, warned southerners, what further calamities might not follow? "If we have social equality, we shall have intermarriage, and if we have intermarriage, we shall degenerate," predicted one man. "Sir, it is a matter of life and death with the Southern people to keep their blood pure." White southerners enforced their demands for segregation through the Ku Klux Klan and its regional variations, like the Knights of the White Camelia, Pale Faces, Red Shirts, and Knights of the Rising Sun.

White Americans united against foreign elements in the population, too. Clergymen and reformers lashed out from pulpit and press to warn Americans that foreign ideas and customs would dilute the nation's heritage and splinter the people into bickering, warring ethnic factions. "Only by fusing all foreign elements into our common nationality," warned a clergyman in 1869, "and making our entire population in spirit and intent Americans, shall we preserve our unity and concord as a nation." The Irish had posed the biggest threat to American unity before the war, but, by the 1860s, "nativist" sentiment against "Paddy" and "Bridget" had softened. A more treacherous enemy, most people agreed, was the Chinese. As non-whites and non-Christians, the Chinese frightened Americans. Americans regarded them as slovenly, ignorant, and heathen barbarians, whose chief virtues were "their fitness for servile duties and their want of social ambition." Businessmen approved of Chinese immigration because thousands of "coolies"—a form of indentured servitude dating from the eighteenth century in which contractors offered passage money to Chinese workers in return for their labor—filled jobs in western mines and on western railroads. Everyone else felt nervous about the 160,000 Chinese who entered the United States during the Civil War era.

Their concerns differed. A few people, convinced that contract coolie labor represented a new form of slavery, opposed the immigration on humanitarian grounds. More troublesome to other people were confirmed reports that two thousand coolies on a plantation in Peru had rebelled and, "armed with clubs, knives, and axes, murdered the families of the plantation owners, and then prepared to sack a small village." Still others feared the "terrible diseases of Asia" that all Chinese were said to transmit. Some of these diseases went nameless, largely because they existed only in imagination. Others, however, such as cholera, leprosy, and syphilis, were well known (though not particularly "Asian") and feared. By implication, a disease like "Chinese syphilis" was more potent, ravaging, and impervious to treatment than run-of-the-mill American syphilis. Additionally, Americans believed the Chinese to be incorrigible dope addicts, with "opium dens" serving as the center of Chinese life. Chinese men, said accepted wisdom, lived in filth, feasted on rodents, gambled, worshiped hideous idols, smoked opium, and lusted after white women.

Competition for jobs became another potent stimulus to anti-Chinese feeling. The harshest words and most violent actions came out of the West, where the overwhelming majority of Chinese lived. In October 1869, white miners in Virginia City, Nevada, drove out two hundred Chinese workers. "The Chinese all fled at their approach," claimed a witness. "They declare that no Chinaman shall work at mining or any similar occupation in Storey County." Such scenes multiplied in the 1870s, as western labor unions conducted vicious anti-Chinese campaigns. California laws prohibited Chinese children from attending public schools and blocked immigration of Chinese women who could not prove their good character. San Francisco law forbade anyone to carry baskets on long poles, a common practice in Chinatown. But as coolies arrived to work in eastern states as farmhands, launderers, railroad workers, and cigar makers, the panic spread. Anti-Chinese riots broke out in many cities, and virtually every labor organization in the country opposed further immigration.

# 10

ENJOYING LIFE

D ESPITE their daily woes, Americans knew how to enjoy themselves. Sometimes quiet, family-oriented activities filled their needs. Parlor games and croquet, church socials and family picnics provided congenial remedies for a hard day in field, factory, or office. Hunting and fishing remained popular pastimes, even though they were not often necessary for survival. On other occasions, only public pleasures and amusements, enjoyed amidst jolly crowds, could cure the doldrums and personal tragedies created by wars, economic depressions, tyrannical employers, and gloomy weather. As one carpenter explained in 1871, he and his friends wanted stimulating recreations, something "to make them feel good." To meet the demand, Americans devised a sparkling cavalcade of fraternal orders, sporting events, theatricals, musical entertainments, fairs, circuses, and public holidays. Even a bare sampling shows a people that knew how to have a good time.

Americans have been called a nation of joiners, noted for their group activities and community spirit. The nation's most intense period of fraternization would not dawn until the 1880s and 1890s, but a thoughtful observer in the Civil War era could have anticipated the binge. Churches, of course, continued to serve as important centers for group activity, but growing numbers of secular organizations, including civic groups, fraternal bodies, ethnic societies, women's clubs, political clubs, and labor unions, offered exciting alternatives. By the mid-1870s, hundreds of thousands of Americans belonged to at least one lodge, club, fraternity, or society. Even a distant western town like Virginia City, with a population of under twenty thousand in 1870, supported chapters of the Sons and Daughters of Temperance, Good Templars, Band of Hope, Order of the Red Men, Fenian Brotherhood, Anti-Chinamen, Grand Army of the Republic, Turnverein, Hebrew Benevolent Society, and German Benevolent Society.

Most of these organizations stressed a serious side, having been created to promote high moral and ethical values, community spirit, patriotic fervor, social reform, "self-improvement," or some other noble end. Some of the nation's oldest fraternal groups, for instance, had been organized by immigrants seeking to relieve anxieties caused by life in a new land. The Ancient Order of Hibernians, Sons of Hermann, and Independent Order of B'nai Brith joined with immigrant churches, schools, and newspapers to preserve distinct ethnic traditions and cultures. Similarly, native-born Americans joined fraternities like the Freemasons, Independent Order of Odd Fellows, Knights of Pythias, Elks, and Ancient Order of United Workmen to support high ideals and simplify the complexities of an increasingly hectic world. Women, in particular, entered a new world of secular female association, as an independent women's club movement began in earnest in the late 1860s and provided opportunities for broader roles in social reform, cultural pursuits, and public life.

On the other hand, clubs and fraternities could be fun, too. They sponsored parades, picnics, banquets, and balls to celebrate various occasions and holidays. The elaborate rituals, handshakes, passwords, regalia, and hierarchies of many fraternities, contrasting so sharply with the workaday world of shop, factory, and field, gave members pleasure as well as a sense of exclusiveness. Literary societies and political clubs, volunteer fire companies and philanthropic associations gave men and women a chance to relax, to escape the pressures of work and household cares.

Typical of many associations was the Patrons of Husbandry, founded in 1867. Most societies and clubs flourished in towns and cities, but the "Grange," as it was popularly known, provided farmers with the benefits of association. Over 760,000 people had joined the Grange by 1875. Its greatest strength rested in the Midwest, but local "granges" could be found in every state of the Union. Members represented a cross section of rural America, with men and women, teenagers and octogenarians, dirt farmers and prosperous magnates joining hands in Grange halls everywhere. Only blacks remained excluded. The Grange offered farmers very tangible educational, financial, and political benefits, but members responded most to its social activities.

In addition to regular weekly or monthly meetings and the usual berry parties, barbecues, and picnics, most local granges organized four specific social occasions each year. "Harvest Day" observances celebrated the most important event in a farmer's life with a weekend-long revel of dancing, singing, eating, and occasional prayers of thanksgiving. An annual "Children's Day," usually in spring, celebrated the family and the contributions of children to rural life. Games, prizes, singing, and "good things" to eat characterized this festive fling. December 4, anniversary of the order's founding, produced further revelry. In 1874, for instance, the brothers and sisters of West Fork, Liberty, and Crawford, Arkansas, met at a local schoolhouse for a banquet and dance. "There were nice boiled hams, turkeys, chickens, and a variety of meats, cakes of all kinds, and a general supply of 'knick-knacks' and everything that [the] heart could wish," declared one participant. The affair, declared another member, would be "long remembered . . . as a day pleasantly and profitably spent." Finally, no Grange social calendar would have been complete without an Independence Day parade and picnic.

Outside the Grange halls and literary club teas, individual amusements could be quite simple. Farm families enjoyed driving their flat-bed wagons into town on Saturday morning to buy supplies, sell produce, pick up mail, and catch up on local gossip. Everyone had a special mission. Father headed for the blacksmith shop, general store, or feed store. If attending some special Saturday night event, he might pause at the barbershop, not so much for a haircut as a good ten-cent shave. Mother did her shopping and enjoyed "woman's talk" at the milliner's shop. The children played in the town square or went window-shopping. If they behaved themselves, each child might be allowed to select a handful of penny candy at the general store. In large towns, the whole family could quench its thirst with carbonated water at a "soda fountain." Lemon seemed to be the most popular flavor, but strawberry, pineapple, vanilla, and ginger beer had loyal followings, and a Philadelphia pharmacist, Charles E. Hires, added a new selection, "root beer," in the 1870s. A few towns even had ice-cream parlors. Vanilla ice cream reigned as the favorite, but it had to compete with a variety of new flavors, including banana, coffee, coconut, apricot, and tutti-frutti.

The more active citizens joined the sports craze that became such a notable feature of American life in the 1860s. Americans had long been devoted to spectator sports, like prizefighting and horse racing; but widespread participation in sporting and athletic contests was quite new. Numerous coeducational activities, such as croquet, bicycling, skating, lawn tennis, and archery, enjoyed immense popularity in the 1870s. Similarly, the YMCA and German Turnverein launched interest in gymnastics. Amateur athletic clubs promoted track and field meets. Colleges began to sponsor athletic teams. National magazines devoted to sports, including *Sporting Times* and *Sports and Games*, appeared on newsstands. Many people joined the craze out of concern for the "invalid habits" of America's fat and flabby citizens. "Noble, athletic sports, manly outdoor exercises . . . which strengthen the mind by strengthening the body, and bring man into a generous and exhilarating communion with nature . . . are too little cultivated in town and country," lamented one critic. Strange to say, the same activities would have been considered extravagant wastes of time only a few years earlier; but Americans had discovered another benefit of sports: they were fun.

The principal pioneer, and the sport destined for supremacy, was baseball. Baseball had been played in a variety of forms (cricket, rounders, town ball) for at least a century. Not until the late 1850s, however, did the National Association of Base Ball Players formalize rules and sponsor twenty-five amateur teams east of the Mississippi River, including clubs in New York, Philadelphia, Washington, Detroit, Chicago, and New Orleans. The game received a tremendous boost during the Civil War, when many northern and southern soldiers became exposed to it. Returning home, these veterans formed teams where none had existed, so that by 1866, the National Association included 202 teams in seventeen states. "Since the war, it has run like wildfire," exclaimed an observer in 1868. By 1872, a writer in *Sports and Games* had stated categorically that baseball had become "the national game of the United States." His appraisal overlooked the fact that in 1867 the National Association had officially barred black players from membership.

Increasing competition soon spawned professionalism. It began on a small scale, as local amateur teams began to woo gifted players by offering them good-paying jobs in their communities. A Chicago team offered young Albert G. Spalding, the future sporting goods manufacturer, $40 a week, ostensibly to work as a wholesale grocery clerk, but really to be their pitcher. In 1869, the Cincinnati Red Stockings ended the charade and hired the first professional players at salaries ranging from $800 to $1,400 to tour the country. When the Red Stockings beat every team they faced that summer (trouncing one hapless opponent 103 to 8), the benefits of professionalism became apparent. Spalding led his Rockford, Illinois, team on tour the next summer, winning 51 of 65 contests. The National Association opposed professionalism, but lost control of the game in the 1870s to the newly organized National League of Professional Baseball Clubs.

Neither amateur nor professional used very much equipment or played with a marked degree of skill before the 1880s. Fielders used bare hands to catch the ball. Not until 1877 did catchers use a mask or lightly padded glove. Add to this a large and lively six-ounce elastic ball, famous for its erratic bounces, and professional scores of 103 to 80 were not uncommon. Early players had scant respect for rules. How to break the rules without getting caught became the standard approach to every contest. Umpires (only one, standing behind either pitcher or catcher) had nominal control of games, but unless they were impressively large men with a local reputation for pugilism, most umpires cut pathetic figures. Players and hostile "fans" abused them mercilessly, sometimes mobbing them after particularly unpopular calls. Even the sports tabloids, which began publishing box scores, details of important games, and biographical sketches of star players, made sarcastic remarks about the umpires.

But baseball through the 1870s remained largely a sport for amateurs and children. On city streets and village greens, baseball reigned supreme. In May 1867, an Algona, Iowa, newspaper announced that anyone interested in forming a local team should meet at the town square at 3 P.M. that Saturday. Within weeks, enthusiasts had laid out a diamond and begun practice. That summer, rival teams squared off every Wednesday at 5 P.M. and every Saturday at 2 P.M. A New York paper complained, in 1868, that boys "will play . . . in spite of all travel and obstruction." Boys' leagues soon appeared in every part of the country, and as early as 1873 parents in Wichita, Kansas, helped organize a "young ladies' club." Most children used makeshift equipment, especially balls. Parents frequently helped them by unraveling old woolen socks, winding the strands tightly into a ball of proper size, and covering it with leather from an old boot or shoe.

Baseball also became a popular way for spectators to relax on a weekend afternoon or a weekday evening. Americans enjoyed the excitement and rivalry as towns or villages pitted their best men against all comers. They appreciated the grace, speed, and increasing skill of the players. They welcomed the escape from daily cares. Professional teams drew 800 to 1,500 spectators per game in the 1870s. Amateurs attracted smaller crowds, but the sidelines might well include every man, woman, and child in a community. Baseball served as a form of boosterism, with communities taking immense pride in the victories of their "nine." Albert Spalding called one early promoter of baseball in the Windy City "a typical Chicago man, [who] never spoke of what he could do, or what his club would do, but it was always what Chicago would do." When a team from Monroe, Wisconsin, suffered a 66-to-39 defeat at the hands of Freeport, in 1869, the town's newspaper editor wrote an elaborate defense of the team. He pointed out that the score had been tied 31-31 at the end of five innings, but that Freeport had used three pitchers while Monroe's lone hurler had tired in the late innings.

Football also gained popularity during the 1870s, although it remained a strictly amateur affair. Like baseball, football evolved from earlier prototypes that were refined and reshaped into an American style. Princeton and Rutgers played the first recorded intercollegiate contest in 1869. In 1876, representatives from Harvard, Yale, Princeton, and Columbia drew up rules derived from English rugby. The American refinements included reducing the number of players from fifteen to eleven; assigning players to specific positions; changing rules for running, kicking, and passing the ball; and replacing the rugby huddle, or "scrummage," with a clearly defined line of "scrimmage." Spectator interest was immediate, particularly for games involving the Big Three of eastern colleges—Harvard,

Yale, and Princeton. Their Thanksgiving Day games became high points of the fall season.

Then, as now, prowess in football allowed young men to earn the respect of their peers. Consider the young North Carolinian, son of a Confederate family, who, in 1873, journeyed to upstate New York to attend college. "Mean-spirited" northern classmates taunted the lad about his Confederate lineage. They called him "conceited," "dull," and "uncultivated"; they ridiculed his "Southern pride." The young man usually bit his tongue, ignored their insults, and attended to his studies. "Ah!" he confessed on one occasion, "but I like to show these Yankees what a 'Reb' can do on the foot-ball field. I, made desperate by their ways, made frequent alarming charges, and their cries of 'Good enough' kind of soothe my feelings."

Horse racing had long been a popular spectator sport. Only New Englanders seemed to spurn it. Everyone else, especially southerners and westerners, sponsored endless racing seasons. The surroundings and atmosphere varied from place to place. Some cities, like New York, Baltimore, Louisville, Cincinnati, Nashville, and New Orleans, had very fashionable racetracks. Popular resort areas in the Northeast, including Long Branch and Saratoga, won renown for their summer racing. Smaller communities offered less extravagant surroundings. Their tracks usually lacked grandstands, and rail fences marking the course (usually a quarter mile) wanted whitewash. On the other hand, people visiting these tracks did not have to beware of the professional pickpockets, gamblers, and bookmakers who infested larger tracks. "The event every Saturday afternoon in Wichita is a horse race," reported a citizen of that unpretentious Kansas town. "The track is just north of, and in plain view of the town. Last Saturday the race was between a Texas horse and a Wichita mare. The mare won the race, and it is said over a thousand dollars changed hands." The amount won in wagers equaled the size of the crowd. "So great was the rush," reported one spectator, "that Main Street for an hour or so seemed almost deserted."

Nor was racing confined to formal events. Two strangers meeting on a public road and eyeing each other's mount might decide to judge the superior piece of horseflesh then and there. Neighbors, weary of hearing each other brag about their horses, challenged rivals to contests that would settle the issue. Some townspeople protested this passion for racing as a public nuisance. "An excellent way to fix a street," maintained one disgruntled editor in 1874, "is to plow a deep ditch across it. It prevents horse racing." Most towns and cities passed ordinances against careless and reckless driving, a step necessitated by a penchant among delivery boys and draymen for racing their horses and wagons along public thoroughfares.

Prizefighting, along with horse racing, had dominated as a spectator sport before the baseball boom. Fighting—one could not properly call it boxing—was a brutal, bare-knuckles, murderous sort of entertainment through the 1870s. It reigned as the premier "underground" activity in most towns and cities, outlawed by local ordinances and condemned by the clergy. Even championship fights had to be staged clandestinely in out-of-the-way places. Not until adoption of the Marquis of Queensbury rules, in the 1880s, did prizefighting begin to lose something of its stigma. Even then, many people continued to condemn its association with gambling.

Even out West, where cowboys, miners, and farmhands engaged in open brawls, prizefighting remained a clandestine activity. Fun seekers, however, knew where to go for the action. "I stopped to see a regular knock down in a crib ... called P. McCarthy's saloon," reported a Virginia City man. "The doors were fastened, but I got a chance to peek in [the] window—they were stripped to their drawers & had fought several rounds already.... [They were] bloody as butchers—both badly punished." Even fights with championship implications had to be held "in the hills about 4 miles SE of [the] ... city." One fight, for a purse of $105, attracted 1,500 spectators and continued for sixty-four rounds (nearly two-and-a-half hours). "Both men were badly disfigured," reported a disapproving local paper, "and it is to be hoped that mankind will one day arrive at a more civilized state, when such animal brutality will no longer be tolerated."

People who preferred more refined entertainment flocked to a wide assortment of theatrical fare, the nation's favorite form of public amusement. And such variety. Drama, melodrama, comedy, burlesque, vaudeville, opera, and minstrel shows kept town and city theaters packed at most times of the year, even though fall and winter formed the official theatrical "season." Most theaters could be categorized either as "temples of amusement," catering to popular tastes in drama and variety for ten to thirty cents per seat, or "temples of art," specializing in Shakespeare, the classics, and contemporary drama, for twenty-five-cents to one-dollar admission. Both categories drew on two competing systems of casting. Stock companies, the traditional means of producing shows, used talented but unknown actors, actresses, and performers. The newer "star" system relied on a single popular male or female performer to draw customers. Top stars, like Edwin Booth, Edwin Forrest, and Joseph Jefferson, commanded as much as five hundred dollars a performance. About a dozen lesser stars earned one hundred to two hundred dollars per week, while the standard wage in New York stock companies hovered between fifteen and twenty dollars a week.

Classical drama held its own in the theater world of most communities. Then, as now, New York reigned as the nation's theatrical center, and most people acknowledged Edwin Booth's magnificent Renaissance-style theater on Sixth Avenue as the nation's supreme house. "The plays presented here are superbly put on the stage," reported one patron. "The scenery is strictly accurate when meant to represent some historic locality, and is the finest to be found in America." An 1869 production of *Hamlet,* with Booth in the title role, "held the boards" for over a hundred nights, and critics raved about the magnificent scenery, costumes, and "make up."

Most Americans, however, preferred melodrama to classics. In New York, the Old Bowery Theatre catered to local demand for "blood and thunder dramas." "The titles are stunning," observed one man, "the plays themselves even more so." These sizzling panoramas of death and destruction differed little in plot and characters. Each included four acts with some twenty-odd scenes and a cavalcade of lilting heroines, courageous heroes, wicked villains, flirtatious soubrettes, and comic buffoons. Most melodramas provided a moral, but the message was usually lost amidst extravagant overacting and vivid portrayals of murder, arson, and burglary. Only rape and seduction were never shown, although they might be implied. Audiences at theaters like the Bowery could be as fascinating as the plays. "Every nook and cranny is occupied," recounted one witness. "The suckling infant. . . . The youngster rubbing his sleepy eyes. The timid Miss, half frightened with the great mob and longing for the fairy world to be created. Elder boys and elder sisters. Mothers, fathers, and the wrinkled old grand-sire." Toss in a few sailors with their "black-eyed Susans," some shop girls, clerks, and tradesmen, and the audience provided a pretty good cross section of the working classes. People were not bashful about joining in the action either. They cheered when the hero rescued his sweetheart from the jaws of death; they hissed when the mustache-twirling villain slunk onto the stage. Finally, wandering through this animated audience, came red-shirted peanut vendors. "Almost every jaw in the vast concern is crushing nut-shells," complained one patron. "You fancy you can hear it in the lulls of the play like a low unbroken growl."

Comedies and less sensational melodramas provided entertainment at respectable middle-class theaters, or "opera houses." Every community with pretensions to gentility had an opera house, although they staged few operas in them. Because

actors were notorious for licentious living, respectable populations in American towns would not think of having a disreputable "theater" tarnish civic honor. They built, instead, opera
houses, which became community centers for every sort of
pageant and play. The opera house in Adrian, Michigan, hosted
a slate of local activities in 1869, including a Catholic festival,
an Episcopal fair, strawberry and peach festivals, a magic show,
school graduation ceremonies, an acrobatic troupe, a temperance meeting, several dances, and an amateur play. Most communities, especially towns not large enough to attract touring
professionals, organized amateur theatrical groups. The average production, from the acting to the scenery, was decidedly
second rate, but people with greasepaint in their blood would
not be denied.

Despite the prejudice against actors and theaters, local thespians and traveling stock companies found eager audiences
wherever they appeared. Residents of Virginia City, Nevada,
could enjoy comedies, melodramas, and classical productions
every week at either Maguire's Opera House or Piper's Opera
House. Edwin Booth, Thomas Keene, James A. Hearne, and
Joseph Jefferson were among the many stars to appear there.
"Evening at Maguire's," reported one regular theatergoer.
"Crowded house in every part—all standing room occupied—
great number of ladies." The same gentleman reported seeing
twelve different productions in 1869, including *Rip Van Win-
kle, The Ragpicker of Paris, Camille, Lucrezia Borgia, Oliver
Twist, Blow for Blow,* and *After Dark,* the last being identified
as "a sensational piece like 'Under the Gaslight.' "

"Sensational" scarcely described the daring new melodrama
that opened at New York's Niblo's Gardens in 1866. *The Black
Crook,* a six-hour musical production based loosely on the Faust
legend, featured lavish sets and a ballet troupe of a hundred
scantily clad young ladies (in tights and tutus) to give Americans
a spectacle of unparalleled splendor and unabashed sensuality.
Stage productions earlier in the decade had sometimes featured

young ladies in tights; but, with the exception of the somewhat
kinky closing scene in *Mazeppa, or The Wild Horse,* in which
a young lady clad in light gauze chiffon and strapped to the side
of a snorting stallion galloped off stage, nothing compared to
*The Black Crook.* "The scenery and the legs are everything,"
reported Mark Twain. "Girls—nothing but a wilderness of girls
. . . dressed with a meagerness that would make a parasol blush."
Clergymen were beside themselves; men's opera glasses sold
like hotcakes.

Producers exploited the play's success with a host of imitations. "Ballet, spectacle, machinery, and pink legs" formed the
chief ingredients of one such clone entitled *The White Faun.*
"The dialogue is senseless, the plot undiscoverable, and the
music commonplace," claimed one critic. The sets and costumes, he conceded, were "novel and lavish," yet the play's
success depended ultimately "on the well-formed lower extremities of female humanity." Hard on the heels of such American productions, a Parisian opéra bouffe company featuring
Jacques Offenbach's operettas and the skirt-flinging "can-can"
took the country by storm. It was followed, in 1868, by Lydia
Thompson's British burlesque troupe of plump, blond
showgirls.

Burlesque, a collage of dance, song, comedy, and scantily clad
women, became the era's most popular form of adult entertainment. Critics called it a "disgraceful spectacle of padded legs
juggling and wriggling in the insensate follies and indecencies
of the hour." A Bostonian labeled the dances "wanton excess"
with "nothing of innocent intent." The songs were "coarse,"
complained one actress, the dialogue filled with slang and double entendres. Devotees called it art. "When we went through
the United States in 1869 and again in 1872," recalled Lydia
Thompson of her American tours, "it was like a triumphant
march. The entire male citizenry of your republic rose up and
threw open their arms everywhere to us in a welcoming embrace." Female reaction acknowledged the impact, too, as thou-

sands of American girls peroxided their hair in imitation of Lydia's "British Blondes." Respectable women even began attending the less risqué shows—not the ones staged in saloons and dance halls—to see what all the commotion was about. A very mixed New York audience included "comfortable, middle-aged women from the suburbs and from the remoter country, their daughters, groups of children, a few professional men . . . [and] a clergyman or two."

Vaudeville, a form of theater that appealed to all ages and both sexes, appeared in the 1870s. Vaudeville combined elements of legitimate theater, variety acts, and burlesque, but with the burlesque element elevated to "a high plane of respectability and moral cleanliness." The "variety" portion included minstrel acts, ballads, comic songs, gymnastics, jugglery, dancing, and dramatic and comic skits. Nine acts usually played on "the bill," and provided continual entertainment for fifteen, thirty-five, or fifty cents, depending on the seat. When one act finished, another leaped onto the boards. A "dumb act"—a dance routine or animal act—usually opened the show in order to catch people's attention and allow latecomers to take their seats without seriously disrupting the action. A ventriloquist or singer came next, a comedy act third. The fourth and fifth spots were big music and dance productions. An intermission following these show stoppers gave the audience time to catch its breath. The show resumed with a magician or juggler redirecting people's attention toward the stage. A dramatic sketch followed, setting up the eighth and principal act. This was usually a "star" singer who specialized in light comedy. A grand finale, often a trapeze act, sent people out of the theater still buzzing about the spectacle. Each show generally played two or three times daily.

Besides providing good family entertainment, vaudeville appealed to city folk because its songs and skits frequently dealt with city life. They told of love in the city, the plight of the working girl, the joys of the beer garden. Modern audiences might consider some of the humor rather sharp, particularly its racial and ethnic stereotypes. Yet the brawling Irishmen, lazy Negroes, tight-fisted Scots, beer-guzzling Germans, sharp-witted Jews, devious Chinamen, and country bumpkins of vaudeville, like the stock figures of melodrama, had meaning to audiences of the time.

Minstrel shows, an important part of early vaudeville, had already reached their peak of popularity before the Civil War. Thereafter, they began a gradual decline, which accelerated as vaudeville incorporated minstrelsy's comic routines, cheerful patter, clever dancing, and tuneful melodies in its own "black face" acts. Black minstrelsy remained a popular form of "native theatrical," with some thirty minstrel shows still touring in the 1860s; but it began to mellow. The old minstrel shows had been rather earthy and unsentimental. By the 1870s, they had come to resemble the burlesque and vaudeville shows with which they competed, and the introduction of non-Negro characters and sketches diluted their integrity. On the other hand, they also spawned several genuinely black performing groups, not whites in blackface, as most minstrel shows had been. Black minstrel troupes appeared more frequently, always stressing their credentials as "authentic," "genuine," and "bona-fide." Black colleges in the South formed choral groups and toured the East and Midwest as a means of raising funds for struggling schools like Fisk University and Hampton Institute. They performed a genuinely black repertoire, relying heavily on spirituals and plantation melodies, interspersed with a few rousing minstrel "breakdowns."

Americans also packed theaters to hear lectures. Lecture topics varied as widely as stage productions. Henry Ward Beecher, Frederick Douglass, and Susan B. Anthony addressed important "issues of the day." Popular humorists, like Mark Twain and Artemus Ward, spoke in a lighter vein, and serious literary figures, such as Charles Dickens, gave dramatic readings. Several entrepreneurs even organized lecture bureaus to schedule tours for popular speakers. Some lecturers began to accompany their talks with stereopticon, or "magic lantern," shows in the 1860s. In 1874, the Chautauqua movement, a nationwide series of cultural and educational lectures, closely aligned with church groups and ladies' aid societies, became a mainstay of small-town America. Held locally for a week each summer, Chautauqua provided intellectual and inspirational grist for communities that had little hope of hearing Mark Twain or Charles Dickens.

Humorists drew the largest audiences. When Artemus Ward arrived in Virginia City to deliver a series of three lectures, the congeniality of the citizens and their response to his lectures so overwhelmed him that he stayed three weeks. Mark Twain, who had earlier lived and worked in the silver country of Nevada, met with a similar response. "Crammed house," reported a member of Twain's Virginia City audience in 1866. "I heard it all—mighty good. Lecture 1½ hours long—perhaps a bit more." Next day's newspaper declared Twain an "immense success." It praised his "peculiar and inimitable style" and marveled at the way he punctuated "passages of drollest humor" with "lofty flights of descriptive eloquence."

Meanwhile, opera houses, music halls, and village greens echoed to the sound of music. Musical entertainment, after the theater, ranked as America's favorite amusement, and in some places it led the way. Every middle-class home had a piano or organ, and the number of local singing clubs, choral societies, and church musical associations was beyond counting. Americans flocked to concert halls, music academies, outdoor bandstands, any facility where they might hear singing or instrumental music.

Americans of the Civil War era felt only a mild attraction for "cultivated music"—that is, opera, symphonies, and the like. New Orleans ranked as the most lively operatic center, largely because of its French influence. Of course, other large cities, such as New York and Boston, entertained touring European companies, but opera failed to flourish in most cities, and it never took root in the hinterland. Symphonic orchestras were nearly as rare as opera companies. Only New York supported a permanent symphony orchestra before 1881. Smaller, privately organized orchestras and chamber groups existed, most of them along the Atlantic coast. Theodore Thomas directed the nation's best-known orchestra. Founded in 1864 and based in New York, Thomas's orchestra performed regularly at the Academy of Music and outdoors in Central Park; but it also toured widely through the East and Midwest.

Still, touring choral groups, orchestras, and virtuoso performers (dubbed "musical missionaries" by snobbish easterners) received enthusiastic welcomes wherever they appeared. Some people attended as devotees of good music. Others went because the opera house had a reputation for being the place "to be seen." Not a few went from curiosity or "to drive away care." In 1869 and 1870, Boston's Mendelssohn Quintette Club, one of the nation's most popular touring attractions, traveled over nine thousand miles and gave over 150 concerts in the principal towns of Michigan, Indiana, Illinois, Wisconsin, Minnesota, Iowa, Kansas, Missouri, and Kentucky. Their programs, like a modern "pops" concert, included both classics and popular pieces, and introduced many audiences to the first "really artistic music" they had ever heard. A typical program offered operatic selections, orchestral overtures, extracts from symphonies, English ballads, and American popular songs, such as "Turkey in the Straw," "Home, Sweet Home," "Yankee Doodle," and "O Susannah." A few people resented the light program as a "degradation of themselves," but less sensitive souls welcomed the effort. "We left the hall grateful," admitted a resident of Macon, Georgia, after hearing a touring northern group perform in his town. "Grateful that these refined musicians had not passed us by, and that we had been mildly, not wildly entertained for one evening with music not severely artistic, but adapted to a people as yet untutored in musical classics."

Other people grumbled about the lack of musical and social sophistication displayed at supposedly sophisticated events. A Chicagoan, commenting on a performance of the Mendelssohn Quintette in his city, noted that, while eager audiences filled "the house" for every performance, they showed "less enthusiasm than on some less pretentious occasions." They also seemed uncertain when to applaud unless an aria concluded with "a grand flourish of cadenzas." Even in established music centers like New York, commentators complained about the "ill manners and unmusical demonstrations" of concert audiences. Old men reading newspapers, dowagers gossiping and knitting, and assorted people of both sexes dozing and snoring distracted more attentive members of the audience. One perturbed customer complained that New York Philharmonic Society concerts might better be titled "Flirt-Harmonic" concerts, because of the outrageous way in which young people tried to impress members of the opposite sex.

Americans seemed more attentive when listening to popular music. Sentimental songs and standard hymns, the tunes of vaudeville and burlesque, these provided the melodies that people played on their parlor pianos and whistled as they worked in field and factory. The nation also preferred brass bands to string orchestras. Every proper hamlet had its own band to perform at school commencement ceremonies, Fourth of July parades, concerts on the village green, and other public occasions. Marches, quicksteps, waltzes, and polkas served as the staples for band music, with trumpets and cornets the favored solo instruments. Because Americans had a prejudice against purely instrumental concerts ("How well music does go with singing" was how a Saint Louis woman expressed it), at least one vocal soloist adorned the standard concert bill. Printed programs meticulously numbered each musical piece in a concert, thus initiating the colloquial expression "number" for a popular music composition.

Music also provided facades for less respectable pleasures in concert saloons and dance halls. Concert saloons, opened only in the evening, employed "abandoned women" to serve cheap drinks while "a low order of music" provided the entertainment. "It may be an old cracked piano, with a single, half-drunken performer," explained one visitor, "or a couple or more musicians who cannot by any posible means draw melody from their wheezy instruments." Few patrons noticed, for they focused their attention primarily on drinking and the opposite sex. Large cities were infested with dozens of these saloons, but they enjoyed their widest popularity as haunts for miners and cowboys in western towns. Dance halls differed from concert saloons only in that they ranked "one grade lower both as regards the inmates and the visitors" (particularly sailors in port cities). Critics also believed the dancing, when added to the temptations of drink and frisky waitresses, increased the possibilities of sin. "Respectable people," declared one opponent of both saloons and dance halls, "have no business in such places."

Music proved particularly useful in relieving the tedium of rural and village life. More often even than sporting events, church activities, lodge meetings, and quilting parties, dances and musicales provided a popular form of group amusement in the countryside. Every farming community knew how to prepare a barn or meeting hall for a Saturday night fling. They did not require large—or even proficient—bands. A lone fiddler would do just fine. "It was a joy to watch him 'start the set,' " recalled a midwesterner of his county's star fiddler and "caller." "With a fiddle under his chin he took his seat in a big chair on the kitchen table in order to command the floor." One mighty stomp of his boot on the tabletop, a slicing sweep of his bow across the taut strings, and a command of "Honors tew your partners—right and left Four!" and the dance began.

Even religiously conservative communities, with a prejudice against fiddles and dancing, had "play parties." Young people would choose their partners and skip through floor work similar

to that of a square dance, schottische, or polka, but without
instrumental accompaniment. Revelers kept time by singing
tunes like "Miller Boy" and "Skip to Ma Lou," and the lack of
music seldom dampened youthful spirits. "The violin [fiddle]
was taboo," recalled one man of rural parties in his part of
Indiana, "but we sang songs and danced to them and hugged
the girls until they would often grunt as we swung them clean
off the floor or ground, in the barn or house or on the green."
Among the favorite country dance songs, with or without fiddles, were "Turkey in the Straw," "Irish Washerwoman," "Old
Dan Tucker," "Billy Boy," and "Buffalo Gals":

> Oh Buffalo gals, ain't you comin' out to-night,
> Ain't you comin' out to-night, ain't you comin' out to-night;
> Oh Buffalo gals, ain't you comin' out to-night,
> To dance by the light of the moon?

Besides all these conventional forms of amusement, Civil
War–era Americans also enjoyed an array of bizarre, off-beat,
and unclassified public spectacles. "There have been unusual
attractions down town for the past two days," reported a young
lady in the village of Canandaigua, New York. "About 5 P.M. a
man belonging to the Ravel troupe walked a rope stretched
across Main street from the third story of the Webster House to
the chimney of the building opposite." After walking back and
forth several times along the rope, the artist performed "some
extraordinary feats," including walking blindfolded, pushing a
wheelbarrow, and performing from a trapeze. "There were at
least 1,000 people in the street and in the windows gazing at
him," the girl reported. "Grandmother says that she thinks all
such performances are wicked, tempting Providence to win the
applause of men."

A similar spectacle could be enjoyed on the other side of the
continent. "I went down & saw Miss Ella LaRue walk a rope
stretched from the brick building corner of D and Union streets
to the balcony of the Opera House—about 160 feet," reported

a resident of Virginia City. "About 30 to 40 feet above the ground—1,500 or 2,000 people witnessed it." Miss LaRue does not seem to have been quite so flamboyant as Mr. Ravel, but her sex and the setting made Miss LaRue's performance a memorable one. "Bright moonlight, bonfire in the street, and red fire burnt at each end of the rope—beautiful sight," swore the witness. "She was dressed in short frock, tights & trunks. . . . [G]reat 'shape'—more of it than I ever saw in any female. Immense across the hips—huge thighs."

The circus ranked as the most popular occasional entertainment of the 1860s and 1870s. Although Phineas T. Barnum had toured the country with his Grand Colossal Museum and Menagerie in the 1850s, not until the 1870s did the circus realize its enormous potential. "Each year one came along from the east," recalled an Iowan, "trailing clouds of glorified dust and filling our minds with the color of romance." Barnum, who joined forces with William C. Coup in 1871, still personified the "Greatest Show on Earth." With Coup, he assembled the nation's largest collection of wild animals, curiosities, acrobats, equestrian performers, and clowns: giraffes from Africa, cannibals from the Fiji Islands, midgets and bearded women, herds of elephants, men shot from cannons, even a hippopotamus (advertised as the "blood-sweating Behemoth of Holy Writ"). His "big top" covered the largest enclosed performing area in the world. The entire company of men, women, and animals toured by rail in sixty-one special cars.

Not that Barnum lacked competition. Numerous traveling shows, varying much in size and quality, rambled across the country. Two circuses visited Virginia City in 1869. One of them, Dan Costell's Circus, sported the largest tent anyone in Nevada had ever seen. "Had to pitch it in baseball ground," reported one man; "fully 2,500 present and lots couldn't get in." Many of the audience, however, went away disappointed. "Nothing new, except elephant and a few animals which no one could see," grumbled a spectator. "Some five or six dens of them, lions, tigers, leopards, zebra, monkeys etc. The circus part was poor—poor riders and tumblers, one or two good trained horses. Not a single new feature. A dam big bilk, for $1.50." On the other hand, this same gentleman judged Wilson's Great World Circus, which visited town that same summer, "pretty good," perhaps because it included a minstrel show (for twenty-five cents extra) and some unexpected excitement in the big top. "At one time during the Circus," he explained, "a trained pony got exasperated with being whipped, and jumped the ring & plunged among the audience in the seats—several got bruised, and one man had to be carried out—considerably hurt." The observer attended Wilson's show three days running.

The popularity of the circus may be explained by its exotic nature. "The tumult was benumbing," recalled a midwesterner, as he described the white tents, fluttering flags, sideshows, concession booths, caged animals, and swarming crowd. "The color, the glitter, the grace of gesture, the precision of movement, all so alien to the plains—so different from the slow movement of stiffened old farmers and faded and angular women, as well as from the shy and awkward manners of the beaux and belles of country dances" captivated rural residents in particular. Small wonder so many boys talked of running away with the circus. "Oh, to be one of those fine and splendid riders," sighed one farm boy, "with no more corn to plough, or hay to rake, or corn to husk."

As if that were not sufficient entertainment, most circuses, like the one at Virginia City, followed the big top performance with a minstrel show, sometimes in a different tent and for a slight additional charge. Many townspeople regarded the minstrel show as vital a part of the day as acrobats and elephants. It provided them, once every year, with the latest songs, dances, and jokes from the city. A minstrel show, testified one man, "brought to our ears the latest band pieces and taught us the popular songs. It furnished us with jokes. It relieved our dullness. It gave us something to talk about."

Residents of a few big cities had sideshows, of sorts, all year round in the form of "museums." Colonel Joseph H. Wood's museum in Chicago and Barnum's museum in New York (although destroyed by fire in 1865) ranked as the most famous of the species. Wood advertised "150,000 curiosities of every kind," from fossils and sea lions to paintings and antique china. Wood labeled many of his exhibits "educational," and underscored the high character of his establishment by opening an adjoining lecture hall; but most people went to see the freaks and curiosities. The same was true for Barnum's, which became a Mecca for residents and rural visitors alike. "Barnum's . . . is ever worth a visit of 25 cents," asserted one New Yorker. "To see the West Indian fish and the snakes is alone worth the money. . . . We must not forget to mention the interesting couple, a giant and giantess, and the Lilliputian mannikin."

Towns and villages distant from the circus routes (which followed the railroad lines) had to be content with modest itinerant sideshows. Patent medicine shows became the most familiar rural diversion. While most medicine men called themselves "doctor" or "professor," few had any legitimate claim to the title. In springboard wagons and covered wagons, medicine men prowled the countryside selling their wares and preying on the desire of hard-working folk to rid themselves of aches and pains that local physicians had been unable to cure. Whether calling door to door in isolated areas or setting up a formal tent show in town, the medicine man's "pitch" always sounded the same. He claimed that his magic tonics, which might contain anything from colored sugar water to crude oil and sold for fifty cents to one dollar per three-ounce bottle, relieved colds, piles, rheumatism, cancer, and croup. Some vendors had a variety of products, including salves, ointments, tonics, and elixirs, and not a few men sold cheap jewelry, patent soap, and cigars on the side. Most professors were smooth talkers of innate charm. Some of them traveled with sizable companies and attracted crowds from miles around with tent shows that featured magic tricks, displays of marksmanship, and testimonials from "satisfied customers."

Public celebrations also helped break the monotony of daily working lives. The Gulf Coast, especially Louisiana, had its Mardi Gras Carnival, during which all businesses closed down and carnival authorities assumed control of the towns. "They direct the police," marveled a northern visitor to New Orleans; "they arrest the mayor, and he delivers to them the keys, while the chief functionaries of the city declare their allegiance to 'Rex,' " the king of the festival. Meanwhile, in a different sort of local event, a westerner reported nearly one thousand people in attendance at a local "Turn Verein" picnic. "Big tent with dancing floor," he elaborated, "some 40 ft square, crowded with dancers." A brass band supplied the dance music, and two glee clubs, one singing in German and the other in English, offered additional musical fare. Beer proved the most popular beverage of the day, with 250 gallons being consumed.

In rural districts, county fairs, usually held in late summer or early autumn, provided a major excuse for closing up shops and "knocking off" work for a day. Before the Civil War, county fairs, as well as state and regional ones, had been sponsored by local agricultural societies (some 1,200 of them by 1860) and had fostered a serious purpose. Exhibits of prize cows, pigs, and poultry; awards for the biggest pumpkins, juiciest tomatoes, and tastiest pies; and plowing contests all ostensibly focused attention on the merits of scientific farming: crop rotation, careful breeding, seed selection, and proper fertilizers. Amusements, while not lacking, had been strictly subordinated to instruction. Postwar fairs shifted the balance. Judges still awarded prizes for the biggest and best animals and produce; the Grange, agricultural societies, and manufacturers of farm machinery still distributed literature on new fertilizers and seed drills; but a carnival atmosphere steadily overwhelmed the fair's earlier serious intent.

If not as large and rousing as a circus, local fairs certainly borrowed heavily from circus sideshows. Even in the 1850s, numerous fakirs, lager beer stands, fat ladies, snake charmers, and caged monkeys had appeared near, if not on, the fair grounds. After the war, they swiftly became part of the fair, as did balloon ascensions, glassworks, monkey shows, shooting galleries, minstrel troupes, medicine shows, organ grinders, and merry-go-rounds. Representative of these changes was the new role of horse racing. Racing had long been an important part of fair day, but where past races had been staged primarily to determine the swiftest and sturdiest local stock, postwar races became major betting concerns, with trotters and thoroughbreds entered from across the region. Entrepreneurs organized racing circuits for the fair season, and fair directors constructed formal racetracks and grandstands to attract spectators.

Numerous national holidays provided opportunities for picnics and parties. New Year's Eve and Day started the year out right, with young people free from the rigors of school and adults attending gala suppers and dances. Valentine's Day, while not an official holiday, still gave an excuse for dances and kissing games. George Washington's Birthday, a traditional day for relaxing and celebrating, had begun to decline in popularity by the mid-1870s; but Memorial Day, first commemorated in honor of Civil War dead, rapidly filled the void and soon rivaled the Fourth of July as a patriotic holiday. Brass bands, picnic lunches, baseball games, and general merrymaking soon attached themselves to the new holiday, as it became as much a celebration of spring as a commemoration of the nation's honored dead. Numerous ethnic holidays, including Saint Patrick's Day and the German Schutzenfest, spread with the growing immigrant population.

Even Christmas, largely a private, family-oriented holiday, had its public side. Christian churches held worship services, carolers roamed the streets, and most towns sponsored holiday pageants. "Singing, declamation, dialogues, tableaux—very good & interesting entertainment," asserted one man of a local Methodist program. "When old Santa Claus came marching in dressed in skins, etc, with lots of presents, he made nice little speech to children—gave all his presents to be distributed with the rest, from the tree, which was most beautifully trimmed, & arranged as usual." Some people shot off guns and firecrackers to celebrate. Young men sometimes roamed the streets on Christmas Eve visiting one saloon after another, but most people stayed home to sing carols, exchange gifts, and trim trees with strings of popcorn and cranberries, hand-crafted ornaments, and candles. All students, from grammar school to college, enjoyed at least a week's vacation, and everyone tried to get "home" for the holidays. Most modern Christmas traditions were already firmly entrenched by the 1860s, including Santa Claus, Christmas trees, greeting cards, mistletoe, and massive turkey or goose dinners. Children hung stockings over the fireplace or in the branches of the Christmas tree in hopes that Saint Nick would fill them with candies, nuts, and oranges.

Without question, the Fourth of July, the Glorious Fourth, remained the nation's principal holiday. An orgy of patriotic speeches, parades, picnics, dances, and sporting events characterized the day. "We celebrated the day here with far more than usual spirit," reported one westerner, "as is shown by the records of the police court the next day, although the officers took none to the station house except those who were disorderly as well as very drunk." While some people made too many trips to the punch bowl, most Americans celebrated in a wholesome family fashion. One Iowa town, typical of a thousand others, began the day by sounding anvils, cannons, guns, and bells shortly after sunrise. By 9 A.M., impatient people crowded onto Main Street waiting for the parade. They had strung their storefronts and houses with red, white, and blue bunting; they had festooned doorways and windows with eagles and national flags. Soon, an array of brass bands, floats illustrating patriotic themes, town officials in shining carriages, volunteer firemen, militia companies, and members of local fraternal, patriotic, and ethnic organizations passed in review. There seemed to be as many marchers as spectators.

The parade over, townspeople continued on to nearby picnic grounds for a day-long celebration. The first of many patriotic speeches, made from a makeshift platform, received rousing and spontaneous applause; but after several hours of droning pontification, most of the once-attentive audience concentrated on eating dinner. Some communities left each family to fend for itself; others asked that everyone contribute food to a common table. At Concordia, Kansas, in 1870, a table seventy feet long accommodated four shifts of diners. Some parts of the country, most notably the South and West, held monster barbecues. Meanwhile, as the speakers spoke and the diners dined, a full schedule of sack races, wheelbarrow races, horse races, horseshoe matches, wrestling matches, and baseball games kept people active. By late afternoon, brass bands and glee clubs began serenading the multitudes with patriotic and popular songs. As evening approached, everyone watched the skies in anticipation of a great fireworks display. "Nothing more picturesque, more delightful, more helpful," recalled one midwesterner of those Independence Day festivities, "has ever arisen out of American rural life."

# EPILOGUE:

# THE SECOND CENTURY

D IE-HARD Confederates refused to celebrate Independence Day during the 1860s and 1870s. "Being good Christians," reported a Georgian in summary fashion, "we did not join in the celebration of the 4th." But by 1876, most Americans, North and South, had sensed that the centennial of American independence might be an appropriate time to put the years of civil war and political reconstruction behind and look to the future. Besides, a continuing economic depression and the still-unfolding scandals of the Grant administration cried out for some sort of diversion. Americans responded by staging a monster celebration in Philadelphia. They called it the Centennial Exposition and invited the world to help celebrate their one-hundredth birthday party. The Centennial, people predicted, would demonstrate American progress since the war; it would proclaim the nation's new unity, growing strength, returning prosperity, and unabashed optimism. It would also remind observant Americans that they lived in a very different world from the one of fifteen years earlier.

Physically, the Centennial impressed everyone. Its 167 buildings and 30,000 exhibits covered 236 acres in Fairmount Park. The Main Exhibition Building, housing the principal exhibits of manufactured products and scientific achievements, measured 1,800 feet long and 464 wide, the largest building in the world.

Four other great halls—Machinery Hall, Agricultural Hall, Horticultural Hall, and Memorial Hall—formed the nucleus of the principal exhibition centers. The titles of the first three buildings explained their functions. Memorial Hall, called "the most imposing and substantial of all the Exhibition structures," housed international displays of painting, sculpture, engraving, photography, and crafts. Other prominent structures included the United States Government Building, which housed displays illustrating the work of various federal agencies, an exhibit of military hardware, and a functioning post office. A Woman's Building showcased "the results of woman's labors." Seventeen of thirty-nine participating states erected buildings to spotlight their history and accomplishments. Nine foreign governments erected buildings, and a total of thirty-five foreign nations provided exhibits or entertainment in one form or another. Additional exhibits included the Singer Sewing Machine Building, Photograph Gallery, Turkish Coffee Building, Shoe and Leather Building, Bible Pavilion, New England Log House, Nevada Quartz Mine, Woman's School House, Brewer's Hall, Butter and Cheese Factory, and the Campbell Printing Press Building. Scattered throughout the grounds one found cigar booths, beer gardens, popcorn stands, ethnic restaurants, and assorted statues and monuments, including likenesses of Christopher Columbus and Elias Howe, and the Torch of Liberty from the yet-unfinished Statue of Liberty.

"Dear Mother," one young woman wrote after first seeing the grounds, "Oh! Oh! O-o-o-o-o-o-o-o-o!!!!!!" Somewhat more articulately, another visitor recorded, "How the American heart thrills with pride and love of his land as he contemplates the vast exhibition of art and prowess here." These two satisfied customers joined over eight million other people who paid fifty cents apiece to see the fair, and nearly ten million people entered the fairgrounds. Never had any single attraction brought together such large, enthusiastic crowds from across the nation. The Centennial replaced Niagara Falls that summer as the principal honeymoon spot. Railroad companies encouraged a visit by reducing round-trip fares by one-fourth. While still expensive for the average citizen, this meant that travel to the fair from Chicago cost only $34.50, from New Orleans $68.02, from Denver $106.50, and from San Francisco $204. On May 10, 200,000 people poured through the fairgrounds' 106 entrances to witness President Grant, the emperor of Brazil, and a host of politicians, military officers, and other dignitaries officially open the Centennial for its six-month run. They heard Theodore Thomas conduct an orchestra and chorus in several marches, hymns, and cantatas composed expressly for the occasion by the likes of Richard Wagner, John Knowles Paine, and Dudley Buck. John Greenleaf Whittier, New England Quaker and abolitionist, wrote the lyrics for Paine's Centennial Hymn, while ex-Confederate Sidney Lanier, of Georgia, supplied the words for Buck's cantata. The climax came when Thomas led orchestra and chorus in a rousing rendition of Handel's "Hallelujah Chorus" as an American flag unfurled from atop the main building and a hundred cannons fired in salute.

From the perspective of our own century, the Centennial offers a fine summary of everyday American beliefs, hopes, assumptions, and fears as the Civil War era drew to a close. Even before opening day, the Centennial's directors, the press, and the American people had engaged in a heated debate over whether the exposition should remain open on Sundays. The directors finally bowed to the "national habit" and kept the Sabbath holy. On the other hand, demonstrating a more "liberal" attitude, the directors permitted sale of beer and liquor on the fairgrounds, this at a time when few country fairs, state fairs, circuses, or other places of family amusement would have permitted such a thing. As for the exhibits, the vast majority celebrated the industrial and mechanical transformation of everyday American life. This focus did not happen by chance. In planning the Centennial, one director urged that the celebration demonstrate how "the mass of the people whilst engaged in their daily and necessary pursuits, enjoy a larger measure of personal comfort and dignity than those of any other nation."

Wherever they turned, visitors caught glimpses of everyday American life. Long avenues of plows and mowers, row upon row of farm products, two buildings devoted entirely to kindergarten training, a newspaper printing plant, manufacturing demonstrations of everything from carpets to bricks, operating exhibits of typewriters and pneumatic tubes, a narrow-gauge railroad to transport fairgoers from one great building to another, botanical exhibits ranging from palms to cacti, Alexander Graham Bell personally demonstrating his new electric telephone, Thomas Edison explaining his new automatic telegraph, all of these suggested the context and direction of American life. Everyone found something familiar; few failed to discover something new and fantastic, something never seen or imagined. It was overwhelming. "To remember one [exhibit]," complained a dazed visitor, "was to forget a thousand."

Although one visitor, with some justification, called Agricultural Hall "the most exclusively American" building at the Centennial, nowhere could the nation's future be seen more clearly than at Machinery Hall. At center stage stood that mighty "athlete of steel and iron," the Corliss engine. Two cylinders 40 inches in diameter with a stroke of 10 feet, a flywheel 30 feet in diameter whirling at 360 revolutions per minute, 40 miles of belting, and 23 miles of shafting allowed this silent giant, the greatest achievement of American steam technology, to power hundreds of other machines on display. Not a few awestruck spectators believed the Corliss symbolized the Centennial and, with it, American civilization. "One thinks only of the glorious triumphs of skill and invention," admitted one visitor confronted by the surging power and shining metal in the hall; "and wherever else the national bird is mute in one's breast, here he cannot fail to utter his pride and content. . . . Yes, it is still in these things of iron and steel that the national genius most freely speaks." Machinery Hall, rhapsodized another visitor, "makes an extraordinary impression upon everybody, and probably those who understand nothing of what they see are more imaginatively affected than those who know all about valves and pistons. The predominating impression is that of manifold movement. One is amazed to see how many sorts of motion there are, and how they can be expressed by those soulless, senseless machines." Then, as a vision of the future burst upon him, the visitor exclaimed, "Surely here, and not in literature, science, or art, is the true evidence of man's creative power; here is Prometheus unbound."

Equally revealing, however, were the missing exhibits. Most noticeably, black Americans had no exhibit they could call their own. Only two black artists, Edmonia Lewis and Edward Bannister, had paintings displayed. Blacks received no mention or acknowledgment in the Woman's Building. Their most prominent exposure came at a concession known variously as "The South" and the "Southern Restaurant," where, guidebooks cheerfully informed the public, "a band of old-time plantation 'darkies' . . . sing their quaint melodies and strum the banjo before visitors in every clime." No blacks had been employed in constructing the fairgrounds and its buildings, despite Philadelphia's extremely large black population. At the fair, blacks worked in stereotypical jobs as entertainers, waiters, hotel clerks, messengers, and janitors. Frederick Douglass, a powerful orator and the most prominent black in the United States, sat on the dignitaries' platform during opening ceremonies, but he was not asked to address the crowd.

The Smithsonian Institution organized a magnificent American Indian display in the United States Government Building, but the conglomeration of pottery, tools, weapons, wigwams, costumes, and life-size wax figures formed more an archaeological exhibit than a presentation of a living race with multiple cultures. Indeed, it portrayed Indians as the antithesis of progress. "The red man, as he appears in effigy and in photograph in this collection, is a hideous demon, whose malign traits can hardly inspire any emotion softer than abhorrence," concluded one visitor. "Novelists with subdued fancies, may sit in their cozy back parlors, and write pretty little stories of the noble red man," observed another man, but let them once see the wax figures of those "red gentlemen, with . . . small, cruel, black eyes, . . . coarse, unkempt locks, . . . and large animal mouth," and they would depict a different breed. That five thousand Sioux and Cheyenne warriors had annihilated George Custer's command in late June did not help the Indian's cause at the Centennial.

Other minorities suffered similar treatment. Displays and exhibits from Japan, China, and Africa drew slight attention and little favorable comment by American fairgoers. Even the Japanese, whom Americans regarded as the most intelligent, industrious, and moral of all Asians, received only backhanded compliments. "The quaint little people," commented a man favorably impressed by gorgeous displays of Japanese bronze, porcelain, basketry, and other art, "with their shambling gait, their eyes set awry in their head, and their grave and gentle ways, how can it be in them . . . to make such wonderful things?" Wherever they went on the fairgrounds, visitors saw and heard xenophobic expressions of prejudice. Foreign-looking people of all races and nationalities, were they Orientals, Turks, Slavs, Egyptians, or Spaniards, were "followed by large crowds of idle boys, and men, who hooted and shouted at them as if they had been animals of a strange species."

Perhaps the most telling contrast to the Centennial's official visions of progress and expressions of superiority was the counterculture "Centennial City" that sprang up outside Fairmount Park. Like the disreputable fringes of most American cities and towns, Centennial City was actually a rough-and-tumble shantytown, its structures hurriedly constructed from wood, tin, and canvas. Along the mile-long strip stood cheap restaurants, small hotels, beer gardens, ice-cream parlors, peanut stands, pie stalls, sausage vendors, lemonade stands, balloon salesmen, and small, circuslike sideshows to refresh, accommodate, and entertain people who could not afford admission to the Centennial grounds. The most popular attraction became a poor man's "museum," which advertised among its many attractions "the wild man of Borneo, and the wild children of Australia, the fat woman . . . heavy enough to entitle her to a place in Machinery Hall, and a collection of 'Feejees,' who were vouched for by the exhibitors as 'pure and unadulterated man-eaters.' "

Centennial City must have been a vaguely unsettling sight to gay holiday visitors at the official Exposition. For despite the aura of brash confidence, immense power, and unparalleled prosperity projected by the fair, many Americans felt not at all confident, powerful, or prosperous. The present seemed bleak and the future more than a little uncertain. Examined closely, the Centennial itself betrayed uncertainty. It lacked any focus or underlying principle, other than the rather broad one of a national birthday party. The country had become so diverse and fluid that no single exhibition could adequately represent the whole. Few societies had ever developed so rapidly as the United States in the decade after the Civil War. It had been a decade of immense preparation for a brave new world. Americans did not lack the courage to confront past, present, or future, but they could not help but wonder if they controlled the future so firmly as once they had.

Like so many American amusements and diversions in the mid-1870s, the Centennial served to disguise and to help people forget the problems and incongruities that continued to haunt, perplex, and hobble the nation. How eliminate the shantytowns? How eradicate racial and ethnic prejudice? How ease the pangs of hunger? How protect rural life from urban growth? How end crime? How curb exploitation? How terminate the Indian menace yet treat fairly with native Americans? Perceptive Americans, as they entered their second century of nationhood, knew that these and many other questions must be answered, but they chose, for the moment, to dismiss their uneasiness and enjoy the best of all possible worlds. They agreed with their everyday poet, Emily Dickinson, who wrote in 1877:

> The Persons of prognostication
> Are coming now—
> We try to show becoming firmness—
> But pompous Joy
> Betrays us, as his first Betrothal
> Betrays a Boy.

# SELECTED BIBLIOGRAPHY

Adams, Andy. *The Log of a Cowboy: A Narrative of the Old Trail Days.* Boston, 1903.

Ahlstrom, Sydney E. *A Religious History of the American People.* New Haven, Conn., 1972.

"Among the Wheat-Fields of Minnesota," *Harper's Monthly* XXXVI (1867–68): 193–201.

Aron, Cindy S. *Ladies and Gentlemen of the Civil Service: Middle-Class Workers in Victorian America.* New York, 1987.

Atherton, Lewis. *Main Street on the Middle Border.* Bloomington, Ind., 1954.

Banner, Lois W. *American Beauty.* New York, 1983.

Barns, Cass G. *The Sod House.* Lincoln, Neb., 1930.

Barron, Hal S. *Those Who Stayed Behind: Rural Society in Nineteenth-Century New England.* Cambridge, Mass., 1984.

Barth, Gunther. *City People: The Rise of Modern City Culture in Nineteenth-Century America.* New York, 1980.

Bartlett, Richard A. *The New Country: A Social History of the American Frontier, 1776–1890.* New York, 1974.

Beecher, Catherine E., and Harriet Beecher Stowe. *The American Woman's Home.* New York, 1869.

Bellew, Frank. *The Art of Amusing.* New York, 1866.

Berthoff, Rowland. *An Unsettled People: Social Order and Disorder in American History.* New York, 1971.

Best, Joel. "Careers in Brothel Prostitution: St. Paul, 1865–1883," *Journal of Interdisciplinary History* XII (1982): 597–619.

Billings, John D. *Hardtack and Coffee; or, the Unwritten Story of Army Life.* Boston, 1887.

Blair, Karen J. *The Clubwoman as Feminist: True Womanhood Redefined, 1868–1914.* New York, 1980.

Blegan, Theodore C., ed. *Land of Their Choice: The Immigrants Write Home.* Minneapolis, 1955.

Branch, Douglas. *The Cowboy and His Interpreters.* New York, 1961.

Bremner, Robert H., ed. *Children and Youth in America: A Documentary History,* 3 vols. Cambridge, Mass., 1970–74.

————. *The Public Good: Philanthropy and Welfare in the Civil War Era.* New York, 1980.

Brody, David. *Steelworkers in America: The Non-Union Era.* New York, 1969.

Brown, Richard Maxwell. *Strains of Violence: Historical Studies of American Violence and Vigilantism.* New York, 1975.

Brown, Ronald C. *Hard-Rock Miners: The Intermountain West, 1860–1920.* College Station, Texas, 1979.

Brownlee, W. Elliot, and Mary M. Brownlee, eds. *Women in the American Economy: A Documentary History, 1675 to 1929.* New Haven, Conn., 1976.

Burton, Orville Vernon. *In My Father's House Are Many Mansions: Family and Community in Edgefield, South Carolina.* Chapel Hill, N. C., 1985.

Butler, Anne M. *Daughters of Joy, Sisters of Misery: Prostitutes in the American West, 1865–1890.* Urbana, Ill., 1985.

Cathell, D. W. *The Physician Himself and What He Should Add to His Scientific Acquirements.* Baltimore, 1882.

Channing, Steven A. *Confederate Ordeal: The Southern Home Front.* Alexandria, Va., 1984.

"Children Who Work," *Scribner's Monthly* I (1870–71): 607–15.

Clark, Clifford Edward, Jr. *The American Family Home, 1800–1960.* Chapel Hill, N.C., 1986.

Clark, Thomas D. *Pills, Petticoats, and Plows: The Southern Country Store.* Norman, Okla., 1963.

Clark, Victor S. *History of Manufactures in the United States,* 3 vols. Washington, D.C., 1929.

Clark, Walter Van Tilburg, ed. *The Journals of Alfred Doten, 1849–1903,* 3 vols. Reno, Nev., 1973.

Coffman, Edward M. *The Old Army: A Portrait of the American Army in Peacetime, 1784–1898.* New York, 1985.

Coggins, Jack. *Arms and Equipment of the Civil War.* New York, 1983.

Commager, Henry Steele. *The Blue and the Gray: The Story of the Civil War as Told by Participants,* 2 vols. Indianapolis, 1950.

Cornish, Dudley T. *The Sable Arm: Negro Troops in the Union Army, 1861–1865.* New York, 1966.

Corson, Richard. *Fashions in Makeup from Ancient Times to Modern.* London, 1972.

Cremin, Lawrence A. *American Education: The National Experience, 1783–1876.* New York, 1980.

Cunnington, Cecil W., and Phillis Cunnington. *The History of Underclothes.* London, 1951.

Curti, Merle. *The Making of an American Community: A Case Study of Democracy in a Frontier County.* Stanford, Calif., 1959.

Danhof, Clarence H. *Change in Agriculture: The Northern United States, 1820–1870.* Cambridge, Mass., 1969.

Danker, Donald F., ed. *Mollie: The Journal of Mollie Dorsey Sanford in Nebraska and Colorado Territories, 1857–1866.* Lincoln, Neb., 1959.

Davies, Margery W. *Woman's Place Is at the Typewriter: Office Work and Office Workers, 1870–1930.* Philadelphia, 1982.

Davis, William, ed. *The Image of War: 1861–1865,* 6 vols. Garden City, N.Y., 1982.

Dawley, Alan. *Class and Community: The Industrial Revolution in Lynn.* Cambridge, Mass., 1976.

Dedmon, Emmett. *Fabulous Chicago.* New York, 1953.

Degler, Carl N. *At Odds: Women and the Family in America from the Revolution to the Present.* New York, 1980.

Demos, John. *Past, Present, and Personal: The Family and the Life Course in American History.* New York, 1986.

Dick, Everett. *The Sod-House Frontier, 1854–1890.* New York, 1937.

Doyle, Don Harrison. *The Social Order of a Frontier Community: Jacksonville, Illinois, 1825–70.* Urbana, Ill., 1978.

Dudden, Faye E. *Serving Women: Household Service in Nineteenth-Century America.* Middletown, Conn., 1983.

Dulles, Foster Rhea. *America Learns to Play: A History of Popular Recreation, 1607–1940,* 2nd edition. New York, 1965.

Ebbutt, Percy G. *Emigrant Life in Kansas.* London, 1886.

Egleston, Nathaniel Hillyer. *Villages and Village Life.* New York, 1878.

Ehrlich, Richard L., ed. *Immigrants in Industrial Ameria, 1850–1920.* Charlottesville, Va., 1977.

Emhoff, Floy L., ed. "A Pioneer School Teacher in Central Iowa: Alice Money Lawrence," *Iowa Journal of History and Politics* XXXIII (1935): 376–95.

Erickson, Charlotte. *Invisible Immigrants: The Adaptation of English* and Scottish Immigrants in Nineteenth-Century America. Coral Gables, Fla., 1972.

Farrell, James J. *Inventing the American Way of Death, 1830–1920*. Philadelphia, 1980.

Ferguson, Charles W. *Fifty Million Brothers: A Panorama of American Lodges and Clubs*. New York, 1937.

Fite, Emerson David. *Social and Industrial Conditions in the North During the Civil War*. New York, 1909.

Fite, Gilbert C. *Cotton Fields No More: Southern Agriculture, 1865–1980*. Lexington, Ky., 1984.

Foner, Philip S. *Organized Labor and the Black Worker, 1619–1973*. New York, 1974.

———. *Women and the American Labor Movement: From Colonial Times to the Eve of World War I*, 2 vols. New York, 1979.

Forbis, William H. *The Old West: The Cowboys*. New York, 1973.

Friedman, Jean E. *The Enclosed Garden: Women and Community in the Evangelical South, 1830–1900*. Chapel Hill, N.C., 1985.

Friedman, Lawrence M. *A History of American Law*. New York, 1973.

Fuller, Wayne E. *The American Mail: Enlarger of the Common Life*. Chicago, 1972.

———. *The Old Country School: The Story of Rural Education in the Middle West*. Chicago, 1982.

Garland, Hamlin. *Boy Life on the Prairie*. New York, 1899.

———. *A Son of the Middle Border*. New York, 1917.

Garner, John S. *The Model Company Town: Urban Design through Private Enterprise in Nineteenth-Century New England*. Amherst, Mass., 1984.

Gates, Paul W. *Agriculture and the Civil War*. New York, 1965.

Giedion, Siegfried. *Mechanization Takes Command: A Contribution to Anonymous History*. New York, 1948.

Goldman, Marion S. *Gold Diggers and Silver Miners: Prostitution and Social Life on the Comstock Lode*. Ann Arbor, Mich., 1981.

Gompers, Samuel. *Seventy Years of Life and Labour*, 2 vols. New York, 1925.

Gorsline, Douglas. *What People Wore: A Visual History of Dress from Ancient Times to Twentieth-Century America*. New York, 1952.

Graham, Hugh Davis, and Ted Robert Gurr, eds. *Violence in America: Historical and Comparative Perspectives*, rev. ed. Beverly Hills, Calif., 1979.

Greever, William S. *The Bonanza West: The Story of the Western Mining Rushes, 1848–1900*. Norman, Okla., 1963.

Grover, Kathryn, ed. *Dining in America, 1850–1900.* Amherst, Mass., 1987.

Haller, John S., Jr. *American Medicine in Transition, 1840–1910.* Urbana, Ill., 1981.

Haller, John S., Jr., and Robin Haller. *The Physician and Sexuality in Victorian America.* Urbana, Ill., 1974.

Hammond, Harold Earl, ed. *Diary of a Union Lady, 1861–1865.* New York, 1962.

Handlin, David P. *The American Home: Architecture and Society, 1815–1915.* Boston, 1979.

Handlin, Oscar, and Mary F. Handlin. *Facing Life: Youth and the Family in American History.* Boston, 1971.

Hareven, Tamara K., ed. *Transitions: The Family and the Life Course in Historical Perspective.* New York, 1978.

Harrison, Lowell H. "The Cattle-Sheep Wars," *American History Illustrated* III (1968): 20–27.

Harvey, Katherine A. *The Best-Dressed Miners: Life and Labor in the Maryland Coal Region, 1835–1910.* Ithaca, N.Y., 1969.

Hayden, Dolores. *The Grand Domestic Revolution: A History of Feminist Designs for American Homes, Neighborhoods, and Cities.* Cambridge, Mass., 1981.

Hitchcock, H. Wiley. *Music in the United States: A Historical Introduction.* Englewood Cliffs, N.J., 1969.

Hooker, Richard J. *Food and Drink in America: A History.* Indianapolis, 1981.

Horn, Huston. *The Old West: The Pioneers.* New York, 1974.

Howells, William Dean. "A Sennight of the Centennial," *Atlantic Monthly* XXXVIII (1876): 92–107.

"In a Country Store," *Harper's Monthly* XL (1869–70): 825–33.

"In a Tobacco Factory," *Harper's Monthly* XLVII (1873): 713–19.

Jackson, Charles O. *Passing: The Vision of Death in America.* Westport, Conn., 1977.

Jackson, Kenneth T. *Crabgrass Frontier: The Suburbanization of the United States.* New York, 1985.

Jeffrey, Julie Roy. *Frontier Women: The Trans-Mississippi West, 1840–1880.* New York, 1979.

Juster, Norton. *So Sweet to Labor: Rural Women in America, 1865–1895.* New York, 1979.

Kett, Joseph F. *Rites of Passage: Adolescence in America, 1790 to the Present.* New York, 1977.

King, Edward. *The Great South.* Edited by W. Magruder Drake and Robert R. Jones. Baton Rouge, 1972.

Klement, Frank L. *Dark Lanterns: Secret Political Societies, Conspiracies, and Treason Trials in the Civil War.* Baton Rouge, 1984.

Langdon, William Chauncy. *Everyday Things in American Life, 1776–1876.* New York, 1941.

Lasansky, Jeannette. *To Draw, Upset & Weld: The Work of the Pennsylvania Rural Blacksmith, 1742–1935.* Lewisburg, Pa., 1980.

Leavitt, Judith Walzer. *Brought to Bed: Childbearing in America, 1750 to 1950.* New York, 1986.

Lebergott, Stanley. *Manpower in Economic Growth: The American Record Since 1800.* New York, 1964.

Lebhar, Godfrey M. *Chain Stores in America, 1859–1959.* New York, 1959.

Leng, John. *America in 1876.* Dundee, Scotland, 1877.

Lerner, Gerda, ed. *The Female Experience: An American Documentary.* Indianapolis, 1977.

Light, Walter. *Working for the Railroad: The Organization of Work in the Nineteenth Century.* Princeton, N.J., 1983.

Linderman, Gerald F. *Embattled Courage: The Experience of Combat in Civil War.* New York, 1987.

Lingeman, Richard. *Small Town America: A Narrative History, 1620 to the Present.* New York, 1980.

Litwack, Leon F. *Been in the Storm So Long: The Aftermath of Slavery.* New York, 1979.

Long, Clarence D. *Wages and Earnings in the United States, 1860–1890.* Princeton, N.J., 1960.

Lynes, Russell, *The Domesticated Americans.* New York, 1963.

———. *The Tastemakers.* New York, 1954.

McCabe, James D., Jr. *Lights and Shadows of New York Life.* Philadelphia, 1872.

McCarthy, Carlton. *Detailed Minutiae of Soldier Life in the Army of Northern Virginia, 1861–1865.* Richmond, Va., 1882.

McClellan, Elisabeth. *History of American Costume, 1607–1870.* New York, 1942.

McDannell, Colleen. *The Christian Home in Victorian America, 1840–1900.* Bloomington, Ind., 1986.

McKelvey, Blake. *The Urbanization of America, 1860–1915.* New Brunswick, N.J., 1963.

McKeown, Martha Ferguson. *Them Was the Days: An American Saga of the '70's.* Lincoln, Neb., 1961.

McMurry, Sally. "City Parlor, Country Sitting Room: Rural Vernacular Design and the American Parlor, 1840–1900." *Winterthur Portfolio* XX (1985): 261–80.

McNamara, Brooks. *Step Right Up: An Illustrated History of the American Medicine Show*. Garden City, N.Y., 1976.

McPherson, James M. *The Negro's Civil War: How American Negroes Felt and Acted During the War for the Union*. New York, 1965.

Macrae, David. *The Americans at Home*. New York, 1952.

Massey, Mary Elizabeth. *Bonnet Brigades: American Women and the Civil War*. New York, 1966.

Mayhew, Edgar deN., and Minor Myers, Jr. *A Documentary History of American Interiors from the Colonial Era to 1915*. New York, 1980.

Miller, Stuart Creighton. *The Unwelcome Immigrant: The American Image of the Chinese, 1785–1882*. Berkeley, Calif., 1969.

Montgomery, David. *Beyond Equality: Labor and the Radical Republicans, 1862–1872*. New York, 1967.

Morris, Lloyd. *Incredible New York: High Life and Low Life of the Last Hundred Years*. New York, 1951.

Morris, Robert C. *Reading, 'Riting, and Reconstruction: The Education of Freedmen in the South, 1861–1870*. Chicago, 1981.

Mott, Frank Luther. *A History of American Magazines*, 5 vols. Cambridge, Mass., 1938–68.

Myers, Robert Manson, ed. *The Children of Pride: A True Story of Georgia and the Civil War*. New Haven, Conn., 1972.

Nevins, Allan. *The Emergence of Modern America, 1865–1878*. New York, 1955.

Nevins, Allan, and Milton Halsey Thomas, eds. *The Diary of George Templeton Strong*, 4 vols. New York, 1952.

Nordin, D. Sven. *Rich Harvest: A History of the Grange, 1867–1900*. Jackson, Miss., 1974.

Olson, James Stuart. *The Ethnic Dimension in American History*. New York, 1979.

"On the Tobacco Plantation," *Scribner's Monthly* IV (1872): 651–66.

Orpen, Adela E. *Memories of the Old Emigrant Days in Kansas, 1862–1865*. Edinburgh, 1926.

Partridge, Bellamy, and Otto Bettman. *As We Were: Family Life in America, 1850–1900*. New York, 1946.

Penny, Virginia. *Five Hundred Employments Adapted to Women*. Philadelphia, 1868.

Pessen, Edward, ed. *Three Centuries of Social Mobility in America.* Lexington, Mass., 1974.

Peterson, Harold L. *Americans at Home: From the Colonists to the Late Victorians.* New York, 1971.

Powderly, Tewrence V. *The Path I Trod.* New York, 1940.

Rabinowitz, Howard N. *Race Relations in the Urban South, 1865– 1890.* Urbana, Ill., 1980.

Ramsdell, Charles W. *Behind the Lines of the Southern Confederacy.* Baton Rouge, 1944.

Randel, William Peirce. *Centennial: American Life in 1876.* Philadelphia, 1969.

Ransom, Roger L., and Richard Sutch. "The Labor of Older Americans: Retirement of Men on and off the Job, 1870–1937," *Journal of Economic History* XLVI (1986): 1–30.

Rickey, Don, Jr. *Forty Miles a Day on Beans and Hay: The Enlisted Soldier Fighting the Indian Wars.* Norman, Okla., 1963.

Riegel, Robert C. *America Moves West,* 3rd ed. New York, 1956.

Rorabaugh, W. J. *The Craft Apprentice: From Franklin to the Machine in America.* New York, 1986.

Rosenberg, Charles E. *The Cholera Years: The United States in 1832, 1849, and 1866.* Chicago, 1962.

———. "The Practice of Medicine in New York a Century Ago," *Bulletin of the History of Medicine* XLI (1967): 223–53.

Ross, Steven J. *Workers on the Edge: Work, Leisure and Politics in Industrializing Cincinnati, 1788–1890.* New York, 1985.

Rothman, Ellen K. *Hands and Hearts: A History of Courtship in America.* New York, 1984.

Rothstein, William G. *American Physicians in the Nineteenth Century: From Sects to Science.* Baltimore, 1972.

Rydell, Robert W. *All the World's a Fair: Visions of Empire at American International Expositions, 1876–1916.* Chicago, 1984.

Sablosky, Irving. *What They Heard: Music in America, 1852–1881. From the Pages of "Dwight's Journal of Music."* Baton Rouge, 1986.

Schlebecker, John T. *Whereby We Thrive: A History of American Farming, 1607–1972.* Ames, Iowa, 1975.

Schnapper, M. B. *American Labor: A Pictorial Social History.* Washington, D.C., 1972.

Shannon, Fred A. *The Farmer's Last Frontier: Agriculture, 1860–1897.* New York, 1968.

Smith, David. "Middle Range Farming in the Civil War Era: Life on a Farm in Seneca County, 1862–1866," *New York History* XLVIII (1967): 339–52.

Smith, George Winston, and Charles Judah, eds. *Life in the North During the Civil War: A Source History.* Albuquerque, N. M., 1966.

Smith, Henry Nash, ed. *Popular Culture and Industrialization, 1865–1890.* New York, 1967.

Smith, Page. *As a City Upon a Hill: The Town in American History.* New York, 1971.

————. *Daughters of the Promised Land: Women in American History.* Boston, 1970.

Spaeth, Sigmund. *Read 'Em and Weep: The Songs You Forgot to Remember.* New York, 1939.

Stallard, Patricia. *Glittering Misery: Lives of Dependents of the Indian-Fighting Army.* Fort Collins, Colo., 1978.

Stannard, David E., ed. *Death in America.* Philadelphia, 1975.

Steffens, Lincoln. *The Autobiography of Lincoln Steffens,* 2 vols. New York, 1931.

Stern, Bernhard J., ed. *Young Ward's Diary.* New York, 1935.

Strasser, Susan. *Never Done: A History of American Housework.* New York, 1982.

Stratton, Joanna L. *Pioneer Women: Voices from the Kansas Frontier.* New York, 1981.

Sutherland, Daniel E. *Americans and Their Servants: Domestic Service in the United States, 1800–1920.* Baton Rouge, 1981.

————. *The Confederate Carpetbaggers.* Baton Rouge, 1988.

Taylor, Joe Gray. *Eating, Drinking, and Visiting in the South: An Informal History.* Baton Rouge, 1982.

Taylor, Philip. *The Distant Magnet: European Emigration to the U.S.A.* New York, 1971.

Thornton, Peter. *Authentic Decor: The Domestic Interior, 1620–1920.* New York, 1984.

Toll, Robert C. *On with the Show: The First Century of Show Business in America.* New York, 1976.

Trelease, Allen W. *White Terror: The Ku Klux Klan Conspiracy and Southern Reconstruction.* New York, 1971.

Trollope, Anthony. *North America.* Edited by Donald Smalley and Bradford Allen Booth. New York, 1951.

United States Bureau of the Census. *The Statistical History of the United States from Colonial Times to the Present.* New York, 1976.

Upton, Dell, and John Michael Veach, eds. *Common Places: Readings in American Vernacular Architecture*. Athens, Ga., 1986.

Utley, Robert. *Frontier Regulars: The U.S. Army and the Indians, 1866–1891*. New York, 1973.

Wainwright, Nicholas B., ed. *A Philadelphia Perspective: The Diary of Sidney George Fisher Covering the Years 1834–1871*. Philadelphia, 1967.

Walker, Robert H. *Life in the Age of Enterprise, 1865–1900*. New York, 1971.

Walkowitz, Daniel J. *Worker City, Company Town: Iron and Cotton-Worker Protest in Troy and Cohoes, New York, 1855–84*. Urbana, Ill., 1978.

Weaver, Robert B. *Amusements and Sports in American Life*. Chicago, 1939.

Wheeler, Keith. *The Old West: The Townsmen*. New York, 1975.

Wilcox, R. Turner. *The Mode in Footwear*. New York, 1948.

———. *The Mode in Hats and Headdress*. New York, 1948.

Wiley, Bell I. *The Life of Billy Yank: The Common Soldier in the Civil War*. Baton Rouge, 1978.

———. *The Life of Johnny Reb: The Common Soldier of the Confederacy*. Baton Rouge, 1978.

Wright, Gwendolyn. *Building the Dream: A Social History of Housing in America*. New York, 1981.

Wyman, Mark. *Hard-Rock Epic: Western Miners and the Industrial Revolution, 1860–1910*. Berkeley, Calif., 1979.

# BIBLIOGRAPHICAL ESSAY FOR THE

# UNIVERSITY OF ARKANSAS PRESS EDITION

Much has been written since the late 1980s about what might loosely be called the "social" history of the Civil War era, but there has been no new synthesis that takes the same nut-and-bolts perspective on everyday life used in *Expansion*. Dorothy D. Volo and James M. Volo come closest to the mark in *Daily Life in Civil War America* (Westport, Conn., 1998), but these authors devote more space to the army, slavery, politics, and the abolitionist movement than they do to the daily routines of the majority of Americans. Volo and Volo also restrict themselves to the war years and to the region east of the Mississippi River. A second book, *Victorian America and the Civil War* (Cambridge, England, 1992), by Anne C. Rose, touches on several broad themes of daily life—specifically religion, work, leisure, family, and politics—but it is more of an intellectual than a social/cultural history. Professor Rose seeks to "explore the connection between culture and war" and to investigate the "meaning" of the Civil War (pp. 1–2), an analysis she carries into the early twentieth century.

Still, there has been an enormous amount of material published on topics related to the daily lives of Americans in the 1860s and 1870s. Were I starting this book from scratch, or even undertaking a significant revision, I could benefit from a wealth of new insights. For example, the experiences and attitudes of Civil War soldiers have received a lot attention from historians. Consequently, Larry J. Daniel, *Soldiering in the Army of Tennessee: A Portrait of Life in a Confederate Army* (Chapel Hill, N.C., 1991); Reid Mitchell, *The Vacant Chair: The Northern Soldier Leaves Home* (New York, 1993); James M. McPherson, *For Cause and Comrades: Why Men Fought in the Civil War* (New York, 1997); and Earl J. Hess, *The Union Soldier in Battle: Enduring the Ordeal of Combat* (Lawrence, Kans., 1997) would all be worth consulting and adding to my original bibliography. For African-American soldiers, Noah Trudeau, *Like Men of War: Black Troops in the Civil War, 1862–1865* (Boston, 1998) would be very useful, as would Elizabeth D. Leonard, *All the Daring of the Soldier: Women of the Civil War Armies* (New York, 1999), for women.

Moving to the home front, Phillip Shaw Paludan's broadly conceived *"A People's Contest": The Union and the Civil War, 1861–1865* (New York, 1988) offers valuable information about some aspects of daily life, especially for industrial and agricultural laborers. Similarly useful, although lacking Paludan's breadth, is J. Matthew Gallman, *The North Fights the Civil War: The Home Front* (Chicago, 1994).

Research on women, children, and family life has grown dramatically in the past decade. The fruit of those labors has produced an impressive amount of work, which, if not always directed toward material culture and the routines of daily living, do frequently shed light on personal relationships, social values, customs, and the matrix of everyday life. Some important contributions to this literature include Sally G. McMillan, *Motherhood in the Old South: Pregnancy, Childbirth, and Infant Rearing* (Baton Rouge, La., 1990); Joan E. Cashin, *A Family Venture: Men and Women on the Southern Frontier* (New York, 1991); Carol Bleser, ed., *In Joy and Sorrow: Women, Family, and*

*Marriage in the Victorian South* (New York, 1991); Catherine Clinton and Nina Silber, eds., *Divided Houses: Gender and the Civil War* (New York, 1992); Drew Gilpin Faust, *Mothers of Invention: Women of the Slaveholding South in the American Civil War* (Chapel Hill, N.C., 1996); Elliott West, *Growing Up with the Country: Children on the Far-Western Frontier* (Albuquerque, N.M., 1989); Karin Calvert, *Children in the House: The Material Culture of Early Childhood, 1600–1900* (Boston, 1990); Wilma King, *Stolen Childhood: Slave Youth in Nineteenth-Century America* (Bloomington, Ind., 1995); and James Marten, *The Children's Civil War* (Chapel Hill, N.C., 1998).

Along similar lines, much work has recently appeared on gender relations, social conventions, and courtship, including Karen Lystra, *Searching the Heart: Women, Men, and Romantic Love in Nineteenth-Century America* (New York, 1989); Mark Carnes and Clyde Griffin, eds., *Meaning for Manhood: Constructions of Masculinity in Victorian America* (Chicago, 1990); John F. Kasson, *Rudeness and Civility: Manners in Nineteenth-Century Urban America* (New York, 1990); Linda Gordon, *Women's Body, Woman's Right: A Social History of Birth Control in America* (2nd. ed.; New York, 1990); Janet Brodie, *Contraception and Abortion in Nineteenth-Century America* (Ithaca, N.Y., 1994); Thomas P. Lowry, *The Story the Soldiers Wouldn't Tell: Sex in the Civil War* (Mechanicsburg, Pa., 1994); Michael Kimmel, *Manhood in America: A Cultural History* (New York, 1996); Martha Hodes, *White Women, Black Men: Illicit Sex in the Nineteenth-Century South* (New Haven, Conn., 1997); Virginia Jeans Laas, *Love and Power in the Nineteenth Century: The Marriage of Violet Blair* (Fayetteville, Ark., 1998); and C. Dallett Hemphill, *Bowing to Necessities: A History of Manners in America, 1620–1860* (New York, 1999).

Concerning benevolent work and religion, valuable information about the era may be found in Anne M. Boylan,

*Sunday School: The Formation of an American Institution, 1790–1880* (New Haven, Conn., 1988); Lori D. Ginzberg, *Women and the Work of Benevolence: Morality, Politics, and Class in Nineteenth-Century United States* (New Haven, Conn., 1990); Marilyn I. Holt, *The Orphan Trains: Placing Out in America* (Lincoln, Neb., 1992); Charles H. Lippy, *Being Religious, American Style: A History of Popular Religiosity in the United States* (Westport, Conn., 1994); and Jeanie Attie, *Patriotic Toil: Northern Women and the American Civil War* (Ithaca, N.Y., 1998).

Informative work has also been done on daily amusements, entertainments, and fashions. Especially useful are Mark E. Lender and James K. Martin, *Drinking in America: A History* (New York, 1987); Patricia M. Click, *The Spirit of the Times: Amusements in Nineteenth-Century Baltimore, Norfolk, and Richmond* (Charlottesville, Va., 1989); George B. Kirsch, *The Creation of American Team Sport: Baseball and Cricket, 1838–1872* (Urbana, Ill., 1989); Ann Fabian, *Card Sharps, Dream Books, & Bucket Shops: Gambling in 19th-Century America* (Ithaca, N.Y., 1990); Kathryn Grover, *Hard at Play: Leisure in America, 1840–1940* (Amherst, Mass., 1992); David Dary, *Seeking Pleasure in the Old West* (New York, 1995); R. L. Shep, ed., *Civil War Ladies: Fashions and Needle Arts of the Early 1860's* (Mendocino, Calif., 1987); and Joan L. Severa, *Dressed for the Photographer: Ordinary Americans and Fashion, 1840–1900* (Kent, Ohio, 1995).

At a more theoretical level, yet quite valuable for understanding the nation's mood, several important books explain changing social values and cultural assumptions. Lewis O. Baum, *The Popular Mood of America, 1860–1890* (Lincoln, Neb., 1990) pays particular attention to religion and death. Louise L. Stevenson, *The Victorian Homefront: American Thought and Culture, 1860–1880* (New York, 1991) explores the intellectual environment of both private and public places, while Lawrence W. Levine, *Highbrow/Lowbrow: The Emergence of Cultural Hierarchy in the United States* (Cambridge, Mass., 1988) provides an excellent discussion of broader themes. Also useful for the urban environment are Stuart M. Blumin, *The Emergence of the Middle Class: Social Experience in the American City, 1760–1900* (Cambridge, England, 1989) and Mary P. Ryan, *Civic Wars: Democracy and Public Life in the American City during the Nineteenth Century* (Berkeley, Calif., 1997).

Architecture and living spaces are important parts of everyday life. Useful recent works on the changing urban landscape of dwellings and commercial buildings include Elizabeth C. Cromley, *Alone Together: A History of New York's Early Apartments* (Ithaca, N.Y., 1990); Daniel Bluestone, *Constructing Chicago* (New Haven, Conn., 1991); Sarah B. Landau and Carl W. Condit, *Rise of the New York Skyscraper, 1865–1913* (New Haven, Conn., 1996); and Mona Domosh, *Invented Cities: The Creation of Landscape in Nineteenth-Century New York and Boston* (New Haven, Conn., 1996). For rural America, Sally McMurry, *Families and Farmhouses in Nineteenth-Century America: Vernacular Design and Social Change* (New York, 1988); and Fred W. Peterson, *Homes in the Heartland: Farmhouses of the Upper Midwest, 1850–1920* (Lawrence, Kans., 1992) are excellent. Also useful for related themes are Kenneth L. Ames, *Death and Dying in the Dining Room and Other Tales of Victorian Culture* (Philadelphia, 1992) and Maureen Ogle, *All the Modern Conveniences: American Household Plumbing, 1840–1890* (Baltimore, 1995).

The story of laboring America is complex and diverse, but the best recent work on the daily lives of workers includes Grace Palladino, *Another Civil War: Labor, Capital, and the State in the Anthracite Region of Pennsylvania, 1840–1868* (Urbana, Ill., 1990); Carole Turbin, *Working Women of Collar City: Gender,*

*Class, and Community in Troy, New York, 1864–86* (Urbana, Ill., 1992); Walter Licht, *Industrializing America: The Nineteenth Century* (Baltimore, 1995); Robert B. Gordon, *American Iron, 1607–1900* (Baltimore, 1996); and Paula Mitchell Marks, *Hands to the Spindle: Texas Women and Home Textile Production, 1822–1880* (College Station, Tex., 1996). Also fascinating for their perspectives on women in the 1860s and 1870s are Marilyn Wood Hill, *Their Sisters' Keepers: Prostitution in New York City, 1830–1870* (Berkeley, Calif., 1993) and Kathleen DeGrave, *Swindler, Spy, Rebel: The Confidence Woman in Nineteenth-Century America* (Columbia, Mo., 1995).

Excellent work on labor and daily routines in rural America has been done by Nancy G. Osterud, *Bonds of Community: The Lives of Farm Women in Nineteenth-Century New York* (Ithaca, N.Y., 1991); John Solomon Otto, *Southern Agriculture during the Civil War Era, 1860–1880* (Westport, Conn., 1994); and Sally McMurry *Transforming Rural Life: Dairying Families and Agricultural Change, 1820–1885* (Baltimore, 1995). Also fitting this category, although with a far broader scope and purpose, is Leslie A. Schwalm, *A Hard Fight for We: Women's Transition from Slavery to Freedom in South Carolina* (Urbana, Ill., 1997).

Interesting perspectives on the business community may be found in Leigh Eric Schmidt, *Consumer Rites: The Buying & Selling of American Holidays* (Princeton, N.J., 1995); Timothy B. Spears, *100 Years on the Road: The Traveling Salesman in American Culture* (New Haven, Conn., 1995); Richard V. Francaviglia, *Main Street Revisited: Time, Space, and Image Building in Small-Town America* (Iowa City, Iowa, 1996); and Robert C. Kenzer, *Enterprising Southerners: Black Economic Success in North Carolina, 1865–1915* (Charlottesville, Va., 1997).

The original printed bibliography for the *Expansion of Everyday Life* was far from comprehensive. Likewise, these relatively few titles acknowledge only a portion of the new literature. Other books could easily be added, and no mention has been made of the periodical literature or of the many personal contemporary accounts in the form of letters, diaries, and memoirs that have been published since 1989. The obstacles to compiling a complete bibliography for a topic of such enormous scope as "everyday life" are numerous, but for a fuller discussion, readers will find Michael J. Marhola, *Everyday Life During the Civil War: A Guide for Writers, Students and Historians* (Cincinnati, 1999), a convenient supplement to the works already mentioned.